Lecture Notes in Computer Science 12548

More information about this subseries at http://www.springer.com/series/7408

José F. Morales · Dominic Orchard (Eds.)

Practical Aspects of Declarative Languages

23rd International Symposium, PADL 2021
Copenhagen, Denmark, January 18–19, 2021
Proceedings

 Springer

Editors
José F. Morales 🆔
IMDEA Software Institute
Pozuelo de Alarcón, Spain

Dominic Orchard 🆔
University of Kent
Canterbury, UK

ISSN 0302-9743   ISSN 1611-3349 (electronic)
Lecture Notes in Computer Science
ISBN 978-3-030-67437-3   ISBN 978-3-030-67438-0   (eBook)
https://doi.org/10.1007/978-3-030-67438-0

LNCS Sublibrary: SL2 – Programming and Software Engineering

This Springer imprint is published by the registered company Springer Nature Switzerland AG
The registered company address is: Gewerbestrasse 11, 6330 Cham, Switzerland

Preface

This volume contains the papers presented at the 23rd International Symposium on Practical Aspects of Declarative Languages (PADL 2021). The symposium was co-located with the 48th ACM SIGPLAN Symposium on Principles of Programming Languages (POPL 2021), and took place during January 18–19, 2021. The conference was planned to be held in Copenhagen, Denmark, but due to the COVID-19 pandemic it took place as a virtual online event.

PADL is a well-established forum for researchers and practitioners to present original work emphasizing novel applications and implementation techniques for all forms of declarative programming, including programming with sets, functions, logics, and constraints. The contributions to PADL 2021 were particulary focused on new ideas and approaches for principled implementation, fuzzing and declarative debugging, domain specific languages, and real-world applications ranging from blockchain to web programming.

Originally established as a workshop (PADL 1999 in San Antonio, Texas), the PADL series developed into a regular annual symposium; previous editions took place in San Antonio, Texas (1999), Boston, Massachusetts (2000), Las Vegas, Nevada (2001), Portland, Oregon (2002), New Orleans, Louisiana (2003), Dallas, Texas (2004), Long Beach, California (2005), Charleston, South Carolina (2006), Nice, France (2007), San Francisco, California (2008), Savannah, Georgia (2009), Madrid, Spain (2010), Austin, Texas (2012), Rome, Italy (2013), San Diego, California (2014), Portland, Oregon (2015), St. Petersburg, Florida (2016), Paris, France (2017), Los Angeles, California (2018), Lisbon, Portugal (2019), and New Orleans, Louisiana (2020).

This year, the Program Committee accepted 10 full papers and 1 short paper (extended abstract), selected from 21 submissions. Each submission was reviewed by at least three Program Committee members and went through a five-day online discussion period by the Program Committee before a final decision was made. The selection was based only on the merit of each submission and regardless of scheduling or space constraints.

We would like to express thanks to the Association of Logic Programming (ALP) and the Association for Computing Machinery (ACM) for their continuous support of the symposium, and Springer for their longstanding, successful cooperation with the PADL series. We are very grateful to the 18 members of the PADL 2021 Program Committee and external reviewers for their invaluable work. Many thanks to Marco Gavanelli, the ALP Conference Coordinator. We are happy to note that the conference was successfully managed with the help of EasyChair.

We note that this was an unusual year due to the COVID-19 pandemic. Many (if not most) members of our research community have been adversely affected, in a variety of ways. This has undoubtedly had an impact on the amount of scientific activity that people have been able to engage in. We are therefore even more thankful to our reviewers for their time and care, and to all contributors to this year's PADL.

January 2021   José F. Morales
                                                                     Dominic Orchard

Organization

Program Committee Chairs

José F. Morales   IMDEA Software Institute, Spain
Dominic Orchard   University of Kent, UK

Program Committee

Mario Alviano   University of Calabria, Italy
Nada Amin   Harvard University, USA
Edwin Brady   University of St. Andrews, UK
Joachim Breitner   DFINITY, Germany
Youyou Cong   Tokyo Institute of Technology, Japan
Mistral Contrastin   Facebook London, UK
Sandra Dylus   University of Kiel, Germany
Esra Erdem   Sabancı University, Turkey
Martin Gebser   Alpen-Adria-Universität Klagenfurt, Austria
Gopal Gupta   U. Dallas, USA
Ekaterina Komendantskaya   Heriot-Watt University, UK
Henrik Nilsson   University of Nottingham, UK
Enrico Pontelli   New Mexico State University, USA
K. C. Sivaramakrishnan   IIT Madras, India
Paul Tarau   University of North Texas, USA
Jan Wielemaker   Free University Amsterdam, Netherlands
Ningning Xie   University of Hong Kong, Hong Kong SAR, China
Neng-Fa Zhou   City University of New York, USA

Additional Reviewers

Kinjal Basu
Jan Christiansen
Matthew Daggitt
Fang Li
Sarat Chandra Varanasi

Contents

Foundations and Programming Concepts

A Family of Unification-Oblivious Program Transformations and Their Applications

Paul Tarau[✉]

Department of Computer Science and Engineering, University of North Texas,
Denton, USA
paul.tarau@unt.edu

Abstract. We describe a family of program transformations that compile a Horn Clause program into equivalent programs of a simpler and more regular structure.

Our transformations, seen as morphisms between term algebras, commute with unification, clause unfoldings and Prolog's LD-resolution, thus preserving the operational semantics of the Horn Clause programs.

As applications, the resulting programs have simpler execution algorithms and can be compiled to minimalist instruction sets.

Keywords: Term algebras · Horn Clause unfoldings · Program transformations · Minimalist canonical forms of logic programs · Simplified instruction sets · Lightweight prolog run-time systems

1 Introduction

Prolog's core execution algorithm works as a search mechanism on Horn Clauses programs. It combines unification, backtracking and it is wrapped together as LD-resolution, a specialization of SLD resolution [7,8] selecting for expansion the leftmost goal in the body of clause, in depth-first search order. It is this core execution algorithm that makes Prolog a general-purpose, Turing-complete programming language by contrast to SAT, SMT or ASP solvers. Adding built-ins, tabling and constraints or extending execution to incorporate sound handling of negation and co-inductive constructs entail orthogonal (and often minor) changes, from an implementor's perspective, to the underlying core execution mechanism.

Program transformations (including partial evaluation) operating on Horn Clause programs also relate to this core execution mechanism. In particular, unfolding of the leftmost goal in the body of a Horn clause mimics a single step in Prolog's LD-resolution.

Multiple equivalent views of Prolog's semantics e.g., via Herbrand models/-fixpoints [7], working with ground terms or non-ground terms (e.g., S-models, C-models) [4] can all be seen as derived from this core execution mechanism.

© Springer Nature Switzerland AG 2021
J. F. Morales and D. Orchard (Eds.): PADL 2021, LNCS 12548, pp. 3–19, 2021.
https://doi.org/10.1007/978-3-030-67438-0_1

Most of the literature covering such transformations, at least in terms of discovering new ones, dates from the 80's and 90's. The same applies to actual implementation models, initially derived empirically [18], although (sometime) consolidated later as formally accurate [11].

Our goal in this paper, after revisiting Prolog's core execution algorithm and making it as self-contained as possible while also formally uniform, is to discover some theoretically interesting and at the same time easily implementable reductions to unusually simple canonical forms. In a way, our program transformations will bring Horn Clause logic to a simplicity comparable to expressing lambda calculus in terms of the S and K combinators, from where, as it happened in functional programming [16], an actual implementation can be derived. As with combinator-based implementations in functional programming, this simplicity has a performance cost. We will show that in our case this performance hit can be significantly reduced.

As applications, we derive extremely lightweight proof-of-concept implementations, in a *few hundred lines* in **Python**, **Swift**, **Julia** and **C**, usable as starting points for deploying logic programming systems in resource-limited environments (e.g., IOT or wearable devices).

The SWI-Prolog [19] implementation of the transformers as well as open-source runtime-systems written in Prolog, Swift, Julia and C are available online[1].

We will proceed as follows. First, we simplify as much as possible the theory behind LD-resolution by reworking the data types inherited from predicate calculus in formally lightweight term algebras. As part of this "refactoring" we transform terms to an equivalent binary tree form via a bijection that commutes with unification. Next, starting from a set of Horn Clauses, via a sequence of semantics-preserving program transformations, we derive simpler equivalent Horn Clause programs. In particular, we revisit the binarization transformation [15] that we use to derive clauses with at most one goal in their body. Finally we convert to an equational form in which unification operations are expressed as triplets, ready to be turned into virtual machine instructions. Together with a *define* and a *proceed* instruction, we obtain our minimalist assembly language of 3-instructions, for we will describe a proof-of-concept Python implementation and discuss aspects of porting it to programming languages like Swift, Julia and C, while being able to delegate last call optimization and garbage collection to the underlying implementation-language.

The rest of the paper is organized as follows: Sect. 2 introduces the term algebras used in our transformations. Section 3 introduces the unfolding monoids defining our LD-resolution computation steps. Section 4 covers several composable transformations on term algebras and Horn Clause programs. Section 5 overviews applications to lightweight run-time system implementations, based on our transformations. Section 6 discusses related work and Sect. 7 concludes the paper.

---

2 Term Algebras

2.1 The General Term Algebra

We define a *Term Algebra* $\mathbb{T}$ as triple $<C, V, T>$ where C is a set of constant symbols, V is set of variable symbols and T is a set of terms for which the following construction rules hold:

1. if $a \in C$ then $a \in T$
2. if $X \in V$ then $X \in T$
3. if $f \in C$ and $T_1, T_2..., T_n \in T$ then $f(T_1, T_2..., T_n) \in T$.

Note that, as this is the norm in logic programming languages, we accept overloading of function symbols with different arities. Note also that, for the same reason we will use constant symbols interchangeably as predicate and term constructors and have variables as goals in atom in clause bodies. When needed, we also assume that an additional $\bot$ element, that's not part of its set of constants or variables, is added to a term algebra.

2.2 The Binary Term Algebra

We define a *Binary Term Algebra* $\mathbb{B}$ as a triple $<C, V, B>$ where C is a set of constant symbols, V is set of variable symbols and B is a set of terms for which the following construction rules hold:

1. if $a \in C$ then $a \in B$
2. if $X \in V$ then $X \in B$
3. if $B_1, B_2 \in B$ then $B_1 \Rightarrow B_2 \in B$.

For convenience, we assume that the "$\Rightarrow$" constructor is right associative i.e., we will write $A \Rightarrow B \Rightarrow C$ instead of $A \Rightarrow (B \Rightarrow C)$. In fact, one can see a Binary Term Algebra simply as a term algebra where terms are only built by using the symbol "$\Rightarrow$" with exactly two terms as its arguments. Note that the resulting language is essentially that of types for simply typed lambda terms + constants, or equivalently, via the Curry-Howard isomorphism [5], that of the implicational subset of intuitionistic propositional calculus. That also hints to our (otherwise arbitrary) choice of "$\Rightarrow$" as the binary constructor symbol for the algebra $\mathbb{B}$.

3 Unfolding Monoids

We assume that the reader is familiar with the most general unifier mgu of two terms [8]. We denote $u(T_1, T_2)$ the result of applying $\theta = mgu(T_1, T_2)$ to any of them (as $T_1\theta = T_2\theta$) if the mgu exists and $\bot$ otherwise. We assume also that

$$\forall T \ u(T, \bot) = \bot \ \textbf{and} \ \mathbf{u}(\bot, \mathbf{T}) = \bot \tag{1}$$

Theorem 1. *The following associativity property holds:*

$$\forall A \ \forall B \ \forall C \ \ u(A, u(B, C)) = u(u(A, B), C) \tag{2}$$

Proof sketch. It follows from known properties of the mgu (see [8]) and assumption (1).

3.1   The Monoid of Horn Clause Unfoldings

LD-resolution is SLD-resolution [8], specialized to Prolog's selection of the first atom in the body of clause. Its basic step can be described as an *unfolding* operation between two Horn Clauses.

A *Horn Clause* $(A_0 :\text{-} A_1, \dots, A_m)$ with *head* A_0 and (non- empty) *body* $A_1, \dots, A_m$ is built of terms $A_i \in \mathbb{T}$ where $\mathbb{T}$ is a term algebra.

Horn Clause *unfolding* is defined as follows:

$$(A_0 :\text{-} A_1, A_2, \dots, A_m) \odot (B_0 :\text{-} B_1, B_2, \dots, B_n) = (A_0' :\text{-} B_1', B_2', \dots B_n', A_2', \dots, A_m') \tag{3}$$

where A_i' and B_j' are the result of applying the most general unifier of A_1 and B_0 to A_i and B_j, respectively, for all $i = 0, \dots, m$ and $j = 1, \dots, n$. We define the result of $\odot$ as the special term $\perp$ if the unification of A_1 and B_0 fails. We assume also that $\perp$ acts as a *zero element* (more generally, an *absorbing element*):

$$\forall X \quad \perp \odot X = X \odot \perp = \perp \tag{4}$$

Computing an answer to a program for a query G can be seen as iterated unfoldings, starting from a clause $G :\text{-} G$, with fresh instances of clauses in the program. At the end, variable bindings in G correspond to answers to the query and reaching $G :\text{-} true$ marks a successful derivation.

Theorem 2. *Horn Clauses form a monoid with the unfolding operation $\odot$. The $\odot$ operation is associative and the clause $V :\text{-} V$ where V is a variable acts as its identity element.*

Proof sketch: As u is associative (2) it follows that $\odot$ is associative. Propagation of failure follows from (4), given the action of $\odot$ on $\perp$.

As an intuition, note that the structure is similar to that on $\mathbb{N}$ with multiplication, where 1 acts as identity and 0 acts as a zero element, except, of course, for commutativity of multiplication in $\mathbb{N}$.

The monoid structure associated to a term algebra $\mathbb{T}$ can also be seen as a *category with a single object* on which its unfolding operations act as morphisms.

3.2   The Monoid of Binary Clause Unfoldings

We consider a term algebra $\mathbb{T}$ extended with a bottom element $\perp$. Binary Clauses are Horn Clauses of the form $H :\text{-} B$ with $H, B \in \mathbb{T}$.

A composition operation on binary clauses is defined as unfolding, specialized to binary clauses:

$$(A_0 :\text{-} A_1) \odot (B_0 :\text{-} B_1) = (A_0' :\text{-} B_1') \tag{5}$$

where A_0' and B_1' are the result of applying the most general unifier (*mgu*) of A_1 and B_0 to A_0 and B_1, respectively. We define the result of $\odot$ as the special term $\perp$ if the unification of A_1 and B_0 fails. We assume also that $\perp$ acts as a *zero element*:

$$\forall X \quad \perp \odot X = X \odot \perp = \perp \tag{6}$$

Theorem 3. *Binary Clauses form a monoid with the unfolding operation $\odot$. The $\odot$ operation is associative, $V :- V$ (where V is a variable) acts as the identity element and $\bot$ acts as a zero element.*

Proof sketch: It follows from Theorem 2, as a special case.

The monoid can be also seen as a category with a single object with morphisms provided by the $\odot$ operation.

4   The Logic Program Transformers

We will now focus on program transformations that can be see as *morphisms* between our term algebras or as morphisms between the Horn Clause programs built on them.

4.1   Binarization: From Horn Clauses to Binary Clauses

Let $HC_\mathbb{T}$ denote the set of Horn Clauses with terms in a given term algebra $\mathbb{T}$ and $BC_\mathbb{T}$ the set of Binary Clauses (clauses having at most one term in their body).

The binarization transformation $bin_\mathbb{T} : HC_\mathbb{T} \to BC_\mathbb{T}$ maps a Horn Clause to a continuation passing Binary Clause as follows.

$$bin((A_0 :- A_1, A_2, \ldots, A_m)) = (A_0 \triangleright C :- A_1 \triangleright A_2 \triangleright \ldots, A_n \triangleright C) \qquad (7)$$

where

$$f(A_1, \ldots, A_m) \triangleright B = f(A_1, \ldots, A_m, B) \qquad (8)$$

and C is a variable not occurring in $A_0: -A_1, A_2, \ldots, A_m$.

Example 1. *Binarization of rules and facts. Note that $\triangleright$ embeds the second operand as last argument of the first.*

```
bin(a:-b,c,d) = a(Cont) :-b(c(d(Cont)))

bin(a(f(A)):-b(c,A),d(g(A))) = a(f(A), Cont):-b(c,A,d(g(A), Cont))

bin(f(a,b)) = f(a,b,Cont):-Cont
```

Note also that in the case of a fact, the continuation forming the body of its transformation via *bin* is a variable.

Theorem 4. $bin_\mathbb{T} : HC_\mathbb{T} \to BC_\mathbb{T}$ *is a injection and its left inverse bin^{-1} can be used to restore answers computed by the binarized program. Prolog's LD-resolution computation acting on a program P (seen as iterated unfoldings in $HC_\mathbb{T}$) is equivalent to LD-resolution of binary clauses (seen as iterated unfoldings in $BC_\mathbb{T}$), where $\mathbb{T}$ is the term algebra built with the set of constants and variables occurring P.*

Proof sketch. With computations proceeding via $\odot$ on the two sides, note that each computation in $BC_{\mathbb{T}}$ corresponds via bin^{-1} to a computation step in $HC_{\mathbb{T}}$ as the morphism $bin_{\mathbb{T}} : HC_{\mathbb{T}} \to BC_{\mathbb{T}}$ (also seen as a functor between the corresponding one-object categories) obeys the following relations:

$$bin_{\mathbb{T}}(C_1 \odot C_2) = bin_{\mathbb{T}}(C_1) \odot bin_{\mathbb{T}}(C_2) \tag{9}$$

$$C_1 \odot C_2 = bin_{\mathbb{T}}^{-1}(bin_{\mathbb{T}}(C_1) \odot bin_{\mathbb{T}}(C_2)) \tag{10}$$

To summarize, this means that *LD-resolution is oblivious to binarization,* in the sense that the same answers will be computed with it or without it.

4.2   The LD-Resolution-Oblivious Bijection Between $\mathbb{T}$ and $\mathbb{B}$

Let $\mathbb{T}$ be a Term Algebra and $\mathbb{B}$ a Binary Term Algebra on the same set of constants and variables.

We define a bijection $bt : \mathbb{T} \to \mathbb{B}$ as follows:

1. if c is a constant, then $bt(c) = c$
2. if v is a variable, then $bt(v) = v$
3. if $x = f(x_1, \ldots, x_n)$ then $bt(x) = (bt(x_1) \Rightarrow bt(x_2) \ldots \Rightarrow bt(x_n) \Rightarrow f)$

Theorem 5. *The transformation $bt : \mathbb{T} \to \mathbb{B}$ is a bijection.*

Proof sketch. By induction on the structure of $\mathbb{T}$ and the structure of $\mathbb{B}$ for its inverse bt^{-1}.

Example 2. *Bijective transformation to binary tree*
```
bt( f(A,g(a,B),B) ) = A=>(a=>B=>g)=>B=>f .
```

Theorem 6. *Let us denote the result of unifying two terms and applying the unifier (in the respective term algebras) to either as the binary operator u. Then*

$$bt(u(A, B)) = u(bt(A), bt(B))$$

Proof sketch. Note that on both sides, we have the same variables. Thus a substitution of A with a term X on one side corresponds to a substitution with term $bt(X)$ on the other side. One can proceed by induction on size of the terms, keeping in mind that the multiway trees representing terms of $\mathbb{T}$ are in bijection with the binary trees representing them in $\mathbb{B}$, and that unifications are expressed as compositions of substitutions.

As an intuition, bt is similar to (and inspired by) *currying* in functional programming, in the sense that applying a function symbol to its arguments is equivalent to applying closures repeatedly.

Theorem 7. *Let $\mathbb{T}$ be a Term Algebra and $\mathbb{B}$ a Binary Term Algebra sharing the same sets of constants and variables. Let $HC_{\mathbb{T}}$ be a set of Horn Clauses and $HC_{\mathbb{B}}$ the result of applying bt to each A_i in each clause A_0 :- $A_1, \ldots, A_n$ in $HC_{\mathbb{T}}$. Then for $C_1, C_2 \in HC_{\mathbb{T}}$ the following holds:*

$$bt(C_1 \odot C_2) = bt(C_1) \odot bt(C_2) \tag{11}$$

$$C_1 \odot C_2 = bt^{-1}(bt(C_1) \odot bt(C_2)) \tag{12}$$

Proof sketch. It follows from Theorems 8 and 6 by applying, inductively, the fact that *bt* commutes with unifications.

4.3   The Lifted One-Function Transformation

Another way to push function symbols into constants is to mark all compound terms with a single functions symbol, not occurring in the term algebra, say \$. Let $T^\$$ be the term algebra $\mathbb{T}$ extended with the constant symbol \$. We define a function $hl : \mathbb{T} \to \mathbb{T}^\$$ as follows:

1. if c is a constant, then $hl(c) = c$
2. if v is a variable, then $hl(v) = v$
3. if $x = f(x_1, \ldots, x_n)$ then $hl(x) = \$(f, hl(x_1), \ldots, hl(x_n))$

Theorem 8. *The transformation $hl : \mathbb{T} \to \mathbb{T}^\$$ is injective and its has a left inverse hl^{-1}. It commutes with unification, and when extended to Horn Clauses, it commutes with LD-resolution and the following relations hold:*

$$hl(C_1 \odot C_2) = hl(C_1) \odot hl(C_2) \tag{13}$$

$$C_1 \odot C_2 = hl^{-1}(hl(C_1) \odot hl(C_2)) \tag{14}$$

where C_1 and C_2 are Horn Clauses.

Proof sketch. By induction on the structure of $\mathbb{T}$ and the structure of $\mathbb{T}^\$$ for its inverse hl^{-1}.

Example 3. *Transformation to lifted one-function terms.*

```
hl( f(A,g(a,B),B) ) = $(f,A,$(f,a,B),B).
```

As all terms have only "\$" in function symbol positions, by omitting them, one can see these terms as multi-way trees with variable or constant labels only at leaf nodes.

4.4   Equational Forms

Equational Forms in Term Algebra $\mathbb{T}$. Given a term $A \in \mathbb{T}$ and an equation of the form $X = A$, it can be deconstructed to an canonical equational form $eqf(X = A)$ as follows:

1. if c is a constant then $eqf(X = c)$ is $X = c$
2. if V is a variable then $eqf(X = V)$ is $X = V$
3. if $A = f(x_1, \ldots, x_n)$ then $eqf(X = A)$ is the nested conjunction

$$X = f(X_1, \ldots, X_n) \, , \, eqf(X_1 = x_1) \, , \, \ldots \, , \, eqf(X_n = x_n)$$

where "=" stands for the unification operation and X_i are variables not occurring in A. Note that equations of the form $X = V$ with both terms variables can be eliminated by uniformly substituting X with V in all the equations it occurs. The same applies to equations of the form $X = c$ with c a constant.

Example 4. *Equational form*

```
eqf(X=f(a,g(V,b,h(c)),V)) =  X=f(a,X2,V),X2=g(V,b,X3),X3=h(c)
```

Equational Form in the Binary Term Algebra $\mathbb{B}$. In particular, given a term $A \in \mathbb{B}$ and an equation of the form $X = A$, its equational form is defined as follows:

1. if c is a constant then $eqf(X = c)$ is $X = c$
2. if V is a variable then $eqf(X = V)$ is $X = V$
3. if $A = (x_1 \Rightarrow x_2)$ then $eqf(X = A)$ is the nested conjunction

$$X = (X_1 \Rightarrow X_2) \ , \ eqf(X_1 = x_1) \ , \ eqf(X_2 = x_2)$$

Note that this suggest applying the composition of the transformations bt and eqf to reduce Prolog terms to a structurally simpler equational form.

Equational Form of a Horn Clause. We extend this to a Horn Clause as

$$eqf(A_0 :\text{-} A_1, \ldots, A_n) = \tag{15}$$
$$p(X_0) :\text{-} eqf(X_0 = A_0), eqf(X_1 = A_1), \ldots, eqf(X_n, A_n), p(X_1), \ldots, p(X_n) \tag{16}$$

where p is a *new constant symbol*, not occurring in the clause. Note that the conjunctions resulting from eqf on the right side can be assumed to be flattened.

Given a program P defined as a set of Horn clauses, its equational form $eqf(P)$ is the set of the equational forms of its clauses.

Theorem 9. *LD-resolution on P computes the same answers as LD-resolution on $eqf(P)$. Moreover, the same applies when permuting the order of the unification equations in any of the clauses.*

Proof sketch. It follows from an equational rewriting of the unification algorithm.

4.5   Composing the Transformations

Theorem 10. *Let ϕ and ψ two transformation that commute with Horn Clause unfoldings (and thus LD-resolution), i.e., such that:*

$$C_1 \odot C_2 \ = \ \phi^{-1}(\phi(C_1) \odot \phi(C_2)) \tag{17}$$

and

$$C_1 \odot C_2 \ = \ \psi^{-1}(\psi(C_1) \odot \psi(C_2)) \tag{18}$$

where C_1 and C_2 are Horn Clauses over their respective term algebras. Let $\xi = \phi \,.\, \psi$ be the composition of the two transformations. Then

$$C_1 \odot C_2 \ = \ \xi^{-1}(\xi(C_1) \odot \xi(C_2)) \tag{19}$$

Proof sketch. Trivial, using the fact that $\xi^{-1} = \psi^{-1} \cdot \phi^{-1}$.

Thus, composition of our transformations enables *compiling* Horn Clause programs to alternative forms which, when executed, will compute the same answers. Moreover, with tweaks for built-ins, IO and other orthogonal language extensions, these can be used to derive actual, possibly much simpler implementations of unification-based logic languages.

5   Applications

5.1   The Triplet Normal Form of Horn Clause Programs

We will show next that composing the transformations like *bin*, *bt* and *eqf* results in a dramatically simple and uniform canonical form for Horn Clause programs.

Theorem 11. *A Horn Clause program can be transformed into an equivalent Horn Clause program (we call it its Triplet Normal Form) that has:*

1. *a single unary tail recursive predicate with Datalog clauses*
2. *a single binary function symbol*
3. *a single non-Datalog fact of arity 3 referring to the function symbol*

Proof sketch. Apply *bin . bt . eqf* (in left to right order). Then, the unification operation "=" can be encapsulated as the predicate u/3 as follows:

```
u(X,Y,(X=>Y)).
```

Clearly, when called as u(A,B,C), it is equivalent to the unification operation (A=>B)=C covering the equational form of a binarized program with terms in $\mathbb{B}$.

Example 5. *Triplet Normal Form of a Horn Clause*

```
?- Cls=(a:-b,c,d), to_tnf(Cls,TopVars,TNF).
Cls =   (a:-b, c, d),
TopVars = [B, E],
TNF = [u(A, a, B)]:[u(A, d, C), u(C, c, D), u(D, b, E)].
```

Note that our code has separated in the result TNF with ":" unification operations expressing the structures of the clause head and clause body.

Note also that u(X,Y,Z) can be split as:

```
u(X,Y,Z):-l(X,Z),r(X,Z).
```

assuming the two binary facts

```
l(X,X=>_).
r(Y,_=>Y).
```

Thus, we can have, alternatively, 2 binary predicates replacing the ternary u/3, given that one can define d/3 as:

```
d(A,B,AB):-l(A,AB),r(B,AB).
```

Theorem 12. *Any reordering of the u/3 (or the l/2 and r/2) operations preserves the LD-resolution semantics of the resulting program.*

Proof sketch. It follows from commutativity of conjunction in the equational form and commutativity and associativity of unifications (see [8]).

5.2   Deriving a Prolog Virtual Machine

Specifying the VM as Prolog Program. We can now use the top variable corresponding to the head to define our unique Datalog predicate p/1 and the top variable corresponding to the body as the recursive last call to the predicate itself.

Example 6. *The predicate p/1 with its self-recursive last call.*

```
?- Cls=(a(f(X)):-b(c,X),d(g(X))), cls2tnf(Cls,TNF), portray_clause(TNF).
p(C) :-
    u(D, f, A),
    u(E, a, B),
    u(A, B, C),
    u(D, g, F),
    u(E, d, G),
    u(F, G, H),
    u(H, b, I),
    u(D, I, J),
    u(c, J, K),
    p(K).
```

Note that one could separate the u/3 unification triplets into ones coming from the head and the ones coming from the body when generating the "assembler" as these are meant exclusively to build terms on the heap with no call to unifications.

By putting the clauses together the resulting code *can be run as a Prolog program*, by adding the definition u(A,B,A=>B) as well as a first clause p(X):-var(X),! or equivalently, by introducing, like in [12,13], a special symbol $true, assumed not to occur in the program, to mark the fact that no continuations are left to unwrap and execute. Reaching this special symbol or unbound variable continuation would also mean that a solution has actually been found, a hint on what a runtime system in a language other than Prolog should do.

The 3-Instruction Assembler. We derive our 3 instruction assembler simply by distinguishing between the entry point to a clause with opcode '**d**' and the recursive call to the predicate p/1 with opcode '**p**'. Together with our unification triples u/3, marked as instructions with opcode '**u**' we obtain our 3-instruction assembler code, ready to run on a VM designed for a procedural implementation language. Thus, the code for the clause:

```
a(f(A)):-b(c, A), d(g(A))
```

becomes:

```
d A
u B f C
u D a E
u C E A
u B g F
```

```
u D d G
u F G H
u H b I
u B I J
u c J K
p K
```

5.3   Sketch of a Virtual Machine, in Python

Our implementation sketch takes advantage of the simplified instruction set generated through the composition of 3 program transformations, resulting in the Ternary Normal Form of a Horn Clause program as stated in Theorem 11, in its 3-assembler instruction form. We refer to the actual implementation[2] for details not covered by this succinct description, focussed on the main ideas behind it.

The General Implementation Concept. To keep things simple we avoid creating our own data types[3]. Variables are represented as Python lists of size 1 (or 2, if keeping names around). We represent the equivalent of Prolog's A=>B term as the Python pair (A,B). Constants could be any other Python types, as all we assume is that they are not Python tuples or lists and have a well defined "==" operation. In practice, we currently have as constants strings, ints and floats as these are also meaningful on the Prolog side where we compile the code.

Unification and dereferencing are standard, except that we use None rather than self-reference to mark unbound variables. Our unification algorithm uses its own local stack and trails variables when "older" than those originating from the current clause.

The main code interpreter consists of an inner loop (the function step() in our code snippet) and a *trampoline* mechanism (function interp() in our code snippet) that avoids recursion and enables last call optimization (LCO).

Besides the *trail*, we use a *todo* stack, accumulating things to do and undo. It is initialized with a term *goal(Answer, Continuation)*. By convention, we assume that the predicate goal/1 has a definition in the sources. The *todo* stack combines goal stack and choice-point stack functions. It manages the current goal and the current next clause index to be tried (if any).

Instead of using a *heap*, for which we would need to write a garbage collector, we assume that the underlying language has a garbage collector, to which we gladly delegate all memory management tasks. Besides Python, languages like Swift, Julia, go, Java or C-sharp qualify, as well as plain C or C++ with the Boehm conservative garbage collector [1] enabled.

---

[2] https://raw.githubusercontent.com/ptarau/LogicTransformers/main/tnf2okAssocUnif.py.

[3] For most of our Python implementation variants. However, we define appropriate data types in Julia, Swift and C either as combinations of struct and union equivalents or by using more efficient tagged unsigned 64 bit integers for both values and array indices or pointers.

As our sketch of Python code will show, we can implement a runtime system supporting the core execution mechanism of Prolog, with key features as LCO and garbage collection "for free", in a host language that automates memory management.

The Inner Clause Selection Loop. As we do not actually manage a heap, the concept of *age* of a variable is undefined. Thus we need to know which variables originate from the current clause, to avoid unnecessary trailing. We achieve that with a lazily built set of new variables (as returned by Python's id() function, held in a register array ("'vars"' in our code snippet).

Trying out a new clause involves creating its data objects from a *template.* We do that using the activate function that lazily copies and relocates elements of the template, while ensuring that variables with the same name correspond to the same variable object, with scopes local to each clause. The inner loop of the step(G,i) function, where G represents the current goal and i represents the clause index next to be tried, decodes our 3-instruction assembler as follows:

- the '**d**' instruction marks the entry to a new clause to be tried against the current goal G. It simply binds its argument, known to be a variable, to the current goal.
- the '**u**' instruction, after inlining some special cases of unification, calls the general unification algorithm, mimicking the equivalent of the Prolog d(A,B,A=>B) fact.
- the '**p**' instruction marks getting to the end of the unification stream marking the success of the current clause. It returns to the *trampoline* a DO instruction implying that there's more work to do or a DONE instruction when no continuation is left to explore and an answer needs to be returned. Note the presence of the NewG variable (to be explored next) as well as the G variable, with which execution would have to resume in case of failure.

At the end of the step() function's loop, if no more clauses are available, a FAIL operation is emitted, usable for tracing purposes but otherwise resulting in no action on the receiving side.

```
FAIL, DONE, DO, UNDO = 0, 1, 2, 3

def step(G, i, code, trail):
  ttop = len(trail)
  while i < len(code):
    unwind(trail, ttop)
    clause,vars = code[i],[]
    i += 1  # next clause
    for instr in clause:
      c = activate(instr, vars)
      op = c[0]
      if op == 'u':
        if not unify((c[1], c[2]), c[3], trail) : break
      elif op == 'd': #assert VAR == type_of(c[1])
```

```
      c[1][0] = G
      trail.append(c[1])
    else: # op==p
      NewG, tg = deref(c[1])
      if NewG == 'true' and CONST == tg: return (DONE, G, ttop, i)
      else: return (DO, NewG, G, ttop, i)
  return (FAIL,)
```

The Main Interpreter and Its "Trampoline" Mechanism. The "trampoline" loop implemented by the function `interp()` calls the `step()` function and handles the `FAIL, DONE, DO` operations returned by it, as well as the `UNDO` operations scheduled for later execution by its `DO` and `DONE` operations. Besides the trail, it uses the `todo` stack that is popped at each step, until empty. The stack holds "trampoline" instructions for scheduling new goals (`DO`), return answers (`DONE`) or to move control to the next unexplored clause (`UNDO`). Its key steps are:

- DO: it executes the recently popped instruction from the `todo` stack, initialized by the original **goal** term (containing the answer pattern as its first argument) and fed by returns from calling the `step()` function. It also schedules a clean-up `UNDO` operation by pushing it on the `todo` stack. Note that for a sequence of successful `DO` operations, their corresponding `UNDO` instructions will get executed in the right order, ensured by the stack's last-in first-out policy.
- DONE: works similarly to `DO`, except that an answer is emitted and no call to the `step()` function is performed. In this case, the **answer** variable (by convention, the first argument of the goal given to the VM) is "ironed" by the function `iron()` into a fully dereferenced term, ready to be yield to the user and insensitive to undoing the binding that lead to it.
- UNDO: unwinds the trail one level below the current one, as instructed by the argument "ttop" and passes control via the `step()` function to the next clause, as instructed by its "i" argument. Note that each new clause to be tried out in `step()` cleans up the mess left by the previous ones, by calling `unwind_trail`. Leaving this to `UNDO` would be too late and result in missing solutions. On the other hand, `UNDO` will be the right instruction to unwind the trail to its appropriate level, as transmitted by the corresponding `DO` instruction.
- FAIL: a no-operation instruction, useful only for tracing. While this is emitted when no clause is left to match a given goal, its clean-up tasks have been delegated to the `step()` function and the `UNDO` instruction as part of the process enabling them to ensure LCO.

```
# trampoline, ensures LCO and eliminates recursion
def interp(code,goal) :
  l=len(code)
  todo,trail=[(DO,goal,None,0,None)],[]
  while todo :
```

```
instr=todo.pop()
op=instr[0]
if DO==op :
  _,NewG,G,ttop,i=instr
  r=step(NewG,0,code,trail)
  todo.append((UNDO,G,ttop,i))
  todo.append(r)
elif DONE==op:
  _, G, ttop, i = instr
  todo.append((UNDO,G,ttop,i))
  yield iron(goal)
elif UNDO==op :
  _, G, ttop, i=instr
  unwind(trail,ttop)
  if i!=None and i<1 : todo.append(step(G,i,code,trail))
else : pass # FAIL == op:
```

Note that with the *trampoline* mechanism we only rely on Python's `yield` operation for passing an answer from the trampoline to the user, something that can be replaced by printing it out, adding it to a queue or sending it over a socket.

Best target implementations are fast, GC-enabled programming languages like Swift, go, Java, C-sharp or Julia. Another possibility is C or C++ relying on the Boehm-Demers-Weiser garbage collector [1]. As applications, this implementation mechanism can enable running Logic Programming systems on network edges, smart IOT, routers, portable devices and GPU-threads.

Note that our proof-of-concept implementations have *no indexing* and the complete program is hosted in *a single predicate* precluding any common Prolog optimizations. Nevertheless, we will list here the progressively better results on computing all solutions for a **10-queens** problem for a few program variants and programming languages, from slower to faster (running on an iMacPro with a Xeon W processor):

VM Implementation	10 queens program|
Python, standard	67.521s
Julia	53.998s
Swift	28.494s
PyPy (JIT compiler for Python)	10.647s
C, unoptimized, with unions and structs	3.530s
C, slightly optimized and with tagged 64 bit pointers	**0.461s**
Prolog-in-Prolog VM, running in SWI-Prolog	1.006s
SWI-Prolog, directly (our baseline)	0.049s
YAP, a usually faster Prolog system	0.032s

While only about twice as fast as running the resulting assembler on an emulated VM in Prolog and one order of magnitude below the native execution speed in SWI-Prolog, our slightly optimized C-implementation shows that the performance penalty for deriving a compiler and a virtual machine for it from our program transformations is manageable. As a side note, the timings might also be an indicator about the price some high-level modern programming languages are willing to pay for language constructs supporting the data types and algorithms needed for executing the core of an unification-based logic programming language.

6 Related Work

Scholarly work on theory and implementation of unification-based logic programming languages and their program transformations covers at this time more than 50 years. We will refer to classic work like [8] for the foundations of the field and [9,10] for a comprehensive overview of some of the transformations we have taken inspiration from. As we have revisited those essential concepts, we have used a uniform and (arguably) much simpler notation, focusing on the commonalities involved in morphing with their help Prolog's core execution mechanism into equivalent alternatives, including the triplet normal form used for deriving our 3-instruction assembler code.

The transformation between $\mathbb{T}$ and $\mathbb{B}$ is new and it was surprising to see that it has not been discovered previously as a general multi-way tree to binary tree bijection. Among possible alternatives, we have looked also at the well-known "Left-child right-sibling binary tree" transformer originating in [6], Section. 2.3.2, which is prone to move variables to function symbol positions and thus it is not commuting with unification operations. At the same time, we have passed also on LISP-based or Micro-Prolog's [3] "everything is a list" representations that, while commuting with unification, are more memory intensive and also prone to conflate Prolog's list data type with a list representation of terms. The uniform treatment of function and constant symbols as a result of the bt or hl transformations can enable similar operations as the use of arbitrary terms in function symbol positions [2], although we have not used this property here to work with higher-order programming constructs, contrary to [14], where such a representation is used. On the other hand, in [14] a representation derived from an equational form similar to eqf is used, but with a goal stacking mechanism instead of binarization and without the simplification brought by the transformation $bt : \mathbb{T} \rightarrow \mathbb{B}$ used here. The binarization transformation is introduced in [15], resulting in the BinProlog system [13], but its implementation is based on a simplified Warren Abstract Machine. More general continuation passing transformations, with goal atoms in argument position, as those raising from binarization as well as several examples of program optimizations using them are described in [10] and an extension to disjunctive continuations is explored via a metainterpreter in [17].

7 Conclusions and Future Work

We have presented a uniform view of a family of unification-oblivious Horn Clause program transformations and sketched an application to build lightweight implementations in several programming languages. The derived triplet normal form and the resulting 3-instruction assembler have opened the door for new implementation techniques for porting unification-based logic programming systems to provide reasoning capabilities on platforms where resource limitations or urgency of implementation might matter, ranging from IOT devices, small drones, CubeSats and smart appliances to wearable devices and portable or implanted medical devices.

An interesting theoretical outcome relies on the following *conjecture*, subject to possible future work.

If a term transformation that has a left inverse and maps variables into variables and constants into constants, then it is oblivious to unification and can be extended into an unfolding monoid on Horn Clauses that commutes with LD-resolution.

Any such a transformation, besides being ready to be used as the "inner language" of a Prolog implementation, would have applications to mechanisms for code serialization, code obfuscation or code encryption.

References

1. Boehm, H., Weiser, M.: Garbage collection in an uncooperative environment. Softw. Pract. Exp. **18**(9), 807–820 (1988)
2. Chen, W., Kifer, M., Warren, D.: HiLog: a first-order semantics for higher-order logic programming constructs. In: Lusk, E., Overbeek, R. (eds.) 1st North American Conference Logic Programming. pp. 1090–1114. MIT Press, Cleveland (1989)
3. Clark, K.L., McCabe, F.G.: Micro-PROLOG - programming in logic. Prentice Hall international series in computer science, Prentice Hall (1984)
4. Falaschi, M., Levi, G., Martelli, M., Palamidessi, C.: A new declarative semantics for logic languages. In: Kowalski, R.A., Bowen, K.A. (eds.) Proceedings of the Fifth International Conference and Symposium on Logic Programming, pp. 993–1005. The MIT Press (1988)
5. Howard, W.: The formulae-as-types notion of construction. In: Seldin, J., Hindley, J. (eds.) To H.B. Curry: Essays on Combinatory Logic, Lambda Calculus and Formalism, pp. 479–490. Academic Press, London (1980)
6. Knuth, D.E.: The art of computer programming, Fundamental Algorithms, vol. I, 3rd edn. Addison-Wesley (1997). https://www.worldcat.org/oclc/312910844
7. Kowalski, R., Emden, M.V.: The semantics of predicate logic as a programming language. JACM **23**(4), 733–743 (1976)
8. Lloyd, J.W.: Foundations of Logic Programming, 1st edn. Springer, Cham (1984)
9. Pettorossi, A., Proietti, M.: Transformation of Logic Programs: Foundations and Techniques. J. Log. Program. **19**(20), 261–320 (1994). https://doi.org/10.1016/0743-1066(94)90028-0
10. Pettorossi, A., Proietti, M.: Transformations of logic programs with goals as arguments. Theory Pract. Log. Program. **4**(4), 495–537 (2004). https://doi.org/10.1017/S147106840400198X, https://doi.org/10.1017/S147106840400198X

11. Russinoff, D.M.: A verified prolog compiler for the warren abstract machine. J. Log. Program. **13**, 367–412 (1992)
12. Tarau, P.: A simplified abstract machine for the execution of binary metaprograms. In: Proceedings of the Logic Programming Conference 1991, pp. 119–128. ICOT, Tokyo, July 1991
13. Tarau, P.: The BinProlog experience: architecture and implementation choices for continuation passing prolog and first-class logic engines. Theory Pract. Log. Program. **12**(1–2), 97–126 (2012)
14. Tarau, P.: A hitchhiker's guide to reinventing a prolog machine. In: Rocha, R., Son, T.C., Mears, C., Saeedloei, N. (eds.) Technical Communications of the 33rd International Conference on Logic Programming (ICLP 2017). OpenAccess Series in Informatics (OASIcs), vol. 58, pp. 10:1–10:16. Schloss Dagstuhl-Leibniz-Zentrum fuer Informatik, Dagstuhl, Germany (2018). https://doi.org/10.4230/OASIcs.ICLP.2017.10, http://drops.dagstuhl.de/opus/volltexte/2018/8453
15. Tarau, P., Boyer, M.: Elementary logic programs. In: Deransart, P., Małuszyński, J. (eds.) PLILP 1990. LNCS, vol. 456, pp. 159–173. Springer, Heidelberg (1990). https://doi.org/10.1007/BFb0024183
16. Turner, D.A.: A new implementation technique for applicative languages. Softw.: Pract. Exp. **9**(1), 31–49 (1979)
17. Vandenbroucke, A., Schrijvers, T.: Disjunctive Delimited Control (2020). https://arxiv.org/abs/2009.04909
18. Warren, D.: An abstract Prolog instruction set. Technical Note 309, SRI International, Stanford, Ca (1983)
19. Wielemaker, J., Schrijvers, T., Triska, M., Lager, T.: SWI-prolog. Theory Pract. Log. Program. **12**, 67–96 (2012). https://doi.org/10.1017/S1471068411000494

On Adding Pattern Matching to Haskell-Based Deeply Embedded Domain Specific Languages

David Young[1(✉)], Mark Grebe[2], and Andy Gill[1]

[1] University of Kansas, Lawrence, USA
{d063y800,andygill}@ku.edu
[2] University of Central Missouri, Warrensburg, USA
grebe@ucmo.edu

Abstract. Capturing control flow is the Achilles heel of Haskell-based deeply embedded domain specific languages. Rather than use the builtin control flow mechanisms, artificial control flow combinators are used instead. However, capturing traditional control flow in a deeply embedded domain specific language would support the writing of programs in a natural style by allowing the programmer to use the constructs that are already builtin to the base language, such as pattern matching and recursion. In this paper, we expand the capabilities of Haskell-based deep embeddings with a compiler extension for reifying conditionals and pattern matching. With this new support, the subset of Haskell that we use for expressing deeply embedded domain specific languages can be cleaner, Haskell-idiomatic, and more declarative in nature.

1 Introduction

Embedded domain specific languages (EDSLs) have long been an effective technique for constructing reusable tools for working in a variety of different problem domains. Haskell is a language which is particularly well-suited to EDSLs due to its lazy evaluation, first-class functions and lexical closures. Despite these advantages Haskell provides for creating EDSLs, there are a few constructs for which representations have proven illusive. One prominent example is that of a `case` expression. Pattern matching is a convenient way to implement control flow structures and to inspect data structures, so it is frequently a desirable feature for many EDSLs. Additionally, lambdas can also be difficult to implement in EDSLs. A major reason for this is that control flow constructs which are typically *outside* the EDSL, such as pattern matching and tail recursion, can make it challenging to "look inside" the lambda. When these control structures are reified within the EDSL, it is easier to also reify lambdas using the dummy argument technique described in [10].

© Springer Nature Switzerland AG 2021
J. F. Morales and D. Orchard (Eds.): PADL 2021, LNCS 12548, pp. 20–36, 2021.
https://doi.org/10.1007/978-3-030-67438-0_2

The following contributions are made by this paper:

- A representation of pattern matching in a Haskell EDSL (Sect. 3)
- A representation of lambdas (Sect. 5) in the EDSL, utilizing the fact that both pattern matching and tail recursion are already captured in the EDSL.
- A GHC Core plugin which transforms a subset of standard Haskell code into this EDSL for pattern matching, extended with tail recursion, lambdas and primitive operations (Sect. 7)
- An implementation of an interpreter for a reference semantics of the EDSL (Sect. 6).

Readers who are primarily interested only in the encoding of pattern matching itself can direct most of their attention to Sects. 2, 3 and 6. Most of the technical aspects of the transformation performed by the Core plugin are described in Sect. 7.

1.1 Motivation

A major benefit of the Haskell language is that it is frequently possible to derive a Haskell implementation from a specification, either partially or fully. In [3], a collection of algorithms is presented with implementations derived in this manner. The work in [13] describes many of the mathematical tools underlying such program derivations. Recent examples of this technique include the work in [8], where an implementation of automatic differentiation is derived from a specification of derivatives. Similarly, the work in [9] derives an implementation of a generalized form of convolution from a specification. When it is not possible to fully derive an implementation, it is often easier to check a Haskell implementation against a specification than it is in many imperative languages due, in part, to the management of side effects in Haskell. This is more difficult to do using an imperative language such as C, as they provide no restrictions on where side effects can occur.

Haskell EDSLs that support powerful language features like pattern matching allow these advantages to be brought to problem domains where it is currently either difficult or impossible to use a language that has these benefits. However, there is no support for capturing pattern matching builtin to the Haskell language itself. As a result, EDSLs which capture pattern matching must do so via a plugin in a Haskell compiler such as GHC. For each such EDSL, this mechanism has needed to be reimplemented each time. Additionally, the task of implementing this is difficult and error-prone. In this paper, we describe a *reusable* framework for capturing pattern matching, as well as lambdas and tail recursion.

1.2 Overview

In this EDSL, the type representing values in the expression language is E t and there are two basic functions which translate values to and from this expression language with the following type signatures (omitting type class constraints for the moment):

```
rep :: a -> E a
abs :: E a -> a
```

Additionally, the following functions mark the parts of the code which the Core plugin will target:

```
internalize :: E a -> a
externalize :: a -> E a
```

The E type is the type of expressions in the EDSL. In this paper, the data constructors of this type will be described incrementally as they are needed.

1.3   Translation Example

In the example below, the Core plugin transforms `example` into `example'`. Note that `example'` is an EDSL expression which is then used by the EDSL interpreter function `abs` to produce the final result, `example''`:

```
x :: Either Char Int
x = Left 'a'

example :: E Int
example =
  externalize (case x of Left c -> ord c; Right i -> i)

example' :: E Int
example' = CaseExp (LeftExp (CharLit 'a'))
  (SumMatchExp
    (OneProdMatch (Lam 1 (Ord (Var 1))))
    (OneSumMatch (OneProdMatch (Lam 2 (Var 2)))))

example'' :: Int
example'' = abs example'
```

2   Representing Algebraic Datatypes

Briefly, an algebraic type T with an automatically generated ERep instance is given a representation in terms of Either, (,), () and Void. This "standardized" type representation is given by ERepTy T. ERepTy is a type family associated to the type class ERep. This type will be called the *canonical type* of T.

Only the "outermost" type will be deconstructed into these fundamental building blocks, and further deconstruction can take place on these pieces later on. For example, consider this type:

```
data ComplexPair =
  ComplexPair (Complex Double) (Complex Double)
  deriving (Generic, Show)

instance ERep ComplexPair
```

Note the instance definition is automatically generated from the `Generic` instance.

Given this code, the following type equality holds:

```
ERepTy ComplexPair ~ (Complex Double, Complex Double)
```

Here is an example that demonstrates why this is more useful than if it *fully* deconstructed each type into `Either`, `(,)` and `()`:

```
sumComplexPair :: ComplexPair -> Complex Double
sumComplexPair p =
  internalize (externalize
    (case p of ComplexPair a b -> a + b))
```

If `ERepTy ComplexPair` were fully deconstructed into `((Double, Double), (Double, Double))`, we would need a `Num` instance for `(Double, Double)`. What we really want is to use the fact that a `Num` instance already exists for `Complex Double`. This is exactly what preserving this type information allows us to do. We can later use this preserved type information in backends, through the corresponding `Typeable` instances (for instance, to provide special support for arithmetic on complex numbers).

It is important to note that we are still able to further deconstruct this type with further pattern matches, since `ERepTy (Complex Double) ~ (Double, Double)`:

```
realSum :: ComplexPair -> Double
realSum p =
  internalize (externalize
    (case p of
      ComplexPair a b ->
        case a of
          a_real :+ _ ->
            case b of
              b_real :+ _ ->
                a_real + b_real))
```

The above pattern matches could also be written as a single nested pattern match. Both forms compile down to the same Core representation.

An additional benefit of this is that recursive types require no special handling. For example, consider:

```
data IntList = Nil | Cons Int IntList
  deriving (Generic, Show)

instance ERep IntList
```

Note that `ERepTy IntList ~ Either () (Int, IntList)`. If `ERepTy` attempted to "fully deconstruct" `IntList`, it would send the compiler into an infinite loop.

This allows us to implement functions on such recursive types:

```
isEmpty :: IntList -> Bool
isEmpty t =
  internalize (externalize
    (case t of
       Nil -> True
       Cons x xs -> False))

intListSum :: (Int, IntList) -> Int
intListSum p =
  internalize (externalize
    (case p of (acc, t) -> case t of
       Nil -> acc
       Cons x xs ->
         intListSum
           (x+acc, xs)))
```

2.1   The Three Major Type-Level Pieces

There are three interconnected foundational parts: E, ERep and ERepTy. E is the deep embedding of the EDSL (a GADT [24] that encodes expressions in the DSL language). ERep is a type class which represents all Haskell types which can be represented in the DSL. ERepTy is a type family associated to the ERep type class, which represents a "canonical form" of the given type. This canonical form can be immediately constructed in the EDSL. Canonical form types crucially include Either and (,), which allow all combinations of basic sum types and product types to be encoded, in the manner described at the beginning of Sect. 2.

With GHC Generics, any data type T with a Generic instance has a corresponding Rep T type, which gives a generic representation of T. Conversion between values of this type and values of the original type T is given by the functions to and from. The generic representation Rep T can be traversed by functions which operate solely on the structure of the data type. This generic representation contains additional metadata which we do not need. However, we can automatically generate a ERep instance for any type which has a Generic instance.

As Generic instances are automatically generated, this provides a simple mechanism to automatically generate ERep instances.

This information is brought into the E type via the constructor ConstructRep. The E also contains constructors representing Either and (,) values:

```
data E t where
  ...
  ConstructRep :: (Typeable a, ERep a) =>
    E (ERepTy a) -> E a
  LeftExp :: E a -> E (Either a b)
  RightExp :: E b -> E (Either a b)
```

```
PairExp :: E a -> E b -> E (a, b)
...
```

ERep and ERepTy provide an interface for transferring values between the EDSL expression language and the source Haskell language:

```
class Typeable t => ERep t where
  type ERepTy t
  construct :: t -> E (ERepTy t)
  rep :: t -> E t
  default rep :: (ERep (ERepTy t)) => t -> E t
  rep x = ConstructRep (construct x)
  unrep' :: ERepTy t -> t
  rep' :: t -> ERepTy t
```

The key algebraic instances mentioned before are as follows:

```
instance (ERep a, ERep b) => ERep (Either a b) where
  type ERepTy (Either a b) = Either a b
  construct (Left x)  = LeftExp (rep x)
  construct (Right y) = RightExp (rep y)
  rep (Left x)  = LeftExp (rep x)
  rep (Right y) = RightExp (rep y)
  unrep' = id
  rep'   = id

instance (ERep a, ERep b) => ERep (a, b) where
  type ERepTy (a, b) = (a, b)
  construct (x, y) = PairExp (rep x) (rep y)
  rep (x, y) = PairExp (rep x) (rep y)
  unrep' = id
  rep'   = id
```

3 Representing Pattern Matching

Within the E expression language, a pattern match is represented by the CaseExp constructor:

```
data E t where
  ...
  CaseExp :: (ERep t, ERepTy (ERepTy t) ~ ERepTy t) =>
    E t -> E (SumMatch (ERepTy t) r) -> E r
  ...
```

The equality constraint ($\sim$) ensures that a canonical type is its own canonical type.

The above code block is a slight simplification of the actual implementation, which has an additional type variable which is used at an "intermediate" point. The expanded form is in place to simplify the Core transformation.

The type `SumMatch` is defined as

```
newtype SumMatch a b =
  MkSumMatch { runSumMatch :: a -> b }
```

For the moment, we will primarily use this type as a type tag and ignore the values it can take on.

A value of type `E (SumMatch a b)` represents a computation within the EDSL which destructures a value of type `E a` and produces a value of type `E b`. Therefore, `E (SumMatch (ERepTy t) r)` represents a computation which destructures a value of type `E (ERepTy t)` and produces a value of type `E r`.

3.1 Lists of Branches

The overall structure of a `E (SumMatch a b)` value is a (heterogeneous) list of `E (ProdMatch x b)` values. Each item of this list corresponds exactly to one branch in the original `case` match.

The following constructors generate `SumMatch`-tagged values in the expression language:

```
data E t where
  . . .
  SumMatchExp :: (ERep a, ERep b, ERepTy b ~ b) =>
    E (ProdMatch a r) -> E (SumMatch b r)
      -> E (SumMatch (Either a b) r)

  OneSumMatch ::
    (ERep a, ERep b, ERepTy a ~ a) =>
      E (ProdMatch a b) -> E (SumMatch a b)
  EmptyMatch :: (ERep b) => E (SumMatch Void b)
```

Note the `ERepTy a ~ a` constraints. This constraint ensures that the type `a` is already in canonical form (that is, consists entirely of `Either`, `(,)` and base types).

3.2 Product Matches

`E (ProdMatch s t)` is equivalent to a function from `s` to `t` in the expression language where `s` is a (potentially nested) pair type. For example, `E (ProdMatch (a, (b, c)) r)` is equivalent to `E (a -> E (b -> E (c -> E r)))`.

```
data E t where
  . . .
  ProdMatchExp :: (ERep a, ERep b) =>
    E (a -> ProdMatch b r) -> E (ProdMatch (a, b) r)

  NullaryMatch :: (ERep a) =>
    E r -> E (ProdMatch a r)
```

```
OneProdMatch :: (ERep a) =>
  E (a -> b) -> E (ProdMatch a b)
...
```

The `ProdMatch` type is defined similarly to the `SumMatch` type and is similarly used primarily as a type tag:

```
newtype ProdMatch a b =
  MkProdMatch { runProdMatch :: a -> b }
```

3.3 An Aside on `ProdMatch` and `SumMatch` values

Though `ProdMatch` and `SumMatch` are used throughout this EDSL as type tags, they do have values and they are not trivial values. The reason for this is that it connects the encoded pattern matches (values from the `E`) type to their semantics. A value of type `E (SumMatch a b)` is an expression which takes in a value of type `a` (embedded within the expression language), internally performs some pattern matching, and produces a value of type `b` (again, embedded within the expression language). This is exactly the semantics of a function from `a` to `b`. Likewise for `ProdMatch a b`.

Recall the previously mentioned function

```
abs :: E a -> a
```

Now consider at the type of `abs` when it is specialized to take `E (SumMatch a b)` values:
If we postcompose with `runSumMatch`, we get:

```
runSumMatch . abs    :: E (SumMatch a b) -> (a -> b)
```

The `SumMatch a b` value which `abs` returns is exactly the function which pattern matches according to its input value. Likewise for `ProdMatch a b` values.

4 Representing Tail Recursion

Tail recursion is given a direct-style representation using a simple sum type, using the technique described in [16].

Consider a tail recursive function of the type `f :: a -> b`. Each recursive call can be seen as a simple "update" of the values of the arguments, since these calls are all in tail position. This is why tail recursive functions can be easily compiled to simple loops or conditional jumps.

We can take advantage of this view by transforming a tail recursive function `f :: a -> b` into a function `f' :: a -> Iter b a`. `Iter b a` is a type which can either correspond to an argument "update" (in the sense mentioned previously) or a final result. This type is implemented as a sum of the types `a` and `b`. Recursive calls are transformed to `Step` applications and non-recursive branches are wrapped in `Done` applications.

```
data Iter a b = Step b | Done a
  deriving (Functor, Generic)
```

To use the new f' function, we repeatedly call it until it gives a **Done** value. If it gives a **Step** value, we pass the value wrapped in the **Step** back into f' and continue.

The function runIter provides the reference semantics for executing such a function representing a tail recursive function:

```
runIter :: (ERep a, ERep b)
  => (a -> Iter b a) -> (a -> b)
runIter f = go
  where go x = case f x of
          Done r  -> r
          Step x' -> go x'
```

This technique can be contrasted with the more traditional trampolining technique for implementing tail recursion. Conventional trampolining uses a sum type of the result type and a thunk with the code necessary to continue execution. [12]

In the technique presented here, we do not need to allocate thunks or closures. We do not need to use higher-order functions for this representation, other than runIter itself.

In the **E** type of our DSL, this form of tail recursion representation is given a deep embedding by the following constructors:

```
data E t where
  . . .
  StepExp :: E b -> E (Iter a b)
  DoneExp :: E a -> E (Iter a b)
  TailRec :: (ERep a, ERep b) =>
    E (b -> Iter a b) -> E (b -> a)
  . . .
```

The process of transforming a tail recursive function in the DSL to a representation which could be passed into a backend and used to generate a traditional iterative loop goes as follows.

Starting with the tail recursive function isEven:

```
isEven :: Int -> Bool
isEven x =
  internalize (externalize (
    case x == 0 of
      True -> True
      False ->
        case x == 1 of
          True -> False
          False -> isEven (x - 2)))
```

We first transform this to use the `Iter` type. The lambda is brought inside of the `internalize (externalize ...)` call and wrapped in a call to `runIter`. This inner expression is then eta expanded. Finally, each `case` branch which does not contain a recursive call is wrapped in a `Done` and every recursive call is transformed into an application of the `Step` constructor.

In the following code, `eta` is a fresh variable.

```
isEven' :: Int -> Bool
isEven' =
  internalize (externalize
    (\ eta ->
      runIter (\ x -> case x == 0 of
                      True -> Done True
                      False -> case x == 1 of
                               True -> Done False
                               False -> Step (x - 2))
            eta))
```

After this initial tail recursion transformation, the rest of the plugin brings this result into the expression language. `TailRec` is substituted for `runIter`, `DoneExp` is substituted for `Done` and `StepExp` is substituted for `Step`. Next, the pattern matching transformation occurs, producing the final result:

```
isEven'' :: Int -> Bool
isEven'' =
  internalize (
    (Lam (Var 1)
      (App (TailRec (Lam (Var 2)
            (IfThenElseExp (Equal (Var 2) (rep 0))
              (DoneExp TrueExp)
              (IfThenElseExp (Equal (Var 1) (rep 1))
                (DoneExp FalseExp)
                (StepExp (Sub (Var 2) (rep 2)))))))
          (Var 1))))
```

5 Representing Lambdas

This representation of pattern matching depends on the ability to bring function values into the expression language. This is accomplished with the following constructors:

```
data E t where
  ...
  Lam :: (ERep a, Typeable a) =>
    Name a -> E b -> E (a -> b)
  Var :: (Typeable a) => Name a -> E a
```

The `Typeable` constraints are necessary to lookup correctly typed values in the variable binding environment later on.

The `Name t` type represents a lambda variable identifier together with its type t (Note that the `ScopedTypeVariables` extension is enabled):

```
newtype Name a = Name Int deriving (Eq, Show)

namesEq :: forall a b.  (Typeable a, Typeable b) =>
  Name a -> Name b -> Maybe (a :~: b)
namesEq (Name n) (Name n') =
  case eqT :: Maybe (a :~: b) of
    Just Refl
      | n == n' -> Just Refl
    _           -> Nothing
```

In the Core transformation, each lambda is given a `Name` with a globally unique `Int`, sidestepping any name capture issues.

The following datatypes are used to represent a variable binding environment of typed names to expression language values:

```
data EnvMapping where
  (:=>) :: forall a. Typeable a =>
    Name a -> E a -> EnvMapping
```

This type encodes a single variable binding, with values of the form `n :=> v`, where n is a typed name and v is the value it is bound to.

These bindings are grouped together in the `Env` type:

```
newtype Env = Env [EnvMapping]

emptyEnv :: Env
emptyEnv = Env []

extendEnv :: Env -> EnvMapping -> Env
extendEnv (Env maps) m = Env (m:maps)

envLookup :: Typeable a => Env -> Name a -> Maybe (E a)
envLookup (Env maps) = go maps
  where go []                 = Nothing
        go ((n' :=> e):rest) =
          case namesEq n n' of
            Just Refl -> Just e
            Nothing   -> go rest
```

6   Recovering Reference Semantics for Pattern Matches

The reference semantics for the EDSL is given by `abs`. Two helper functions, `sumMatchAbs` and `prodMatchAbs`, are used to provide the reference semantics for matches on sum types and matches on product types, respectively. These helper functions are based on the mechanism described in Sect. 3.3.

```
abs :: forall t. E t -> t
abs = absEnv emptyEnv

sumMatchAbs :: (ERepTy (ERepTy s) ~ ERepTy s, ERep s)
  => Env -> E (SumMatch (ERepTy s) t) -> s -> t
...
prodMatchAbs :: (ERep s) =>
  Env -> E (ProdMatch s t) -> s -> t
...
```

Recall that the internal representations of SumMatch a b and ProdMatch a b are functions of type a -> b. These types are unwrapped by the functions

```
runSumMatch :: SumMatch a b -> (a -> b)
runProdMatch :: ProdMatch a b -> (a -> b)
```

Given this, the ProdMatchExp case of the prodMatchAbs function can be implemented as follows:

```
prodMatchAbs env (ProdMatchExp f) = \ pair ->
  case pair of (x, y) ->
    runProdMatch (absEnv env f x) y
```

7   Core Plugin

The Core plugin translates marked expressions. Expressions are marked by the externalize function:

```
externalize :: a -> E a
```

For example, externalize x marks the expression x. If an expression already has an EDSL type (a type of the form E a for some a), then the marking procedure ignores it and does not wrap it with externalize (see M in Fig. 2).

These externalize marks are pushed through the input program, starting at the outermost level. The plugin repeatedly runs over each newly marked node in the abstract syntax tree, applying the appropriate rewrite rules as it goes. This process pushes the marks through the program until it reaches a base case that has no proper subexpressions, such as a character literal.

The plugin's control flow is described in Fig. 1. When control flow reaches a node, the rewrite rules listed in parentheses are performed. These rewrite rule names correspond to the rules given in Fig. 2. In Fig. 2, ε represents an empty term (in the context of the term rewriting system used in that Figure). Calls to unrep :: E a -> a are only used internally and will not exist in the final result of the transformation.

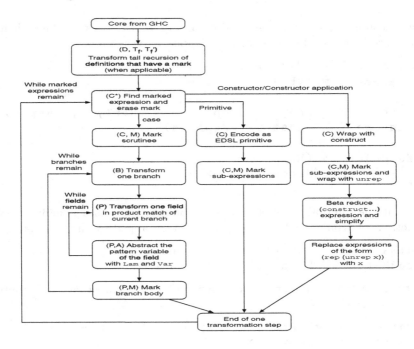

Fig. 1. Control flow of the core plugin

Note that:

- The tail recursion transformation given by D, T_f' and T_f is completely independent of the E type and the transformations associated to the E type. As a result, the tail recursion transformation can be used on its own.
- The total number of marks introduced is upper bounded by the number of subexpressions in the original Core given to the transformation by GHC and each full transformation step (that is, C) eliminates one mark. Therefore, the transformation will terminate.

8   Related Work

The basis of deep embeddings in functional languages is well understood. [10] explains the basic idea, and [14] gives an accessible and more recent account of the area.

A similar EDSL-oriented representation of pattern matching is given in [1, Section 3.3]. In that paper, patterns were given their own representation which allows for compound patterns. This is useful in the context of that work, as the programmer works directly with these patterns.

In the present paper, however, the representation is generated automatically by a compiler plugin. As a result of GHC's desugared Core (which does not have

$D(\texttt{f x = internalize (externalize (case s of \{ ... \})))}$
$\quad \Longrightarrow I(D(\texttt{f x = externalize (case s of \{ ... \})}))$

$D(\texttt{f x = externalize (case s of \{ ... \})})$

$$\Longrightarrow \begin{cases} \texttt{f} = C^*(\texttt{externalize} (\lambda\eta \rightarrow \texttt{runIter} (\lambda\texttt{x} \rightarrow \texttt{case s of \{} T'_t(...) \texttt{ \}}) \eta)) & \text{if } \texttt{f} \text{ occurs free in} \\ & \texttt{\{ ... \}}, \text{where } \eta \\ & \text{is a fresh name} \\ \\ \texttt{f x} = C^*(\texttt{externalize (case s of \{ ... \})}) & \text{otherwise} \end{cases}$$

$I(\texttt{f x = externalize e}) \Longrightarrow \texttt{f x = internalize (externalize e)}$
$I(\texttt{f = externalize e}) \Longrightarrow \texttt{f = internalize (externalize e)}$

$T'_t(\texttt{K x0 ...}_U \texttt{ xN} \rightarrow \texttt{case s of \{ ...}_V \texttt{ \}; ...}_W \texttt{)}$
$\quad \Longrightarrow \texttt{K x0 ...}_U \texttt{ xN} \rightarrow T_t(\texttt{case s of \{ ...}_V \texttt{ \}); } T'_t(\texttt{ ...}_W \texttt{)}$

$T'_t(\texttt{K x0 ...}_U \texttt{ xN} \rightarrow \texttt{body0; ...}_V \texttt{)}$

$$\Longrightarrow \begin{cases} \texttt{K x0 ...}_U \texttt{ xN} \rightarrow \texttt{body0[f} \mapsto \texttt{Step]; } T'_t(\texttt{ ...}_V \texttt{)} & \text{if } \texttt{f} \text{ occurs free in body0} \\ \texttt{K x0 ...}_U \texttt{ xN} \rightarrow \texttt{Done body0; } T'_t(\texttt{ ...}_V \texttt{)} & \text{otherwise} \end{cases}$$

$T'_t(\varepsilon) \Longrightarrow \varepsilon$

$T_t(\texttt{case s of \{ ... \})}$

$$\Longrightarrow \begin{cases} \texttt{case s of \{ } T'_t(\texttt{ ... }) \texttt{ \}} & \text{if } \texttt{f} \text{ occurs free in \{ ... \}} \\ \texttt{Done (case s of \{ ... \})} & \text{otherwise} \end{cases}$$

$$C^*(\texttt{x}) \Longrightarrow \begin{cases} \texttt{x} & \text{if } \texttt{x} \text{ has no subexpressions marked with } \texttt{externalize} \\ C^*(C(\texttt{y})) & \text{if } \texttt{externalize y} \text{ is the first marked subexpression of } \texttt{x} \end{cases}$$

$C(\texttt{runIter f x}) \Longrightarrow \texttt{App (TailRec } M(\texttt{f})) \ M(\texttt{x})$
$C(\texttt{x + y}) \Longrightarrow \texttt{Add } M(\texttt{x}) \ M(\texttt{y})$
$C(\texttt{case scrutinee of \{ ... \}}) \Longrightarrow \texttt{CaseExp } M(\texttt{scrutinee}) \ B(\texttt{ ... })$
$C(\lambda\texttt{x} \rightarrow \texttt{body}) \Longrightarrow A(\lambda\texttt{x} \rightarrow \texttt{body})$
$C(\texttt{K x0 ... xN)}$
$\quad \Longrightarrow \texttt{construct (K (unrep } M(\texttt{x0})) \ ... \ (\texttt{unrep } M(\texttt{xN})))$ (Where K is a constructor)
$C(\texttt{f x}) \Longrightarrow \texttt{App } M(\texttt{f}) \ M(\texttt{x})$
$B(\texttt{K x0 ...}_U \texttt{ xN} \rightarrow \texttt{body0; ...}_V) \Longrightarrow \texttt{SumMatchExp } P(\texttt{x0 ...}_U \texttt{ xN} \rightarrow \texttt{body0}) \ B(\texttt{ ...}_V \texttt{)}$
$B(\texttt{K x0 ... xN} \rightarrow \texttt{body}) \Longrightarrow \texttt{OneSumMatchExp } P(\texttt{x0 ... xN} \rightarrow \texttt{body})$
$B(\varepsilon) \Longrightarrow \texttt{EmptyMatch}$
$P(\texttt{x0 x1 ... xN} \rightarrow \texttt{body}) \Longrightarrow \texttt{ProdMatchExp } A(\lambda \texttt{ x0} \rightarrow P(\texttt{x1 ... xN} \rightarrow \texttt{body}))$
$P(\texttt{x} \rightarrow \texttt{body}) \Longrightarrow \texttt{OneProdMatchExp } A(\lambda \texttt{ x} \rightarrow \texttt{body})$
$P(\rightarrow \texttt{body}) \Longrightarrow \texttt{NullaryMatch } M(\texttt{body})$
$A(\lambda(\texttt{x :: a}) \rightarrow \texttt{body}) \Longrightarrow \texttt{Lam (Name @a uniq) } M(\texttt{body[x} \mapsto \texttt{unrep (Var @a uniq)]})$
$\quad$ (where uniq is a globally unique identifier)
$M(\texttt{unrep x}) \Longrightarrow \texttt{x}$

$$M(\texttt{x :: a}) \Longrightarrow \begin{cases} \texttt{externalize x} & \text{if } \nexists t, a \sim E \ t \\ \texttt{x} & \text{if } \exists t, a \sim E \ t \end{cases}$$

Fig. 2. Rewrite rules

compound patterns), there is no need to directly express compound patterns at the representation-level.

There is other recent work using deep embeddings in functional languages for system development. One example is the Ivory language [11] which provides a deeply embedded DSL for use in programming high assurance systems, However, its syntax is typical of a deep EDSL and requires additional keywords and structures above idiomatic Haskell.

The Feldspar project [2,22] is a Haskell embedding of a monadic interface that targets C, and focuses on high-performance. Both Feldspar and our work mix deep and shallow language constructs [18,19,23].

Svenningsson and Axelsson [22] explored combining deep and shallow embedding. They used a deep embedding as a low level language, then extended the deep embedding with a shallow embedding written on top of it. Haskell type classes were used to minimize the effort of adding new features to the language.

Yin-Yang [17] provides a framework for DSL embedding in Scala which uses Scala macros to provide the translation from a shallow to deep embedding. Yin-Yang goes beyond the translation by also providing autogeneration of the deep DSL from the shallow DSL. The focus of Yin-Yang is in generalizing the shallow to deep transformations, and does not include recursive transformations.

Forge [21] is a Scala based meta-EDSL framework which can generate both shallow and deep embeddings from a single EDSL specification. Embeddings generated by Forge use abstract `Rep` types, analogous to our EDSL's `E` types. Their shallow embedding is generated as a pure Scala library, while the deeply embedded version is generated as an EDSL using the Delite [20] framework.

Elliott developed GHC plugins [4,6] for compiling Haskell to hardware [5], using worker-wrapper style transformations [15] equivalent to the `abs` and `rep` transformations described in Sect. 1.2. These plugins were later generalized to enable additional interpretations [7].

9   Conclusion

In this paper, a representation of pattern matching was given in the form of a GADT called `E`. A GHC plugin is then used to transform code written in a subset of Haskell consisting of algebraic data types, pattern matching, tail recursion and lambdas into values of this GADT. A backend can then use these `E a` values to interpret the Haskell code, compile it or otherwise manipulate it.

Additionally, a uniform representation of algebraic data types in terms of (,), `Either` and (), called `ERepTy`, was outlined for use in the previously mentioned pattern matching representation. This representation of ADTs is determined entirely by the structure of a type, allowing the pattern matching mechanism to act on the structure of values.

References

1. Atkey, R., Lindley, S., Yallop, J.: Unembedding domain-specific languages. In: Proceedings of the 2nd ACM SIGPLAN Symposium on Haskell, Haskell 2009, pp. 37–48. Association for Computing Machinery, New York (2009). https://doi.org/10.1145/1596638.1596644

2. Axelsson, E., et al.: Feldspar: a domain specific language for digital signal processing algorithms. In: MEMOCODE 2010, pp. 169–178 (2010)
3. Bird, R.: Pearls of Functional Algorithm Design. Cambridge University Press, Cambridge (2010). https://doi.org/10.1017/CBO9780511763199
4. Elliott, C.: (2015). https://github.com/conal/lambda-ccc
5. Elliott, C.: (2015). https://github.com/conal/talk-2015-haskell-to-hardware
6. Elliott, C.: (2016). https://github.com/conal/reification-rules
7. Elliott, C.: Compiling to categories. Proc. ACM Program. Lang. 1(ICFP) (2017). https://doi.org/10.1145/3110271. http://conal.net/papers/compiling-to-categories
8. Elliott, C.: The simple essence of automatic differentiation. In: Proceedings of the ACM on Programming Languages (ICFP) (2018). http://conal.net/papers/essence-of-ad/
9. Elliott, C.: Generalized convolution and efficient language recognition (extended version). CoRR abs/1903.10677 (2019). https://arxiv.org/abs/1903.10677
10. Elliott, C., Finne, S., de Moor, O.: Compiling embedded languages. J. Funct. Program. 13(2) (2003). http://conal.net/papers/jfp-saig/. updated version of paper by the same name that appeared in SAIG '00 proceedings
11. Elliott, T., et al.: Guilt free ivory. In: Proceedings of the 8th ACM SIGPLAN Symposium on Haskell, pp. 189–200. ACM (2015)
12. Ganz, S.E., Friedman, D.P., Wand, M.: Trampolined style. In: Proceedings of the Fourth ACM SIGPLAN International Conference on Functional Programming, ICFP 1999, pp. 18–27. Association for Computing Machinery, New York (1999). https://doi.org/10.1145/317636.317779
13. Gibbons, J.: Calculating functional programs. In: Backhouse, R., Crole, R., Gibbons, J. (eds.) Algebraic and Coalgebraic Methods in the Mathematics of Program Construction. LNCS, vol. 2297, pp. 151–203. Springer, Heidelberg (2002). https://doi.org/10.1007/3-540-47797-7_5
14. Gill, A.: Domain-specific languages and code synthesis using Haskell. Commun. ACM 57(6), 42–49 (2014). https://doi.org/10.1145/2605205
15. Gill, A., Hutton, G.: The worker/wrapper transformation. J. Funct. Program. 19(2), 227–251 (2009)
16. Grebe, M., Young, D., Gill, A.: Rewriting a shallow DSL using a GHC compiler extension. In: Proceedings of the 16th ACM SIGPLAN International Conference on Generative Programming: Concepts and Experiences, GPCE 2017, pp. 246–258. ACM, New York (2017). https://doi.org/10.1145/3136040.3136048
17. Jovanovic, V., Shaikhha, A., Stucki, S., Nikolaev, V., Koch, C., Odersky, M.: Yin-yang: Concealing the deep embedding of DSLs. In: Proceedings of the 2014 International Conference on Generative Programming: Concepts and Experiences, GPCE 2014, pp. 73–82. Association for Computing Machinery, New York (2014). https://doi.org/10.1145/2658761.2658771
18. Persson, A., Axelsson, E., Svenningsson, J.: Generic monadic constructs for embedded languages. In: Gill, A., Hage, J. (eds.) IFL 2011. LNCS, vol. 7257, pp. 85–99. Springer, Heidelberg (2012). https://doi.org/10.1007/978-3-642-34407-7_6
19. Sculthorpe, N., Bracker, J., Giorgidze, G., Gill, A.: The constrained-monad problem. In: Proceedings of the 18th ACM SIGPLAN International Conference on Functional Programming, pp. 287–298. ACM (2013). http://dl.acm.org/citation.cfm?doid=2500365.2500602
20. Sujeeth, A.K., et al.: Delite: a compiler architecture for performance-oriented embedded domain-specific languages. ACM Trans. Embedd. Comput. Syst. (TECS) 13(4s), 1–25 (2014)

21. Sujeeth, A.K., et al.: Forge: generating a high performance DSL implementation from a declarative specification. In: Proceedings of the 12th International Conference on Generative Programming: Concepts and Experiences, GPCE 2013, pp. 145–154. ACM, New York (2013). https://doi.org/10.1145/2517208.2517220
22. Svenningsson, J., Axelsson, E.: Combining deep and shallow embedding for EDSL. In: Loidl, H.-W., Peña, R. (eds.) TFP 2012. LNCS, vol. 7829, pp. 21–36. Springer, Heidelberg (2013). https://doi.org/10.1007/978-3-642-40447-4_2
23. Svenningsson, J.D., Svensson, B.J.: Simple and compositional reification of monadic embedded languages. In: Proceedings of the 18th International Conference on Functional Programming, pp. 299–304. ACM (2013)
24. Vytiniotis, D., Weirich, S., Peyton Jones, S.: Simple unification-based type inference for GADTs. In: International Conference on Functional Programming (ICFP 2006). ACM SIGPLAN (2006). https://www.microsoft.com/en-us/research/publication/simple-unification-based-type-inference-for-gadts/. 2016 ACM SIGPLAN Most Influential ICFP Paper Award

Synchronous Message-Passing
with Priority

Cheng-En Chuang$^{(\boxtimes)}$, Grant Iraci, and Lukasz Ziarek

University at Buffalo, Buffalo, NY 14260, USA
{chengenc,grantira,lziarek}@buffalo.edu

Abstract. In this paper we introduce a tiered-priority mechanism for
a synchronous message-passing language with support for selective communication and first-class communication protocols. Crucially our mechanism allows higher priority threads to communicate with lower priority threads, providing the ability to express programs that would be
rejected by classic priority mechanisms that disallow any (potentially)
blocking interactions between threads of differing priorities. We provide
a prototype implementation of our tiered-priority mechanism capable of
expressing Concurrent ML and built in the MLton SML compiler and
runtime. We evaluate the viability of our implementation by implementing a safe and predictable shutdown mechanisms in the Swerve webserver
and eXene windowing toolkit. Our experiments show that priority can be
easily added to existing CML programs without degrading performance.
Our system exhibits negligible overheads on more modest workloads.

Keywords: Priority · Synchronous message passing · Concurrent ML

1 Introduction

Message-passing is a common communication model for developing concurrent
and distributed systems where concurrent computations communicate through
the passing of messages via *send* and *recv* operations. With growing demand
for robust concurrent programming support at the language level, many programming languages or frameworks, including Scala [12], Erlang [13], Go [11],
Rust [14], Racket [1], Android [2], and Concurrent ML [19] have adopted this
model, providing support for writing expressive (sometimes first-class) communication protocols.

In many applications, the desire to express priority over communication
arises. The traditional approach to this is to give priority to threads [17]. In
a *shared memory* model, where concurrent access is regulated by locks, this
approach works well. The trivial application of priority to *message passing* languages, however, fails when messages are not just simple primitive types but
communication protocols themselves (i.e. first-class representations of communication primitives and combinators). These first-class entities allow threads to
perform communication protocols on behalf of their communication partners –

© Springer Nature Switzerland AG 2021
J. F. Morales and D. Orchard (Eds.): PADL 2021, LNCS 12548, pp. 37–53, 2021.
https://doi.org/10.1007/978-3-030-67438-0_3

a common paradigm in Android applications. For example, consider a thread receiving a message carrying a protocol from another thread. It is unclear with what priority that passed protocol should be executed - should it be the priority of the sending thread, the priority of receiving thread, or a user specified priority?

In *message-passing* models such as Concurrent ML (CML), threads communicate synchronously through protocols constructed from send and receive primitives and combinators. In CML synchronizing on the communication protocol triggers the execution of the protocol. Importantly, CML provides *selective communication*, allowing for computations to pick non-deterministically between a set of available messages or block until a message arrives. As a result of non-deterministic selection, the programmer is unable to impose preference over communications. If the programmer wants to encode preference, more complicated protocols must be introduced. Whereas adding priority to selective communication gives the programmer to ability to specify the order in which messages should be picked.

Adding priority to such a model is challenging. Consider a *selective communication*, where multiple potential messages are available and one must be chosen. If the *selective communication* only looks at messages and not their blocked senders, a choosing thread may inadvertently pick a low priority thread to communicate with, when there is a thread with higher priority waiting to be unblocked. Such a situation would lead to priority inversion. Since these communication primitives must therefore be priority-aware, a need arises for clear rules about how priorities should compose and be compared. Such rules should not put undue burden on the programmer or complicate the expression of already complex communication protocols.

In this paper, we propose a *tiered-priority scheme* that defines prioritized messages as first-class citizens in a CML-like *message-passing* language. Our scheme introduces the core computation within a message, an *action*, as the prioritized entity. We provide a concrete realization of our priority scheme called *PrioCML*, as a modification to Concurrent ML. To demonstrate the practicality of *PrioCML*, we evaluate its performance by extending an existing web server and X-windowing toolkit. The main contributions of this paper are:

1. We define a meaning of priority in a *message-passing* model with a *tiered-priority scheme*. To our knowledge, this is the first definition of priority in a *message-passing* context. Crucially we allow the ability for threads of differing priorities to communicate and provide the ability to prioritize first-class communication protocols.
2. We present a new language *PrioCML*, which provides this *tiered-priority scheme*. *PrioCML* can express the semantics of polling, which cannot be modeled correctly in CML due to non-deterministic communication.
3. We implement the language *PrioCML* and evaluate on the Swerve web server and the eXene windowing toolkit.

2   Background

We realize our priority-scheme in the context of Concurrent ML (CML), a language extension of Standard ML [16]. CML enables programmers to express first-class synchronous message-passing protocols with the primitives shown in Fig. 1. The core building blocks of protocols in CML are events and event combinators. The two base events are sendEvt and recvEvt. Both are defined over a channel, a conduit through which a message can be passed. Here sendEvt specifies putting a value into the channel, and recvEvt specifies extracting a value from the channel. It is important to note both sendEvt and recvEvt are first-class protocols, and do not perform their specified *actions* until synchronized on using the sync primitive. Thus the meaning of sending or receiving a value is the composition of synchronization and an event – sync (sendEvt(c, v)) will place the value v on channel c and, sync (recvEvt(c)) will remove a value v from channel c. In CML, both sending and receiving are synchronous, and therefore the execution of the protocol will block unless there is a matching action.

```
sendEvt:'a chan * 'a -> unit event   guard:(unit -> 'a event) -> 'a event
recvEvt:'a chan -> 'a event          wrap:'a event * ('a -> 'b) -> 'b event
sync   :'a event -> 'a               choose:'a event list -> 'a event
```

Fig. 1. CML Primitives

The expressive power of CML is derived from the ability to compose events using event combinators to construct first-class communication protocols. We consider three such event combinators: wrap, guard, and choose. The wrap combinator takes an event e1 and a post-synchronization function f and creates a new event e2. When the event e2 is synchronized on, the actions specified in the original event e1 are executed, then the function f is applied to the result. Thus the result of synchronizing on the event e2 is the result of the function f. Much like wrap provides the ability to specify post-synchronization actions, guard provides the ability to specify pre-synchronization actions.

To allow the expression of complex communication protocols, CML supports selective communication. The event combinator choose takes a list of events and picks an event from this list to be synchronized on. For example sync (choose([recvEvt(c1), sendEvt(c2, v2)])) will pick between recvEvt(c1) and sendEvt(c2, v2) and based on which event is chosen, will execute the action specified by that event. The semantics of choice depends on whether any of the events in the input event list have a matching communication partner available. Simply put, choose picks an available event if only one is available, or nondeterministically picks an event from the subset of available events out of the input list. For example, if some other thread in our system performed sync (sendEvt(c1, v1)), then choose will pick recvEvt(c1). However, if a third thread has executed `recvEvt(c2)`, then `choose` will pick nondeterministically between `recvEvt(c1)` and `sendEvt(c2, v2)`.

3 Motivation

To illustrate the desire for priority in communication, consider a server written in CML. For such a server, it is important to handle external events gracefully and without causing errors for clients. One such external event is a shutdown request. We want the server to terminate, but only once it has reached a consistent state and without prematurely breaking connections to clients. Conceptually, each component needs to be notified of the shutdown request and act accordingly.

Leveraging the first-class events of CML, we can elegantly accomplish this. If a server is encoded to accept new work via communication in its main processing loop, we can add in shutdown behavior by using selective communication. Specifically, we can pick between a shutdown notification and accepting new work. The component can either continue or begin the termination process. However, by introducing selective communication, we also introduce non-determinism into our system. The consequence is we have no guarantee that the server will process the shutdown event if it consistently has the option to accept new work. The solution is to constrain the non-deterministic behavior through the introduction of priority. If we attach a higher priority to the shutdown event, we express our desire that given the option between accepting new work and termination, we would prefer termination. Here priority allows the programmer to express intent and guide the resolution of the non-deterministic behavior.

Where to added priority in the language, however, is not immediately clear. In a message-passing system, we have two entities to consider: computations, as represented by threads, and communications as represented by first-class events. In our shutdown example, the prioritized element is a communication, not a computation. If we directly applied a thread-based model of priority to the system, the priority of that communication would be tied to the thread that created it. We could isolate a communication into a dedicated thread to separate its priority. While simple, this approach has a few major disadvantages. It requires an extra thread to be spawned and scheduled. This approach also is not easily composed, with a change of priority requiring the spawning of yet another thread. A bigger issue is that the introduction of the new thread breaks the synchronous behavior that the CML communication primitives provide. When communication is the only method ordering computations between threads, this is a major limitation on what can be expressed.

Instead, consider what happens if we attach priority directly to communication. In the case of CML, since communications are first-class entities, this would mean prioritizing events. By giving a higher priority to the shutdown event (or a user interaction event), the programmer can express the intent for those to be handled as soon as is possible. If the time between communications is bounded, this provides a guarantee of responsiveness to the application. As soon as we hit the communication point, any available shutdown messages will be processed, even if new computations are available.

While event priority allows us to express communication priority, we still desire a way to express the priority of the computations. In the case of our server, we may want to give a higher priority to the act of serving clients over background tasks like logging. The issue here is not driven by communications between threads but rather competing for computation. As such, we arrive at a system with both event and thread priority.

In a system with message passing, however, this gives rise to priority inversion caused by communication. This happens when communication patterns result in a low priority thread getting scheduled in place of a high priority thread due to a communication choosing the low priority thread over the high priority one. We have no guarantee that the communication priorities agree with the thread priorities. To see this effect, consider the CML program shown in Fig. 2.

T_H : High Priority Thread
T_M : Medium Priority Thread
T_L : Low Priority Thread

```
[T_H] sync (sendEvt (c1, v1))
[T_M] sync (sendEvt (c2, v2))
[T_L] sync (choose [
        recvEvt (c1, LOW),
        recvEvt (c2, HIGH)
      ])
```

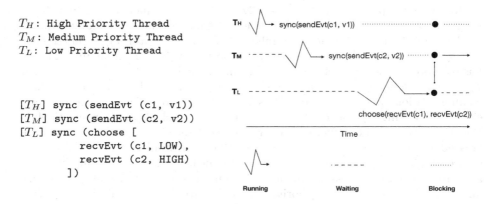

Fig. 2. Priority Inversion by Choice

The programmer is free to specify event priorities that contradict the priorities of threads. Therefore, to avoid priority inversion, we must make **choose** aware of thread priority. A naive approach is to force the thread priority onto events. That is, an event would have the priority equal to that of the thread that created it. At first glance, it seems to solve the problem that shows up in the example above. The choice in T_L now can pick **recvEvt c1** as the matching **sendEvt (c1, v1)** comes from T_H. This approach effectively eliminates event priorities, reviving all of the above issues with a purely thread-based model.

The solution is to combine the priorities of the thread and the event. In order to avoid priority inversion, the thread priority must take precedence. This resolves the problem illustrated in Fig. 2. To resolve choices between threads of the same priority, we allow the programmer to specify an event priority. This priority is considered after the priority of all threads involved. This allows the message in our shutdown example to properly take precedence over other messages from high priority threads.

This scheme is nearly complete but is complicated by CML's exposure to events as first-class entities. Specifically, events can be created within one thread and sent over a channel to another thread for synchronization. When that happens, applying the priority of the thread that created the event brings back the possibility of priority inversion. To see why, consider the example in Fig. 3.

```
[T_H]  sync(sendEvt(c3, sync(sendEvt(c2, v2)))); sync(sendEvt(c1, v1))
[T_M]  sync(recvEvt(c3))
[T_L]  choose(recvEvt(c1), recvEvt(c2))
```

Fig. 3. Priority Inversion Due to Passing of Events

In this example, T_H sends a sendEvt over the channel c2 which will be received and synchronized on by T_M. It is to be noted that this sendEvt will be at the highest priority (which was inherited from its creator T_H) even though it is synchronized on by T_M. T_H then sends out a value v1 on channel c1. T_L has to choose between receiving the value on channel c1 or on channel c2. Since T_H and T_M are both of higher priority than T_L, they will both execute their communications before T_L does. Thus T_L will have to make a choice between either unblocking T_M or T_H (by receiving on channel c2 or c1 respectively). Recall in the current scenario, the priority is determined by the thread that created the event and not by the thread that synchronizes it. Therefore this choice will be non-deterministic; both communications are of the same priority as those created by the same thread. T_L might choose to receive on channel c2 and thus allow the medium priority thread T_M to run while the high priority thread T_H is still blocked - a priority inversion.

The important observation to be made from this example is that priority, when inherited from a thread, should be from the thread that synchronizes on an event instead of the thread that creates the event. This matches our intuition about the root of priority inversion, as the synchronizing thread is the one that blocks, and priority inversion happens when the wrong threads remain blocked.

We have now reconciled the competing goals of user-defined event priority and inversion-preventing thread priority. In doing so, we arrive at a tiered-priority scheme. The priority given to threads takes precedence, as is necessary to prevent priority inversion. A communication's thread priority inherits from the thread that synchronizes on the event, as was shown to be required. When there is a tie between thread priorities, the event priority is used to break it. We note that high priority communications tend to come from higher priority computations. Thus, this approach is flexible enough to allow the expression of priority in real-world systems. In Sect. 5, we show this in the context of a web server and a GUI application in CML.

4   Implementation

To demonstrate our priority mechanism, we have implemented it as an extension to the CML implementation in MLton, an open source compiler for Standard ML. Our implementation consists of approximately 1400 LOC, wholly in ML.

4.1   Priority atop CML

To understand why priority at the CML language level is needed, we first consider a prioritized communication channel built from existing CML primitives.[1] Implementing communication using a prioritized channel requires a two step communication. We need one step to convey the event priority and another to effect the event's communication. The prioritized channel itself is encoded as a server that accepts communications and figures out the appropriate pairings of sends and receives (in this case based on priority).

The sender blocks, waiting to receive a notification from the server that is acting as the priority queue, while it waits for its message to be delivered by the priority queue to a matching receiver. Once the priority queue successfully sends the value to a receiver, it unblocks the sender by sending a message. The mechanism is nearly identical for a receiver, but since we need to return a value, we pass an event generating function to the channel. While the per-communication overhead is undesirable, this encoding captures the behavior of event priority for send and receive. On selective communication, however, this encoding becomes significantly more complicated. A two stage communication pattern makes encoding the clean up of events that are not selected during the choice challenging. We also still lack the ability to extract the priority information from threads. Recall that preventing priority inversions requires reasoning about the priority of both threads and events. Instead, we opted to realize our priority mechanism as a series of small modifications to the existing CML runtime.

4.2   Extensions to CML

The major changes made to CML are to the thread scheduler and channel structure. These changes are exposed through a set of new prioritized primitives, shown in Fig. 4.

```
spawnp      : (unit -> unit) -> threadPriority -> thread_id
sendEvtP    : 'a chan * 'a * eventPrio -> unit event
recvEvtP    : 'a chan * eventPrio -> 'a event
changePrio  : ('a event * eventPrio) -> 'a event
```

Fig. 4. *PrioCML* Primitives

---

[1] Available at: https://gist.github.com/Cheng-EnC/ea317edb62f01f55b85a9406f6093 217.

We extend the thread scheduler to be a prioritized round-robin scheduler with three fixed thread priorities. While other work has explored finer-grained approaches to priority [18], for simplicity, we use a small, fixed number of priority levels. We chose three priority levels as that is enough to encode complex protocols such as the earliest deadline first scheduling [3]. Our implementation could be extended to more priority levels if desired. The new primitive spawnp spawns a new thread with a user-specified thread priority: LOW, MED, or HIGH. Threads within the highest priority level are executed in a round-robin fashion until all are unable to make further progress. This happens when all are blocking on communication. If all high priority threads are blocked, then the medium priority threads are run until either a high priority thread is unblocked or all medium threads block. This process continues with low priority threads. This scheme guarantees that a thread will never be chosen to run unless no thread of higher priority is able to make progress.

Event priority is managed by following primitives: sendEvtP, recvEvtP, and changePrio. The eventPrio is an integer where a larger number implies higher priority. The two base event primitives sendEvt and recvEvt are replaced by their prioritized versions. These functions take in an event priority and tie that priority to the created events. The changePrio function allows the priority of an existing event to be changed. We also note that all CML primitives continue to exist in *PrioCML*. The primitive spawn creates a thread with LOW priority. The base event constructors are given default priority levels and reduce calls to the new prioritized primitives. The combinators continue to work unchanged. In this way, our system is fully backward compatible with existing CML programs.

4.3   Preventing Priority Inversion

To make the local selection, we leverage the channel structure. To see how this is done, first consider the action pairing mechanism in unmodified CML [20]. When an event is synchronized, the corresponding action is placed in a queue over the channel it uses. If there is a match already in the channel queue, the actions are paired and removed. In the case of choice, all potential actions are enqueued. Each carries a reference to a shared flag that indicates if the choice is still valid. Once the first action in a given choice is paired, the flag is set to invalid. If the action has its flag set to invalid upon attempting a match, it is removed, and the next action in the queue is considered. This lazy cleaning of the channel queues amortizes the cost of removal.

Figure 5 shows how a synchronized event is paired. We split the channel queue into three queues in our prioritized implementation: one for each thread priority level. Keeping those three priority queues separate is what allows us to realize our tiered-priority mechanism efficiently. By looking first at the higher thread priority queues, we give precedence to thread priority over the event priority that orders each queue.

Choice is handled similarly to how it was handled before priority. Again, lists are cleared lazily to amortize the costs of removal. The major overhead our scheme introduces is that inserting an action into a channel now requires

```
val send_pqueue = array of three priority queues for pending send events
val recv_pqueue = array of three priority queues for pending recv events
if is_send_event(current_evt) then
   case deque(recv_pqueue[H]) of
     SOME recv_evt => pair with recv_evt
     NONE => case deque(recv_pqueue[M]) of ...
               case deque(recv_pqueue[L]) of ...
                  NONE => enque(send_pqueue[thread_priority(current_evt)],
                                current_evt)
else  (* Same structure as the if branch
         but switch the recv_pqueue to send_pqueue *)
```

Fig. 5. Pairing a synchronized event

additional effort to keep the queues in order. For a choice, this overhead must be dealt with for each possible communication path. The impacts of this are measurable, but minor, as discussed in Sect. 5.1.

4.4   Polling

Polling, a common paradigm in concurrent programming, is fundamentally the ability to do a non-blocking query on an event. The primitives of CML (Fig. 1 from Sect. 2) do not provide the ability to express non-blocking synchronization. The only available synchronization operation is **select**, which is blocking.

This problem is illustrated by Reppy in *Concurrent Programming in ML* [20]. At first glance, the **always** event primitive could provide a non-blocking construction. This event is constructed with a value, and when synchronized on, it immediately yields the wrapped value. By selecting between **always** and **recv** events, the synchronization is guaranteed not to block. This flawed approach, as explained by Reppy, would look as follows:

```
fun pollCh ch = sync (choose [alwaysEvt NONE, wrap (recvEvt ch, SOME)])
```

While it is true that this construction will never block, it may also ignore available communications on the channel. The choose operation in CML is nondeterministic, and could choose the **alwaysEvt** branch, even if the **recvEvt** would not block. This problem led to the introduction of a dedicated polling primitive **recvPoll** in CML. While its use is generally discouraged, it serves as an important optimization in some communications protocols outlined by Reppy.

In our discussion of *PrioCML* thus far, we have omitted discussion of the **always** event for simplicity. The **always** event is different than the communication events as there is no blocked communication partner. It represents a one sided communication. Therefore it is not immediately clear how it fits into our tiered-priority which looks at the thread priorities of two threads. By introducing priority to the **always** event primitive we could capture the polling behavior that would otherwise require a dedicated primitive. We do this by giving `always` events a fixed priority lower than any in the tiered priority system, e.g. `changePrio(alwaysEvt, -1)` while 0 is the lowest priority in event priority. We choose to give it the lowest priority because that expresses our desire to allow another thread to proceed if at all possible. This means during a choice, we will only pick the `always` event if no other events are available. Because of our guarantee that an event is always picked if one is available though, it will still never block. Therefore, under our prioritized implementation, the above example actually works with the intended behavior.

5   Evaluation

To demonstrate that our implementation is practical we have conducted a series of microbenchmarks to measure overheads as well as a case study in a real-world webserver and GUI framework written wholly in CML. The benchmarks and case study were run on our implementation and on MLton 20180207. The benchmarking system had an Intel i7-6820HQ quad-core processor with 16 GB of RAM. We note that MLton is a single core implementation, so although it supports multiple threads these are multiplex over a single OS thread.

5.1   Microbenchmarks

We create microbenchmarks that exercise spawn, send-receive, and choice. In spawn and send-receive, we see constant overheads as shown in Fig. 6 and Fig. 7. We note that the send-receive benchmark performs n communications where n is the number of iterations, so the constant overhead leads to a steeper slope to the line. To benchmark choice, we build a lattice of selective communication. It has a grid of choice cells where a single message is sent at the top and bounces around non-deterministically until it falls out the bottom. To show the growth behavior of this benchmark, we scaled both the height and width, so for a run parameterized by n, there were n^2 choice cells, of which the message would pass through n. From the results shown in Fig. 8, we observe that the runtimes of both CML and *PrioCML* appear quadratic. Our implementation shows a cost higher by a constant factor, and thus a steeper curve. From a static analysis of the open-source Swerve web-server implementation, we believe deeply nested choice operations to be rare in real-world applications. Thus, while our implementation does exhibit noticeable slowdown on the synthetic benchmarks, we expect real-world performance to be unaffected.

5.2   Case Study: Termination in Swerve

To demonstrate that the problem of timely graceful termination is prevalent in message passing programs, we take a look at a large CML project: the Swerve web server. Swerve is full featured, modular web server written using CML with approximately 30,000 lines of code [22]. As noted by [22], Swerve lacks a graceful shutdown mechanism. Currently, shutdown of the webserver is accomplished

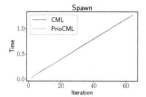
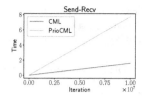
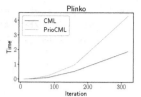

Fig. 6. Spawn   **Fig. 7.** Send-Receive   **Fig. 8.** Plinko (Choice)

by sending a UNIX signal to terminate the process. This approach has several drawbacks. As the process is killed immediately, it does not have the opportunity to flush the asynchronous logging channel. This can lead to incomplete logs near server shutdown. Additionally, clients being served at the time of server shutdown have their connections closed abruptly, without a chance for the server to finish a reply. This can lead to an error on the client side, or in the case that the request was not idempotent, inconsistent or partially updated state server-side. Thus to cleanly exit the server, it is important to allow all currently running tasks to complete, including both flushing the log and handling connected clients. As [22] explains, this can be handled by rejecting all new clients and waiting for existing ones to finish before flushing the logs and exiting the process. We implement such a system in Swerve, the core of which is seen in Fig. 9.

```
select [wrap (recvEvt acceptChan, new_connect),
        wrap (recvEvt lchan, handle_msg),
        wrap (shutdownEvt, fn () => shutdown num_connects)]
```

Fig. 9. Graceful Shutdown in Swerve

Here we select between the three possible actions in the main connection handling loop. We can accept an incoming connection over the channel `acceptChan` by invoking the function `new_connect`. Alternatively, we can handle a client disconnect event, sent as a message on the channel `lchan` via `handle_msg`. Lastly, we can receive a shutdown signal via the event `shutdownEvt`. This event is a receive event on a channel shared with the signal handler registered to the UNIX interrupt signal. Upon receipt of such a signal, the handler will send a message on that channel to indicate the server should begin shutdown. We leverage CML's first class events to encapsulate this mechanism and hide the implementation from the main loop. When the event `shutdownEvt` is chosen, we invoke the shutdown function which stops accepting new connections, waits for all existing connections to close, flushes the log, then removes a lock file and exits.

While this change successfully resolves the possibility of broken connections and inconsistent server state, it still has a notable limitation. We have no guarantee of a timely shutdown. The original approach of killing the process via a

```
select [wrap (recvEvt acceptChan, new_connect),
        wrap (recvEvt lchan, handle_msg),
        wrap (changePrio (shutdownEvt, 0), fn () => shutdown num_connects)]
```

Fig. 10. Prioritized Shutdown in Swerve

signal is effectively instantaneous. However, because we want to complete the currently running server tasks, the server can't shutdown immediately. We do however, want to be sure that the server does not accept additional work after being told to shutdown. Under the existing CML semantics, the server is free to continue to accept new connections indefinitely after the shutdown event has become ready, provided a steady stream of new connections is presented. This is because there is no guarantee as to which event in a choice list is selected, only that it does not unnecessarily block. Since CML only allows safe interactions between threads via message passing, we have no other way for the signal handler to alert the main loop that it should cease accepting new connections. Thus, under heavy load, the server could take on arbitrarily more work than needed to ensure a safe shutdown. We note that the MLton implementation of CML features an anti-starvation heuristic which in our testing was effective at preventing shutdown delays. This approach however is not a semantic guarantee. By adding priority, as shown in Fig. 10, we obtain certainty that our shutdown will be effected in a timely manner.

We verify the operation of this mechanism by measuring the number of clients that report broken connections at shutdown. With a proper shutdown mechanism we would see no broken connections as the server would allow all to complete before termination. As seen in Fig. 13, without the shutdown mechanism in place clients can experience broken connections. When there are very few clients, the chances that any client is connected when the process terminates are low. As the number of clients increases however, the odds of a broken connection do as well. By adding our shutdown mechanism, we prevent these broken connections. We emphasize that the introduction of priority means achieving a guarantee that the shutdown is correct is simple. The implementing code is short and concise because our mechanism integrates nicely with CML and retains its full composability. We note that event priorities are crucial to ensuring this timely shutdown. For example, consider the case where the signal handler was extended to pass on an additional type of signal such as configuration reload. We would still want to ensure that the shutdown event takes precedence. Thus we need to assign more granular priorities than those available based solely on the priority of the communicating thread.

5.3   Case Study: A GUI Shutdown Protocol

To demonstrate that priority can benefit the response time of graceful shutdown, in this section, we present an evaluation of response time measurement with a shutdown protocol in the context of eXene[10], a GUI toolkit in CML. A typical

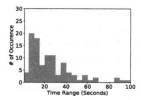

Fig. 11. CML

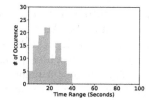

Fig. 12. *PrioCML*

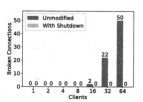

Fig. 13. Swerve

eXene program contains widgets. To realize a graceful shutdown protocol, our eXene program needs to wait for all widgets to close upon receiving a shutdown request. As a result, busy widgets tend to slow down the shutdown protocol. Moreover, the choice's nondeterministic selection degenerates the response time as widgets may overlook a shutdown request. We improve the response time with both shortening and stabilize it by proper encoding of priority in the communication protocol.

We build a widget network in eXene to compute the Fibonacci number. Each widget has a number with the corresponding position in the Fibonacci sequence. Upon a user click, the widget will calculate the corresponding Fibonacci number. By the definition of Fibonacci sequence, a widget of $fib(n)$, except $fib(0)$ and $fib(1)$, needs to communicate with other widgets, which is responsible for computing $fib(n-1)$ and $fib(n-2)$, In the meanwhile, we need to encode the shutdown event so that widget has a chance to receive shutdown request. A widget can be implemented with CML code in Fig. 14

```
select[wrap(recvEvt out_ch_req,   (* Outermost select *)
          fn p => (select[ (* Middle select *)
            wrap(sendEvt(fib_pre1_req, ()),
                 fn () => (let val v1 = recv (fib_pre1_com)
                               val _  = send (fib_pre2_req, ())
                               val v2 = recv (fib_pre2_com)
                           in select [ (* Innermost select *)
                                  wrap(sendEvt(out_ch_com, v1+v2), ...),
                                         shutdownEvt]
                           end)), ...,
              shutdownEvt])),
          shutdownEvt]
```

Fig. 14. Communication Protocol of Fibonacci Widget

Note that in above code we omit the case on the `sendEvt(fib_pre2_req, ())` for brevity. On the outermost `select`, the widget is waiting for either a compute request from `out_ch_req` or a shutdown request. Once receive a compute request, it goes to middle select. The middle select picks between the widgets it needs to communicate and the shutdown event. The code above shows the case the widget of $fib(n-1)$ is available. After we compute the result from $fib(n-1)$, it moves to $fib(n-2)$. Finally, it adds the result and sends it to the output channel in the innermost select, which picks with another shutdown event. As for the shutdownEvt, every widget propagates the shutdown request to the widget of $fib(n-1)$. Hence, the shutdown protocol in the Fibonacci network is a linear chain from the largest Fibonacci widget.

We encode priority in two places. First, the priority of the shutdown event is higher than other events. The use of priority in shutdown events ensures that the shutdown request will be chosen whenever it is available during a selection. Second, we give the priority on send and recv on requesting and receiving the computation of the Fibonacci number. The message priority is higher as the number of Fibonacci is larger in the network. As a result, the widget with a larger number has the priority to request or receive computation. By giving these widgets preference, we boost the shutdown protocol as the linear chain is from largest to smallest widget.

The histogram of CML and *PrioCML* is shown as Fig. 11 and 12 respectively. We run each setting for 100 times and record the time needed to finish the shutdown protocol. We compute a large Fibonacci number to fill the network computation requests so that every widget is saturated with Fibonacci computation before requesting the shutdown protocol. The result shows that the average time spends on shutdown is improved by 26%, from 25.5 s to 18.8 s. Also, it stabilizes the response time by reducing the standard deviation from 20.7 to 9.2. This experiment shows that a shutdown protocol can be improved and become more predictable by properly encoding the priority.

6   Related Work

Priority in Multithreading: Exploration into prioritized computation extends far back into research on multithreaded systems. Early work at Xerox on the Mesa [15] programming language, and its successor project Cedar [23], illustrated the utility of multiple priority levels in a multithreaded system. These systems exposed a fork-join model of concurrency, wherein the programmer would specify that any procedure shall be called by forking a new process in which to run it. The join operation then provides a synchronization point between the two threads and allows the result of the computation to be obtained. This was implemented atop monitors, a form of mutual exclusion primitive. These systems did not consider communication as a first-class entity and only allowed it through the use of monitored objects.

First-Class Communication: Concurrent ML introduced first-class synchronous communication as a language primitive [19]. Since then, there have been multiple incarnations of these primitives, both in languages other than ML (including Haskell [4,21], Scheme [8], Go [11], and MPI [5]). Others adopted CML primitives as the base for the parallel programming language Manticore [9]. Other work has considered extending Concurrent ML with support for first-class asynchrony [24]. We believe our approach to priority would be useful in this context. It would, however, raise some questions regarding the relative priority of synchronous and asynchronous events, analogous to the aforementioned issues with always events. Another extension of interest would be transactional events [6,7]. The introduction of priority would be a natural fit as it provides a precise expression of how multiple concurrently executing transactions should be resolved.

Internal Use of Priority in CML Implementations: As mentioned by [20] in describing the SML/NJ implementation of CML, a concept of prioritization has been previously considered in selective communication [20]. There, the principal goal is to maintain fairness and responsiveness. To achieve this goal, [20] proposes internally prioritizing events that have been frequently passed over in previous selective communications. We note that these priorities are never exposed to the programmer, and exist only as a performance optimization in the runtime. Even if exposed to user, this limited notion of priority only encompasses selective communication and ignores any consideration of the pairing communication. Our realization of priority, and the associated tiered priority scheme is significantly more powerful. This is both due to the exposure of priority to the programmer and the ability of our realization of priority to encompass information from both parties in a communication when considering the priority of an event.

Priority in ML: Recent work has looked at the introduction of priority to Standard ML [18].

To accomplish this, the system [18] propose, PriML, "rejects programs in which a high-priority may synchronize with a lower-priority one." Since all communication in CML is synchronous, in order for a high priority thread to communicate with a lower priority thread, they must synchronize. This is exactly the interaction that is explicitly disallowed by PriML.

7   Conclusion

This paper presents the design and implementation of *PrioCML*, an extension to Concurrent ML that introduces priority to synchronous messages passing. By leveraging a tiered-priority mechanism that considers both thread priority and event priority, *PrioCML* avoids potential priority inversions. Our evaluation shows that this mechanism can be realized to enable the adoption of priority with little effort and minimal performance penalties. The further work is to formalize the priority inversion and provide semantics for *PrioCML*.

Acknowledgment. This work is supported in part by National Science Foundation grants: CRI:1823230 and SHF:1749539. Any opinions, findings, and conclusions or recommendations expressed in this material are those of the author(s) and do not necessarily reflect the views of the National Science Foundation.

References

1. The racket reference (2019). https://docs.racket-lang.org/reference/channel.html
2. Using binder IPC (2020). https://source.android.com/devices/architecture/hidl/binder-ipc
3. Buttazzo, G.: Hard Real-Time Computing Systems: Predictable Scheduling Algorithms and Applications. Springer, New York (2011). https://doi.org/10.1007/978-1-4614-0676-1
4. Chaudhuri, A.: A concurrent ML library in concurrent Haskell. SIGPLAN Not. **44**(9), 269–280 (2009). https://doi.org/10.1145/1631687.1596589
5. Demaine, E.: First class communication in MPI. In: Proceedings of the Second MPI Developers Conference, MPIDC 1996, p. 189. IEEE Computer Society, USA (1996)
6. Donnelly, K., Fluet, M.: Transactional events. J. Funct. Program. **18**(5–6), 649–706 (2008). https://doi.org/10.1017/S0956796808006916
7. Effinger-Dean, L., Kehrt, M., Grossman, D.: Transactional events for ML. In: Proceedings of the 13th ACM SIGPLAN International Conference on Functional Programming, ICFP 2008, pp. 103–114. Association for Computing Machinery, New York (2008). https://doi.org/10.1145/1411204.1411222
8. Flatt, M., Findler, R.B.: Kill-safe synchronization abstractions. SIGPLAN Not. **39**(6), 47–58 (2004). https://doi.org/10.1145/996893.996849
9. Fluet, M., Rainey, M., Reppy, J., Shaw, A.: Implicitly threaded parallelism in manticore. J. Funct. Program. **20**(5–6), 537–576 (2010). https://doi.org/10.1017/S0956796810000201
10. Gansner, E.R., Reppy, J.H.: A Multi-Threaded Higher-Order User Interface Toolkit (1993)
11. Gerrand, A.: Share memory by communicating (2010). https://blog.golang.org/share-memory-by-communicating
12. Haller, P., Odersky, M.: Scala actors: unifying thread-based and event-based programming. Theor. Comput. Sci. **410**, 202–220 (2009)
13. Armstrong, J., Virding, R., Wikström, C., Williams, M.: Concurrent Programming in Erlang, 2nd edn. Prentice-Hall (1996)
14. Klabnik, S., Nichols, C.: The rust programming language (2020). https://doc.rust-lang.org/book/ch16-02-message-passing.html
15. Lampson, B.W., Redell, D.D.: Experience with processes and monitors in Mesa. Commun. ACM **23**(2), 105–117 (1980). https://doi.org/10.1145/358818.358824
16. Milner, R., Tofte, M., Macqueen, D.: The Definition of Standard ML. MIT Press, Cambridge (1997)
17. Mueller, F.: A library implementation of posix threads under Unix. In: USENIX Winter (1993)
18. Muller, S.K., Acar, U.A., Harper, R.: Competitive parallelism: getting your priorities right. Proc. ACM Program. Lang. **2**(ICFP), 1–30 (2018). https://doi.org/10.1145/3236790
19. Reppy, J.H.: CML: a higher concurrent language. In: Proceedings of the ACM SIGPLAN 1991 Conference on Programming Language Design and Implementation, PLDI 1991, pp. 293–305. ACM, New York (1991). https://doi.org/10.1145/113445.113470
20. Reppy, J.H.: Concurrent Programming in ML, 1st edn. Cambridge University Press, New York (2007)

21. Russell, G.: Events in Haskell, and how to implement them. SIGPLAN Not. **36**(10), 157–168 (2001). https://doi.org/10.1145/507669.507655

22. Shipman, A.L.: System Programming with Standard ML (2002)

23. Swinehart, D.C., Zellweger, P.T., Hagmann, R.B.: The structure of cedar. In: Proceedings of the ACM SIGPLAN 85 Symposium on Language Issues in Programming Environments, SLIPE 1985, pp. 230–244. Association for Computing Machinery, New York (1985). https://doi.org/10.1145/800225.806844

24. Ziarek, L., Sivaramakrishnan, K., Jagannathan, S.: Composable asynchronous events. In: Proceedings of the 32nd ACM SIGPLAN Conference on Programming Language Design and Implementation, PLDI 2011, pp. 628–639. Association for Computing Machinery, New York (2011). https://doi.org/10.1145/1993498.1993572

Putting Gradual Types to Work

Bhargav Shivkumar[1,2(✉)] ⬥, Enrique Naudon[1] ⬥, and Lukasz Ziarek[2]

[1] Bloomberg, New York, USA
bhargavs@buffalo.edu
[2] SUNY - University at Buffalo, New York, USA

Abstract. In this paper, we describe our experience incorporating gradual types in a statically typed functional language with Hindley-Milner style type inference. Where most gradually typed systems aim to improve static checking in a dynamically typed language, we approach it from the opposite perspective and promote dynamic checking in a statically typed language. Our approach provides a glimpse into how languages like SML and OCaml might handle gradual typing. We discuss our implementation and challenges faced—specifically how gradual typing rules apply to our representation of composite and recursive types. We review the various implementations that add dynamic typing to a statically typed language in order to highlight the different ways of mixing static and dynamic typing and examine possible inspirations while maintaining the gradual nature of our type system. This paper also discusses our motivation for adding gradual types to our language, and the practical benefits of doing so in our industrial setting.

Keywords: Gradual typing · Type inference · Functional programming

1 Introduction

Static typing and dynamic typing are two opposing type system paradigms. Statically typed languages are able to catch more programmer bugs early in the compilation process, at the expense of a more flexible semantics. On the other hand, dynamically typed languages allow greater flexibility, while allowing more bugs at runtime. The proponents of each paradigm often feel very strongly in favor of their paradigm. Language designers are stranded in the middle of this dichotomy and left to decide between the two extremes when designing their languages.

At Bloomberg, we have felt this pain while designing a domain specific language for programmatically defining financial contracts. For the purposes of this paper, we will call our language Bloomberg Contract Language (BCL). BCL is a statically typed functional language with Hindley-Milner style type inference [4, 17], structural composite types and recursive types. Users of BCL are split into two groups—end users and language maintainers. End users are typically financial professionals whose primary programming experience involves scripting in dynamically typed languages such as Python and MATLAB. On the other hand, language maintainers are Bloomberg software engineers who are most at ease programming in statically typed and often functional languages like OCaml. Whilst it is of paramount importance to provide our end users with

© Bloomberg Finance LP 2021
J. F. Morales and D. Orchard (Eds.): PADL 2021, LNCS 12548, pp. 54–70, 2021.
https://doi.org/10.1007/978-3-030-67438-0_4

an environment in which they are comfortable, our domain—financial contracts—is one in which correctness is of extraordinary importance, since errors can lead to large financial losses. This makes static types appealing, as they catch many errors that dynamic systems might miss. Even though static types provide a more error-free runtime, they do require extra effort from our end users who must learn an unfamiliar system. Our desire to simultaneously satisfy our end users and our language maintainers led us to gradual typing [23], which seeks to integrate static and dynamic typing in one system. Gradual typing in BCL allows language maintainers to stick to static typing and end users to selectively disable static typing when it interferes with their ability to work in BCL.

Since its introduction, gradual typing [23] has been making its way into more mainstream languages [29,30] and more people have acknowledged the varied benefits of mixing static and dynamic typing in the same program. As identified by Siek and Taha [26], there has been considerable interest in integrating static and dynamic typing, both in academia and in industry. There has also been a plethora of proposed approaches, from adding a dynamic keyword [2], to using objects in object-oriented languages [16], to Seik and Taha's gradual typing itself [23]. While there seems to be no one-size-fits-all approach to designing a system that mixes static and dynamic types, Siek and Taha standardize the guarantees [26] we can expect from such a system. For language designers, this provides a more methodical way to approach the integration. Language designers can also draw from a large body of literature exploring the combination of gradual types with other common features, such as objects [24] and type inference [5,25].

While it is typical for dynamically typed languages to go the gradual route in order to incorporate more static type checking, we go the other way and add more dynamism to our already static language. Most static languages that incorporate dynamic typing do so by following in the footsteps of Abadi et al. [2]–C# is a prime example of this [9]. Since BCL already supports type inference and we want to retain the dynamic feel of the language, we implement the inference algorithm described by Siek and Vachhrajani [25], putting us in an interesting position. Our approach promotes the use of a ? annotation to explicitly signify dynamically typed terms while un-annotated terms are (implicitly) statically typed, much like that of Garcia and Cimini [5]. This approach provides a simple escape hatch to end users who want to use dynamic typing as well as avenues to automate this process to ensure backwards compatibility of BCL with legacy code.

Finally, we feel there is a need to study the adaptation of gradual types to an existing language with a substantial user base and lots of existing code. We aim to provide a technical report in this paper that models our design decisions and implementation details of bringing in gradual types to BCL. Our primary contributions include:

- A brief review of other statically typed languages that add dynamic types, to compare and possibly derive inspiration for our own design in Sect. 2.
- Introduce a new use case that shows how a gradually typed language benefits different user groups of a language in Sect. 3.
- An inference algorithm, which is an adaptation of a prominent inference algorithm to add gradual types to a language with type inference in Sect. 4.

Note that throughout this paper we use "gradual" to indicate an implementation that provides gradual guarantees as specified in [26]. While, we do not state this formally for

BCL and leave that to future work, our implementation supports the smooth evolution of programs from static to dynamic typing as prescribed for gradually typed systems.

2 Background

In this section we briefly survey the existing literature to better contextualize our design choices. The incorporation of static and dynamic typing has been extensively studied [8, 15, 23, 26, 28], though usually in the context of a core calculus instead of a full-featured language. There also seems to be a juxtaposition of the literature, which generally follows a static-first approach, and practical implementations, which generally follow a dynamic-first approach[1] [7].

Abadi et al. [2] has been an inspiration for many static languages looking to incorporate dynamic typing. This work is a precursor to gradual typing, and while it does not qualify as gradual à la [23], it is nevertheless a standard when it comes to adding dynamic checks to a static language. Abadi's work uses a dynamic construct to build terms of type Dynamic and a typecase construct to perform case analysis on the runtime type of an expression of type Dynamic. This is similar to the typeof() function in dynamic languages like Python, which resolve the type of an expression at runtime. Siek and Taha observe that translating from their language of explicit casts to Abadi et al.'s language is not straightforward [23]. Nevertheless we believe that it is worthwhile to introduce something like the typecase construct in a static language with gradual types. We identify and discuss some potential applications of this in Sect. 5.

Statically typed object oriented languages like C# and Java have worked to incorporate some form of dynamic typing [6, 16]. C# 4.0 introduced the dynamic type to declare objects that can bypass static type checking [1]. Although this achieves dynamic type checking, there is no indication of it being gradual à la [23]. Moreover, using the dynamic type in a C# program runs the program on the Dynamic Language Runtime (DLR) which is a separate runtime from the Common Language Runtime and which supports dynamic checking.

While works like [18,22] examine gradual type inference from the perspective of removing dynamic checks by performing type inference at runtime, Garcia and Cimini [5] (much like BCL) deals with static reasoning about programs, based on the consistency relation. [5] explores an alternate approach to gradual type inference and presents a statically typed language and its gradual counterpart. Instead of inferring gradual types based on type precision [25], this work limits the inference problem to static types only and requires consistency constraints between gradual types. An interesting feature of their language is that they distinguish between static type parameters and gradual type parameters to tell static parametric polymorphism apart from polymorphism due to the dynamic type.

Our approach is to adopt the properly gradual system defined by Siek and Vachchrajani [25]. That work describes the incorporation of gradual typing into a language with

---

[1] Here, static-first refers elaborating a static surface language to a gradually typed intermediate representation. Conversely, by dynamic-first we mean the opposite: elaborating a dynamic surface language to a gradually typed intermediate representation.

unification-based type inference. Unification-based inference is a common implementation of the Hindley-Milner type system [17], and is the implementation that BCL already uses. This makes our integration work relatively easier and also lets us leverage all the benefits of the standard for gradual typing laid out by Siek and Taha [26].

2.1 Gradual Types and Unification Based Inference

Siek and Vachchrajani [25] (S&V) propose an innovative solution for performing gradual type inference which combines gradual typing with type inference. Their main goal is to allow inference to operate on the statically typed parts of the code, while leaving the dynamic parts to runtime checks. Furthermore, the dynamic type must unify with static types and type variables, so that the static and dynamic portions of code may freely interact. In this section, we summarize their work.

The work of S&V is based on the gradually typed lambda calculus [23]. The gradually typed lambda calculus extends the simply typed lambda calculus ($\lambda_{\rightarrow}$) with an unknown type, ?–pronounced "dynamic"; type checking for terms of this type is left until runtime. The gradually typed lambda calculus ($\lambda_{\rightarrow}^{?}$) allows static and dynamic types to freely mix and satisfies the gradual guarantee [26], ensuring smooth migration between static and dynamic code while maintaining the correctness of the program.

(SVAR) $\dfrac{\Gamma(x) = \tau}{S; \Gamma \vdash x : \tau}$ $\boxed{S; \Gamma \vdash e : \tau}$ (GVAR) $\dfrac{\Gamma(x) = \tau}{S; \Gamma \vdash_g x : \tau}$ $\boxed{S; \Gamma \vdash_g e : \tau}$

(SCNST) $S; \Gamma \vdash c : \mathit{typeof}(c)$ (GCNST) $S; \Gamma \vdash_g c : \mathit{typeof}(c)$

(SAPP) $\dfrac{S; \Gamma \vdash e_1 : \tau_1 \quad S; \Gamma \vdash e_2 : \tau_2 \quad S(\tau_1) = S(\tau_2 \rightarrow \tau_3)}{S; \Gamma \vdash e_1\, e_2 : \tau_3}$ (GAPP) $\dfrac{S; \Gamma \vdash_g e_1 : \tau_1 \quad S; \Gamma \vdash_g e_2 : \tau_2 \quad S \models \tau_1 \simeq \tau_2 \rightarrow \beta \quad (\beta\,\mathit{fresh})}{S; \Gamma \vdash_g e_1 e_2 : \beta}$

(SABS) $\dfrac{S; \Gamma(x \mapsto \tau_1) \vdash e : \tau_2}{S; \Gamma \vdash \lambda x : \tau_1.e : \tau_1 \rightarrow \tau_2}$ (GABS) $\dfrac{S; \Gamma(x \mapsto \tau_1) \vdash_g e : \tau_2}{S; \Gamma \vdash_g \lambda x : \tau_1.e : \tau_1 \rightarrow \tau_2}$

(a) $\lambda_{\rightarrow}^{\alpha}$ (b) $\lambda_{\rightarrow}^{?\alpha}$

Fig. 1. Simply and gradually typed lambda calculus with type variables

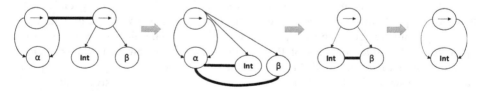

Fig. 2. Huet's unification of $\{\alpha \rightarrow \alpha = Int \rightarrow \beta\}$

Type inconsistencies in $\lambda_{\rightarrow}^{?}$ are caught by a *consistent* relation, instead of equality as in $\lambda_{\rightarrow}$. The *consistent* relation only compares parts of a type that are statically known; it is one of the key contributions of $\lambda_{\rightarrow}^{?}$. All type errors that cannot be statically resolved by the gradual type system are delegated to runtime checks.

Type inference allows programmers to omit type annotations in their programs and have the compiler infer the types for them. Hindley-Milner type inference is often cast as a two step process that consists of generating constraints and then solving them by a unification algorithm [20, 21, 32]. The inference algorithm models the typing rules as equations, called constraints, between type variables, while the unification algorithm computes a substitution S, which is a mapping from type variables to types, such that for each equation $\tau_1 = \tau_2$, we have $S(\tau_1) = S(\tau_2)$.

S&V introduce the gradually typed lambda calculus with type variables ($\lambda_{\rightarrow}^{?\alpha}$), which is $\lambda_{\rightarrow}^{?}$ extended with type variables, α. They define a new relation, *consistent-equal* ($\simeq$), which extends the *consistent* relation from $\lambda_{\rightarrow}^{?}$ to treatment α. Figure 1b compares the typing rules for $\lambda_{\rightarrow}^{\alpha}$, the statically typed lambda calculus with type variables, to the new type system $\lambda_{\rightarrow}^{?\alpha}$. S&V also specify a unification algorithm for $\lambda_{\rightarrow}^{?\alpha}$ which integrates the *consistent-equal* into Huet's unification algorithm [10, 14] which is a popular algorithm that doesn't rely on substitution.

Huet's unification algorithm uses a graph representation for types. For example, a type like $Int \rightarrow \beta$ is represented as a sub graph in Fig. 2. A node represents a type, ground types, type variables or the function type ($\rightarrow$), and edges connect the nodes of types belonging to a $\rightarrow$ type. From this it follows that the unification algorithm is the amalgamation of two graphs present in a constraint equation following the rules of the type system. Huet's algorithm maintains a union find structure [27] to maintain equivalence classes among nodes and thereby types. When node A unifies with node B according to the type rules, the merge results in one of the two nodes becoming the representative of the merge. This signifies that the representative node is the solution to the constraint being unified. Figure 2 shows how the unification of the constraint $\{\alpha \rightarrow \alpha = Int \rightarrow \beta\}$ proceeds.

3   Introduction to BCL

Our motivation to explore gradual types for BCL is rooted in several historical and contextual details, which we discuss in this section. It is first helpful to understand that BCL is predominantly used to model financial contracts, by providing end users with programmatic access to a financial contract library. The library we use is based upon the composable contracts of Peyton Jones, Eber and Seward [19]. Its internal contract data structure is used throughout our broader derivatives system to support various downstream analyses. In this way, BCL serves as an expressive front-end for describing contracts to our derivatives system.

Let us look at a short illustrative example of BCL code. Figure 3 provides an example of the sort of thing for which BCL might be used. The `european_stock_option` function produces a `Contract` which models a European stock option. European stock options grant their holder the right, but not the obligation, to buy or sell stock in a company. The "European" in European stock option

```
let receive currency amount = scale (one currency) amount in

let european_stock_option args =
  let first = stock_price args.effective_date args.company in
  let last = stock_price args.expiry_date args.company in
  let payoff = match args.call_or_put with
    | Call -> (last / first - args.strike)
    | Put -> (args.strike - last / first)
  in
  european args.expiry_date (receive args.currency payoff)
in

european_stock_option
  { company = "ABC Co.",
    call_or_put = Call,
    strike = 100.0,
    currency = USD,
    effective_date = 2021-01-17,
    expiry_date = 2021-01-22 }
```

Fig. 3. European stock option

refers to the fact that, on one specific date, the holder must choose whether or not s/he would like to buy (or sell) the stock. This is in contrast to "American" options, where the holder may choose to buy (or sell) on any date within a specified range of dates.

This stock option is based on several helper functions, defined in [19], which we must examine first. The european function constructs a contract which allows its holder to choose between receiving "something" or nothing on a specified date. receive constructs a contract that pays the specified amount of the specified currency passed as arguments and uses the scale and one primitives. The scale primitive takes an amount of type *Obs Double*–where type *Obs d* represents a time-varying quantity of type *d*–and a contract as arguments and multiplies key values in the contract by the amount. Note that european_stock_option uses - and / operators which are built-ins that operate on *Obs Double* arguments. stock_price is a primitive for looking up the price of the specified stock on the specified date.

european_stock_option starts off by using stock_price to look up the price of the specified company's stock on the "effective" (contract start) and "expiry" (contract end) dates. It uses these stock prices to construct the payoff based on the specified call or put style, and feeds the payoff to receive to construct a contract that pays it. Finally european_stock_option passes the result of receive to the european, which allows the holder to choose between the payoff and nothing. Note that the payoff may well be negative, so the holder's choice is not entirely clear. The end of Fig. 3, provides an example call european_stock_option which constructs a call option on ABC Co. In practice, functions like european_stock_option would be defined in BCL's standard library, and would be called by users who wish to model European stock options directly or who wish to model contracts that contain such options as sub-contracts.

3.1 Motivation for Gradual Types

Given that BCL is mostly used to describe financial contracts, it should come as no surprise that our users are largely financial professionals. In particular, many are financial engineers or quantitative analysts with some programming experience in dynamic languages such as Python and MATLAB. Typically these users need to translate term sheets, plain-English descriptions of a contract, into BCL for consumption by our system. These contracts are mostly one-off and, once finished, are unlikely to be reused as subcontracts to build further contracts. For these reasons, the users of BCL are primarily concerned with development speed. Ideally, they would like to be able to translate a term sheet as quickly as possible, so that they may focus on analyzing the contract's behavior once it has been ingested by our system.

On the other hand, the maintainers of BCL and its standard library are software engineers and functional programmers with extensive experience in OCaml, C++ and other static languages. The main jobs of the BCL maintainers are implementing language extensions and standard library functions. One of the significant constraints that they face is preserving backwards compatibility. All existing user contracts must continue to work as BCL evolves–even minor changes in behavior are unacceptable! Given the broad reuse of the features that BCL's language maintainers implement and the difficulties involved in rolling back features, correctness is the paramount concern of BCL maintainers.

Finally, it is important to note that the version of BCL described here is actually the second version of BCL. The first version of BCL was dynamically typed, so we will distinguish it from the second version by referring to it as Dynamic BCL. Dynamic BCL supports only a few primitive data types, as well as a list composite type; it does not support algebraic types. It also runs only minimal validation before attempting evaluation. This simplicity makes Dynamic BCL well suited to our users who seek to quickly feed contracts into our system, but ill-suited to the library code written by our maintainers. Additionally, some users who encounter runtime type errors while implementing particularly complex contracts would turn to the maintainers for assistance, further increasing the burden on the maintainers. It was in light of these issues, that we developed (Static) BCL.

To address the issues with Dynamic BCL while remaining useful to our users, BCL aims to be a static language that feels roughly dynamic. To this end, BCL supports implicit static types via type inference; we chose Hindley-Milner style inference so that our users could omit type annotations in almost all cases. BCL also supports record and variant types, although they are structural rather than the nominal ones typically seen in OCaml and Haskell. This choice also lends BCL a more dynamic feel.

The goal of BCL's design is to retain enough flexibility for our users, while introducing static types for the benefit of our language maintainers. However, "enough flexibility" is entirely subjective and some users may well feel that any amount of static checking results in a system that is too inflexible. Gradual types address this concern by allowing users to use dynamic types where they like, while also allowing maintainers to use static types where they would like. Importantly, gradual types guarantee that fully dynamic code and fully static code can co-exist, and that static code is never blamed for runtime type errors. Taken together, these two guarantees satisfy both groups, and ensure that the type errors that dynamic users see are isolated to the code that they themselves wrote.

3.2   Core Calculus

BCL's core calculus is the lambda calculus extended with structural composite types and recursive types. Furthermore, BCL is implicitly-typed and supports Hindley-Milner style type inference. This section describes the types and terms of this core calculus. Note, however, that the grammars in this section are abstract representations of BCL's theoretical underpinnings, and do not cover the full set of productions in BCL's grammar.

$$\kappa ::= * \mid \rho \mid \kappa \Rightarrow \kappa \qquad\qquad C ::= \rightarrow \mid \Pi \mid \Sigma \mid \dots$$
$$\tau ::= \alpha \mid C \mid \tau\,\tau \mid l : \tau; \tau \mid \epsilon \mid \mu\alpha.\tau \qquad \sigma ::= \tau \mid \forall\alpha.\sigma$$

Fig. 4. Grammar of types and kinds

Kinds and Types. The grammar of the types and kinds that describe BCL is given in Fig. 4. Our kind system is fairly standard and consists of only three forms. The base kind, $*$, is the kind of "proper" types–Int and $Int \rightarrow Int$, for example–which themselves describe terms. The row kind, ρ, is of course the kind for rows. The operator kind, $\Rightarrow$, is the kind of type operators – $Array$ and $\rightarrow$, for example – which take types as arguments and which do not directly describe terms.

C ranges over type constructors, including the type operators for function types ($\rightarrow$ of kind $* \Rightarrow * \Rightarrow *$), record types ($\Pi$ of kind $\rho \Rightarrow *$) and variant types (Σ of kind $\rho \Rightarrow *$). C may also include additional constructors for base types (e.g. Int and $String$) and more type operators (e.g. $Array$) as desired. However, these additional constructors are not useful for our purposes here, so we make no further mention of them.

Our type system is stratified into monomorphic types and type schemes, per [17]. Monomorphic types, τ, consist of type variables, type constructors, and record, variant and recursive types. Type variables are ranged over by α, β, γ, etc., and are explicitly bound by μ and $\forall$ types, as described below. Rows are written $l : \tau; \tau'$, indicating that the row has a field labeled l of type τ. τ' has kind ρ and dictates the other fields that the row may contain. If τ' is a type variable, the row can contain arbitrary additional fields; if τ' is the empty row, ϵ, the row contains no additional fields; finally if τ' is another type of the form $l : \tau; \tau'$, then the row contains exactly the fields specified therein. Recursive types are written $\mu\alpha.\tau$, where the variable α represents the point of recursion and is bound within τ. BCL's recursive types are equi-recursive, so it does not have explicit constructs for rolling and unrolling recursive types. Finally, type schemes have two forms: monomorphic types and universally quantified schemes. Monomorphic types, τ, are merely the types described above. Universally quantified schemes, $\forall\alpha.\sigma$, bind the variable α within the scheme σ. Naturally, it is through universal quantification that BCL supports parametric polymorphism.

$$t ::= x \mid \lambda x.t \mid t\,t \mid \textbf{let rec } x = t \textbf{ in } t \mid t : \tau \mid \{\overline{l_i : t_i}\} \mid t.l \mid l\,t \mid \textbf{match } t \textbf{ with } \overline{l_i x_i \Rightarrow t_i}$$

Fig. 5. Grammar of terms

Terms. The grammar of the terms in BCL is given in Fig. 5. Most of the term forms are drawn directly from the lambda calculus. Term variables are ranged over by x, y, z, etc., and are introduced by lambda abstraction, let-bindings and match-expressions. Lambda abstraction is written $\lambda x.t$ and binds x within the expression t. Lambda abstractions are eliminated by application, which is denoted by juxtaposition: $t\,t$. Let-bindings are written **let rec** $x = t$ **in** t. The **rec** is optional and, when present, indicates x may be referenced by the expression to the right of the $=$; x may of course always be referenced by the expression to the right of the **in**. Type annotations are written $t : \tau$, and serve to ensure that t has the they τ.

In addition to the forms described above, BCL supports records and variants. Record introduction is written $\{\overline{l_i : t_i}\}$, where t_i evaluates to the value stored in the field l_i. Records are eliminated by field projection. The projection of the field l from the record t is written $t.l$. Variant introduction is written $l\,t$, where the label l is used to tag the variant's payload, t. Variants are eliminated by case analysis, which is written **match** t **with** $\overline{l_i x_i \Rightarrow t_i}$, which evaluates to the branch specified by the tag associated with the variant t.

4   Implementation

We identify three main components required to add gradual typing to a statically typed language with type inference, such as BCL. The first is the ability to annotate terms with types, as these annotations dictate whether a term is type-checked statically or dynamically. The second is the addition of a dynamic type to the existing set of types, and the third is an algorithm to unify the existing types with the newly added dynamic type. Since our grammar, shown in Fig. 5, already supports explicit annotation of terms, we have the means to differentiate between dynamically typed and statically typed code. We add a dynamic type, ?, to our set of types; it serves to indicate that a term that will be dynamically typed. BCL's type inference algorithm statically infers a type for every term, meaning that by default BCL programs are completely statically typed. In order to tell the type system to dynamically type some terms, we must explicitly annotate those terms with the ? type.

For example: a simple increment function can be defined in BCL as follows.

```
let incr x = x + 1 in incr
```

The type system will infer the type $Int \rightarrow Int$ for the incr function. However, we can instead provide an explicit annotation.

```
let incr x = x + 1 in incr : ? -> Int
```

In this case, the inference algorithm retains the annotated type as the type of the function. Any type checks on the argument of the incr function would be put off until runtime. While the type checks pertaining to ? types are delayed, we still need to complete the inference procedure in order to infer the types of the un-annotated portions of the program (like the return type of incr). Siek and Vacchrajani [25] (S&V) extend the standard unification-based inference algorithm to handle the ? type. Their algorithm is based on the *consistent-equal* relation which takes into consideration the type variables that are generated as part of a typical type inference algorithm. Fortunately for us, their algorithm works well for our implementation with only minor adaptations.

Figure 6 shows an outline of our adaptation of S&V's inference algorithm. Unlike the original algorithm by S&V, BCL's does not separate constraint generation and constraint solving.[2] This difference is important, as it means that our inference algorithm does not have access to the whole constraint set prior to unification. Instead the infer function traverses the term, generating and solving constraints on the fly. For example, if it encounters an application $t_1\ t_2$, it figures out the type of the term from the environment (Γ) and generates a constraint like $\{\tau_1 \simeq \tau_2 \rightarrow \alpha\}$, where τ_1 is the type of term t_1, τ_2 is the type of t_2 and α is a fresh type variable. infer sends this constraint to unify, which attempts to satisfy it or raises an error if the constraint cannot be satisfied.

Figure 6 shows the infer case for a term t annotated with the type τ. infer generates a constraint which tries to unify the type inferred for t with the annotated type, τ. We highlight this case for two reasons. First, the only way we can currently introduce a ? type in BCL is through an annotation. Therefore, this is the only point where constraints involving the ? type originate. Second it is critically important that this case returns the annotated type and not the inferred type. Note that in incr the inferred type $Int \rightarrow Int$ differs from–but is *consistent-equal* with–the annotated type $? \rightarrow Int$. We always want the user's explicit annotation to take precedence in this situation.

BCL's unification algorithm is already based on Huet's unification algorithm, which makes adopting the changes suggested by S&V easier. The crux of S&V's algorithm lies in the way the ? type unifies with other types, and particularly with type variables. When ? unifies with a type variable, S&V's algorithm makes ? the representative node. However, when ? unifies with types other than type variables, the other type becomes the representative element of the resulting set. The find and merge functions in Fig. 6 come from the union-find data structure that underlies Huet's unification algorithm. Respectively, they compute a node's representative element, and union two nodes' sets keeping the representative element of the first node's set.

The first six cases of the unify function handle unification with the ? type as laid out by S&V. We say first six because Cases 1 and 2 take care of unifying the ? type with type variables as specified by S&V's algorithm. Cases 3 and 4 handle an edge case in their algorithm. These two cases simulate the operational semantics of Siek and Taha [23], which require constraints like $\{? \simeq \alpha \rightarrow \beta\}$ to be treated as $\{? \rightarrow ? \simeq \alpha \rightarrow \beta\}$. We use new to create a new node different from what was passed in to handle this case.

Cases 8–11 take care of unifying with row and recursive types, neither of which are covered by S&V's solution. However, it is our observation that these types do not require special handling. A constraint like $\{x : Int; \epsilon \simeq ?\}$ would be handled by

---

[2] Put another way, our inference algorithm solves each constraint immediately after generating it, and before generating the next constraint.

```
maybe_copy_dyns (τ₁ ≃ τ₂) =
    τ₁′ ← if was_copied τ₁ then τ₁ else copy_dyn τ₁
    τ₂′ ← if was_copied τ₂ then τ₂ else copy_dyn τ₂
    τ₁′ ≃ τ₂′

unify τ₁″ τ₂″ =
    τ₁ ← find τ₁″
    τ₂ ← find τ₂″
    if was_visited τ₁ and was_visited τ₂ then
      ()
    else case maybe_copy_dyns (τ₁ ≃ τ₂) of
        α ≃ τ | τ ≃ α ⇒ merge τ α (* Case 1 & 2 *)
      | ? ≃ τ₁ → τ₂ | τ₁ → τ₂ ≃ ? ⇒ (* Case 3 & 4 *)
        unify τ₁ (new ?)
        unify τ₂ (new ?)
      | ? ≃ τ | τ ≃ ? ⇒ merge τ ? (* Case 5 & 6 *)
      | τ₁₁ → τ₁₂ ≃ τ₂₁ → τ₂₂ ⇒ (* Case 7 *)
        unify τ₁₁ τ₂₁
        unify τ₁₂ τ₂₂
      | l : τ₁; τ₂ ≃ l′ : τ₁′; τ₂′ if l = l′ ⇒ (* Case 8 *)
        unify τ₁ τ₁′
        unify τ₂ τ₂′
      | l : τ₁; τ₂ ≃ l′ : τ₁′; τ₂′ ⇒ (* Case 9 *)
        α ← fresh_type_variable ()
        unify (l : τ₁; α) τ₂′
        unify (l′ : τ₁′; α) τ₂
      | μα.τ ≃ τ′ | τ′ ≃ μα.τ ⇒ (* Case 10 & 11 *)
        mark_visited (μα.τ)
        unify τ[μα.τ/α] τ′
      | ε ≃ ε ⇒ () (* Case 12 *)
      | _ ⇒ error

infer Γ t =
  case t of
    . . .
    t : τ →
      case (unify (infer Γ t) τ) of
        Error ⇒ Error : inconsistent types
      | _ ⇒ τ
```

Fig. 6. Type inference algorithm

Case 2 and ? would be merged with the row type $x : Int; \epsilon$. Now suppose the ? is present inside the row type like in the following constraint $\{x : ?; \epsilon \simeq x : Int; \epsilon\}$; this will be handled by Case 8 and then Cases 5 and 12 when we recursively call unify with the types within the row. The same holds true for unification with the recursive type. For example, a constraint like $\{List\ Int \simeq List\ ?\}$ will have the following successful unification trace:

$\{List\ Int \simeq List\ ?\}$ (Case 10)

$\to \{\Pi(head : Int; tail : List\ Int; \epsilon) \simeq List\ ?\}$ (Case 11)

$\to \{\Pi(head : Int; tail : List\ Int; \epsilon) \simeq \Pi(head : ?; tail : List\ ?; \epsilon)\}$ (Case 8)

$\to \{\{Int \simeq ?\}, \{List\ Int \simeq List\ ?\}\}$ (Case 6, Case 10)

$\to \cdots$

$\to \{\Pi\ \epsilon \simeq \Pi\ \epsilon\}$ (Case 8)

$\to \{\epsilon \simeq \epsilon\} \to ()$ (Case 12)

Where $List$ is defined as follows.

$List\ \alpha \equiv \mu a.\Sigma(Nil : \Pi\epsilon; Cons : \Pi(head : \alpha; tail : a; \epsilon); \epsilon)$ Note that BCL supports *equi-recursive types*, as mentioned in Sect. 3, so unify tracks the types it visits with mark_visited and was_visited to detect cycles.

The copy_dyn Conundrum: The copy_dyn function is a crucial part of the way ? unifies with other types. In S&V's presentation, copy_dyn ensures that each ? node in the constraint set is physically unique. Without this step, multiple types might unify with the same ? node, and then transitively with each other. This has the potential to cause spurious failures in unify. S&V's solution to this is to traverse the constraint set and duplicate each ? node prior to unification; this is performed by their implementation of copy_dyn. Unfortunately, we do not have access to the full constraint set, because our inference algorithm generates and solves constraints in one step.

Our first attempt at working around this issue was to call copy_dyn as the first step in unification. However, this leads to over copying. For example, consider the constraint $\{\ ? \to \alpha \simeq \alpha \to \tau\ \}$. According to Case 7 of unify, when α unifies with the ? node, copy_dyn is called and a new ? node is created in the union-find structure. But when α then unifies with τ, find looks up ? as α's representative element, and copy_dyn is called once more. τ therefore unifies with the new ? node, instead of the one which unified with α. Thus, we lose the fact that τ and α are the same type.

To rectify this, we implement maybe_copy_dyns, which traverses a constraint and copies each ? node exactly once.[3] The result of this is the same as originally intended by S&V's copy_dyn function. That is, we ensure there is a unique ? node in the union-find structure for every unique use of ?.

4.1 Discussion

In Sect. 2 we gave an overview of how statically typed languages approach this problem of promoting dynamic typing. It is our observation that most statically typed, object-oriented languages approach dynamic typing following Abadi et al. That is, their dynamic type exploits subtype polymorphism to bypass static type checking. This is a natural direction for object-oriented languages which rely heavily on subtyping. In order to inspect the types at runtime, these languages make use of type reflection. Java is one such language where work has been done to add dynamic types using reflection,

---

[3] There are many ways to accomplish this. Our approach was to use one canonical ? node in type annotations, and compare each ?'s address to the canonical node's address before copying.

contracts and mirrors [6]. The Java Virtual Machine supports many dynamic languages like Jython and JRuby, demonstrating that such runtime constructs help static languages add more dynamic type checks. However, these implementations only add dynamic checks, and do not achieve the gradual goal of a seamless mix of static and dynamic types as in [26]. To our knowledge, only Featherweight Java [11] has attempted to support proper gradual typing [12]. In any case, the primary purpose for dynamic types in these languages is inter-operation with other dynamic languages. This differs from our own purpose and the end result does not fit our needs well. Thus we conclude that this approach was not a good design choice for us.

The languages closest to BCL are statically typed functional languages with type inference, such as SML, OCaml, and Haskell. OCaml has incorporated dynamic typing at the library level by leveraging its support for generalized algebraic data types [3]. Similarly, Haskell supports a dynamic type as a derivative of the `Typeable` type class, which uses reflection [13] to look at the runtime representation of types. While these approaches introduce more dynamism, they lack the simplicity of gradual typing, which hide all the nuts and bolts of the type system under a simple ? annotation.

Seamless interoperation of static and dynamic types as promised by gradual typing fits very well with our use case. It lets our end users access both paradigms without knowledge of specialized types or constructs. Furthermore, the approach we use—extending unification-based inference with gradual typing—is a natural extension for languages like BCL, which support static type inference. The addition of dynamic types to the type system easily boils down to how we handle this new type in the unification algorithm, and does not require reworking the entire type system. We attribute this benefit to S&V's proposed inference algorithm, which incorporates the essence of the $\lambda^?_\rightarrow$ type system. This makes it easier to adapt to an existing language with similar constructs.

Garcia and Cimini's work takes a different approach to this problem but their end goal is the same: gradual type inference in a statically typed language. The authors of that work feel that S&V's approach has "complexities that make it unclear how to adopt, adapt, and extend this approach with modern features of implicitly typed languages like let-polymorphism, row-polymorphism and first class polymorphism". Our experience with S&V's approach was different: we found the integration fairly simple without major changes to the original inference algorithm. We leave a deep dive into the differences between these two schemes to future work. Based on Garcia and Cimini's design principle, Xie et al. [34] introduce an inference algorithm with support for higher-rank polymorphism, using a *consistent subtyping* relation. In contrast, BCL only infers rank-1 polymorphic types and doesn't support higher-rank polymorphism.

We recognize an added benefit of going from a static to a dynamic language with explicit ? annotations. Promoting static type checking in a dynamic language without type inference requires the programmer to add annotations to all parts of the code that they want statically checked. Needing to add these annotations is such a burden for the programmer that they often skip some annotations and miss out on static optimizations. These un-annotated types are implicitly dynamic, leading to runtime overhead, despite the fact that on many occasions they could be statically inferred. This in turn has lead to efforts to making gradual typing more efficient [22].

BCL does not have this issue as it provides static inference by default. It therefore enjoys the optimizations of static typing and can skip unnecessary runtime checks.

Moreover, BCL could support a dynamic-by-default mode with an additional compiler flag that implicitly annotates un-annotated terms with the ? type. This makes it even more seamless to go from complete static typing to complete dynamic typing. We might also consider doing this implicit annotation on a file-level or function-level. In cases where it is possible to separate dynamic and static components, this could even lead to cleaner refactoring. These ideas have not yet been implemented in BCL but are something we intend to do as future work.

5   Application of Gradual Types

Gradual typing enables the quick prototyping common in dynamic languages, as well as specialized applications that enable simplification of existing code. In this section, we focus on the latter, due to space constraints. Notice, in Fig. 3, that the `scale` combinator [19] is simply multiplication of a contract by a floating-point *observable*. In a domain specific language like BCL, it is convenient to reuse the `**` multiplication syntax for `scale` as well. We can fit this more general *observable* multiplication operator into the type system with the gradual type $Obs\ Double \rightarrow\ ? \rightarrow\ ?$. Our new multiplication operator can delegate to `scale` when the second argument a $Contract$ at runtime and continue with *observable* multiplication, or raise a runtime type error based on the runtime type of the second argument. With this new operator, the `receive` function can be rewritten thus:

```
let receive currency amount = one currency ** amount in ...
```

There are a variety of extensions to Hindley-Milner that enable this sort of ad-hoc polymorphism statically. Type classes, for example, extend the signature of overloaded functions with classes [31], which our users would need to learn. Similarly, modular implicits introduce a separate syntax for implicit modular arguments [33]. However, these constructs require effort to educate our end users in their use and detract from the dynamic feel of the language. Gradual types, by contrast, are much easier for our end users since they already work in a dynamic environment and it does not require new syntax (save a ? annotation).

It is worth noting that, while the new multiplication operator can be given a valid type in BCL, it cannot currently be implemented in BCL; it can only be implemented as a built-in operator because BCL provides no way to perform case analysis on the runtime type of a dynamic value. However, addressing this is actually quite easy if we reuse BCL's existing support for variants. That is, we could implement a `dynamic_to_type` primitive which consumes a dynamic value and produces a variant describing its runtime type. This would allow us to then branch on this variant with the existing **match** construct. Figure 7 shows a prototype of a function that achieves this effect assuming the `dynamic_to_type` primitive is defined.

`dynamic_to_type` is interesting in light of our discussion in Sect. 2, which describes dynamic programming as the territory of BCL's users and not its maintainers. Clearly, however, the dynamic multiplication operator is something that would live in BCL's standard library and be maintained by the language maintainers. Indeed there are a number of interesting standard library functions which we might add on top of

```
let dyn_obs_mul x y = match dynamic_to_type (y) with
  | Obs Double => x ** y
  | Contract => scale x y
in
    dyn_obs_mul : Obs Double → Dyn → Dyn
```

Fig. 7. Sample of a dynamic observable multiplication function

dynamic_to_type. Another simple example would be a any_to_string function, which could produce a string representation for arbitrary types by traversing their runtime type and delegating to the appropriate type-specific to-string function. Such a function would be very handy for debugging and quick inspection of values.

The any_to_string example is a function which consumes an arbitrary value. However, there are equally compelling use cases for producing arbitrary values. For example, property-based testing frameworks rely on automatically generating values that conform to certain constraints. We could implement a simple property-based testing framework with a function which consumes the output of dynamic_to_type and generates arbitrary values that conform to that type. Such a framework would be especially useful in a domain such as ours, where real money is at stake, and where robust testing is absolutely critical.

6   Conclusion

Dynamic languages are extremely popular with many users. For users with a limited computer science background, for whom ease-of-use is the paramount, this is doubly true. However, despite the flexibility offered by dynamic typing, the safety offered by static typing is helpful in domains where correctness is critical. In such an arena, gradual types are a perfect blend of both paradigms, and they provides a middle ground to please a larger group of users. Given this, it is important for the literature to speak about adapting gradual types to existing languages. As a first step towards that, we write about our experiences adapting gradual typing to our implementation of a statically typed functional language with type inference. We provide context in terms of how others in similar situations approached this problem, and we elaborate our inference algorithm with key insights around what worked for us and what did not. We identify an interesting use case for gradual types here at Bloomberg, where we look to harmonize end users and language maintainers with competing goals. End users want to specify financial contracts without worrying about static typing demands, while language maintainers need a more rigorous type system that ensures that libraries that they write are error-free. Gradual types allow us to satisfy both groups. We also intend to gather feedback from our end users and maintainers about how gradual types are being used, which can give insight into possible tweaks to make this system more amenable to all.

References

1. Using Type Dynamic. https://docs.microsoft.com/en-us/dotnet/csharp/programming-guide/types/using-type-dynamic. Accessed 02 Jan 2021
2. Abadi, M., Cardelli, L., Pierce, B., Plotkin, G.: Dynamic typing in a statically typed language. ACM Trans. Program. Lang. Syst. (TOPLAS) **13**(2), 237–268 (1991)
3. Balestrieri, F., Mauny, M.: Generic programming in OCaml. Electron. Proc. Theor. Comput. Sci. **285**, 59–100 (2018). https://doi.org/10.4204/EPTCS.285.3
4. Damas, L., Milner, R.: Principal type-schemes for functional programs. In: Proceedings of the 9th ACM SIGPLAN-SIGACT Symposium on Principles of Programming Languages, pp. 207–212 (1982)
5. Garcia, R., Cimini, M.: Principal type schemes for gradual programs. SIGPLAN Not. **50**(1), 303–315 (2015). https://doi.org/10.1145/2775051.2676992
6. Gray, K.E., Findler, R.B., Flatt, M.: Fine-grained interoperability through mirrors and contracts. ACM SIGPLAN Not. **40**(10), 231–245 (2005)
7. Greenberg, M.: The dynamic practice and static theory of gradual typing. In: 3rd Summit on Advances in Programming Languages (SNAPL 2019). Schloss Dagstuhl-Leibniz-Zentrum fuer Informatik (2019)
8. Gronski, J., Knowles, K., Tomb, A., Freund, S.N., Flanagan, C.: Sage: hybrid checking for flexible specifications. In: Scheme and Functional Programming Workshop, vol. 6, pp. 93–104 (2006)
9. Hejlsberg, A.: C# 4.0 and beyond by anders hejlsberg. Microsoft Channel, vol. 9 (2010)
10. Huet, G.: Resolution d'equations dans des languages d'order 1, 2,..., ω. these d'etat, University de Paris (1976). https://ci.nii.ac.jp/naid/10006536039/en/
11. Igarashi, A., Pierce, B.C., Wadler, P.: Featherweight Java: a minimal core calculus for Java and GJ. ACM Trans. Program. Lang. Syst. **23**(3), 396–450 (2001). https://doi.org/10.1145/503502.503505
12. Ina, L., Igarashi, A.: Gradual typing for featherweight Java. Comput. Softw. **26**(2), 18–40 (2009)
13. Peyton Jones, S., Weirich, S., Eisenberg, R.A., Vytiniotis, D.: A reflection on types. In: Lindley, S., McBride, C., Trinder, P., Sannella, D. (eds.) A List of Successes That Can Change the World. LNCS, vol. 9600, pp. 292–317. Springer, Cham (2016). https://doi.org/10.1007/978-3-319-30936-1_16
14. Knight, K.: Unification: a multidisciplinary survey. ACM Comput. Surv. (CSUR) **21**(1), 93–124 (1989)
15. Matthews, J., Findler, R.B.: Operational semantics for multi-language programs. ACM Trans. Program. Lang. Syst. (TOPLAS) **31**(3), 1–44 (2009)
16. Meijer, E., Drayton, P.: Static typing where possible, dynamic typing when needed: the end of the cold war between programming languages. Citeseer (2004)
17. Milner, R.: A theory of type polymorphism in programming. J. Comput. Syst. Sci. **17**(3), 348–375 (1978)
18. Miyazaki, Y., Sekiyama, T., Igarashi, A.: Dynamic type inference for gradual Hindley-Milner typing. Proc. ACM Program. Lang. **3**(POPL), 1–29 (2019). https://doi.org/10.1145/3290331
19. Peyton Jones, S., Eber, J.M., Seward, J.: Composing contracts: an adventure in financial engineering (functional pearl). SIGPLAN Not. **35**(9), 280–292 (2000). https://doi.org/10.1145/357766.351267
20. Pottier, F.: A modern eye on ml type inference: old techniques and recent developments (September 2005)
21. Pottier, F., Rémy, D.: The essence of ML type inference, pp. 389–489 (January 2005)

22. Rastogi, A., Chaudhuri, A., Hosmer, B.: The ins and outs of gradual type inference. SIG-PLAN Not. **47**(1), 481–494 (2012). https://doi.org/10.1145/2103621.2103714
23. Siek, J., Taha, W.: Gradual typing for functional languages. In: Scheme and Functional Programming Workshop (2006)
24. Siek, J., Taha, W.: Gradual Typing for objects. In: Ernst, E. (ed.) ECOOP 2007. LNCS, vol. 4609, pp. 2–27. Springer, Heidelberg (2007). https://doi.org/10.1007/978-3-540-73589-2_2
25. Siek, J.G., Vachharajani, M.: Gradual typing with unification-based inference. In: Proceedings of the 2008 Symposium on Dynamic Languages, pp. 1–12 (2008)
26. Siek, J.G., Vitousek, M.M., Cimini, M., Boyland, J.T.: Refined criteria for gradual typing. In: Ball, T., Bodik, R., Krishnamurthi, S., Lerner, B.S., Morrisett, G. (eds.) 1st Summit on Advances in Programming Languages (SNAPL 2015). Leibniz International Proceedings in Informatics (LIPIcs), vol. 32, pp. 274–293. Schloss Dagstuhl-Leibniz-Zentrum fuer Informatik, Dagstuhl (2015). https://doi.org/10.4230/LIPIcs.SNAPL.2015.274
27. Tarjan, R.E.: Efficiency of a good but not linear set union algorithm. J. ACM (JACM) **22**(2), 215–225 (1975)
28. Tobin-Hochstadt, S., Felleisen, M.: Interlanguage migration: from scripts to programs. In: Companion to the 21st ACM SIGPLAN Symposium on Object-Oriented Programming Systems, Languages, and Applications, pp. 964–974 (2006)
29. Tobin-Hochstadt, S., Felleisen, M.: The design and implementation of typed scheme. ACM SIGPLAN Not. **43**(1), 395–406 (2008)
30. Vitousek, M.M., Kent, A.M., Siek, J.G., Baker, J.: Design and evaluation of gradual typing for Python. In: Proceedings of the 10th ACM Symposium on Dynamic Languages, DLS 2014, pp. 45–56. Association for Computing Machinery, New York (2014). https://doi.org/10.1145/2661088.2661101
31. Wadler, P., Blott, S.: How to make ad-hoc polymorphism less ad hoc. In: Proceedings of the 16th ACM SIGPLAN-SIGACT Symposium on Principles of Programming Languages, POPL 1989, pp. 60–76. Association for Computing Machinery, New York (1989). https://doi.org/10.1145/75277.75283
32. Wand, M.: A simple algorithm and proof for type inference (1987)
33. White, L., Bour, F., Yallop, J.: Modular implicits. Electron. Proc. Theor. Comput. Sci. **198**, 22–63 (2015). https://doi.org/10.4204/EPTCS.198.2
34. Xie, N., Bi, X., Oliveira, B.C.D.S., Schrijvers, T.: Consistent subtyping for all. ACM Trans. Program. Lang. Syst. **42**(1), 1–79 (2019). https://doi.org/10.1145/3310339

Applications of Declarative Languages

Application of Different Languages

A Logic Programming Approach to Regression Based Repair of Incorrect Initial Belief States

Fabio Tardivo[✉], Loc Pham, Tran Cao Son, and Enrico Pontelli

New Mexico State University, Las Cruces, NM 88003, USA
{ftardivo,lpham,tson,epontelli}@cs.nmsu.edu

Abstract. This paper explores the challenge of encountering incorrect beliefs in the context of reasoning about actions and changes using action languages with sensing actions. An incorrect belief occurs when some observations conflict with the agent's own beliefs. A common approach to recover from this situation is to replace the initial beliefs with beliefs that conform to the sequence of actions and the observations. The paper introduces a regression-based and revision-based approach to calculate a correct initial belief. Starting from an inconsistent history consisting of actions and observations, the proposed framework **(1)** computes the initial belief states that support the actions and observations and **(2)** uses a belief revision operator to repair the false initial belief state. The framework operates on domains with static causal laws, supports arbitrary sequences of actions, and integrates belief revision methods to select a meaningful initial belief state among possible alternatives.

Keywords: Regression · Action languages · Incorrect beliefs · Prolog

1 Introduction

In reasoning about actions and change, sensing actions have been considered as the mean for agents to *refine* their knowledge in presence of uncertainty and/or incomplete knowledge. In these formalisms, a sensing action helps an agent to determine the truth value of an *unknown* fluent. For example, the action *look* helps the agent to determine whether the light in the kitchen is *on* or off ($\neg on$). If the agent does not know whether the light is on or off, her knowledge about the state of the world is the set of *possible states* that she thinks she might be in, i.e., the set $\{\{on\}, \{\neg on\}\}$. The execution of the *look* action will help the agent to decide whether the current state of the world is $\{on\}$ or $\{\neg on\}$.

Let us assume that S denotes the set of possible states that an agent believes she might be in; the execution of a sensing action a, that determines the truth value of a fluent f, will result in:

© Springer Nature Switzerland AG 2021
J. F. Morales and D. Orchard (Eds.): PADL 2021, LNCS 12548, pp. 73–89, 2021.
https://doi.org/10.1007/978-3-030-67438-0_5

- S if the truth value of f is correct in every state in S;
- a subset $S' \subseteq S$, such that each state in S' has the correct value of f and each state in $S \setminus S'$ has the incorrect value of f.

It is important to observe that a sensing action *does not change the world* and its effect is about the knowledge of the agent. Although this fact is true, previous approaches to dealing with sensing actions in action languages or situation calculus, such as those proposed in [11,15,17], often make a fundamental implicit assumption: the reasoning agent has *correct* information. This also means that these approaches cannot be directly applied to situations in which the reasoning agent has completely *incorrect* information (or beliefs) about the world. Let us illustrate this with an example.

Example 1. Consider a robot which was **told** that the light in the kitchen is off and it needs to turn the light on. According to the given information, a plan for the robot consists of two actions: go the kitchen and turn the light on. For the sake of our discussion, let us assume that the action of turning the light on/off can only be executed when the light is off/on.

If, in reality, the light in the kitchen is on, then the proposed plan of actions will fail. The robot goes to the kitchen and sees that the light is on. The robot reasons and comes up with three[1] possible explanations. The first one is that the light turned on by itself. The second one is that the robot's sensing equipment is defective. The third possibility is that **the robot was told something wrong,** i.e., its initial belief about the state of the world is wrong. To check its sensing equipment and see whether the light turns on by itself, the robot flips the switch and sees that the light is off. It waits and then flips the switch again and sees that the light is on. It concludes that its sensing equipment is in good condition and that the light cannot turn on by itself. It realizes that the third possibility is the only acceptable explanation for the *inconsistency* between its beliefs and the real state of the world. It corrects its initial beliefs and moves on.

This simple example illustrates the usefulness of sensing actions in helping an agent to revise their beliefs in real-world situations. Generalizing this idea, it means that agents need to be able to incorporate observations and update their beliefs while executing a plan. In this paper, we propose an approach that combines regression (or reasoning about previous states) and belief revision (or updating the beliefs when new information is available) to allow agents to correct their initial belief state. The main contributions of this paper can be summarized as follows: **(1)** we formalize a general framework based on regression and revision for repairing false beliefs in dynamic domains and develop algorithms for a concrete implementation of the framework; **(2)** we consider the formalization to include support for static causal laws and sensing actions; **(3)** we present an implementation for computing the initial correct belief state.

---

[1] We ignore the possibility that some other agent turns on the light while the robot is moving to the kitchen. This could be identified with the first option.

2   Background: The Action Language $\mathcal{B}_S$

We use a simplified version of the semantics for $\mathcal{B}_S$ in [4] that is similar to the semantics of the language $\mathcal{A}_S$ in [11]. In $\mathcal{B}_S$, an action theory in $\mathcal{B}_S$ is defined over two disjoint sets, a set of actions **A** and a set of fluents **F**. A *fluent literal* is either a fluent $f \in \mathbf{F}$ or its negation $\neg f$. A *fluent formula* is a propositional formula constructed from fluent literals.

An action theory is composed of statements of the following forms:

$$e \text{ if } \{p_1, \ldots, p_n\} \qquad (1) \qquad a \text{ causes } \{e_1, \ldots, e_n\} \text{ if } \{p_1, \ldots, p_m\} \qquad (2)$$

$$a \text{ executable\_if } \{p_1, \ldots, p_n\} \quad (3) \qquad\qquad a \text{ determines } f \qquad (4)$$

where a is an action, f is a fluent, e, e_i are fluent literals representing *effects* and p_i are fluent literals indicating *preconditions*. (1) represents a *static causal law*; it conveys that whenever the fluent literals $p_1, \ldots, p_n$ hold in a state, then e will also hold in the state. (2) represents a *dynamic causal law*. It states that if $p_1, \ldots, p_m$ hold in a state and action a is executed, then the literals $e_1, \ldots, e_n$ will hold in the resulting state after the execution. (3) encodes an *executability condition* for action a. It states that action a can only be executed in a state where the literals $p_1, \ldots, p_n$ hold. (4) is called a *knowledge producing law*. The execution of the *sensing action* a will ensure that in the resulting state the truth value of f is known.

For simplicity, we assume that sensing actions do not occur in dynamic causal laws. To simplify the notation, we often drop the set notation from the laws; we indicate with R_a the set of laws of the form $a \text{ causes } \{e_1, \ldots, e_n\} \text{ if } \{p_1, \ldots, p_m\}$. Given a static or dynamic law r, we indicate with $e(r)$ its effects and with $p(r)$ its preconditions.

An *action theory* is a pair (D, Ψ_0) where Ψ_0 is a fluent formula, describing the *initial state*, and D, called *action domain*, consists of laws of the form (1)–(4). For convenience, we sometimes denote the set of laws of the form (1) by D_C.

2.1   Transition Function

The semantics of $\mathcal{B}_S$ is based on a transition function; its definition requires some introductory concepts. Given a domain D in $\mathcal{B}_S$, a literal is either a fluent $f \in \mathbf{F}$ or its negation $\neg f$; a set of literals s is said to be *consistent* if for each $f \in \mathbf{F}$ we have that $\{f, \neg f\} \not\subseteq s$. A set of literals s is *complete* if for all $f \in \mathbf{F}$ we have that $f \in s \vee \neg f \in s$.

A consistent set of literals s is *closed* under a set of static causal laws $C \subseteq D_C$ if, for all $c \in C$ we have that $p(c) \subseteq s \Rightarrow e(c) \subseteq s$. With $Cl_C(s)$ we denote the smaller consistent set of literals that contains s and is closed under C. To simplify the notation we omit C when $C = D_C$.

A set of literals s is a *state* when it is complete and closed under D_C. A *belief state* is a set of states; intuitively, a belief state represents the states that an agent thinks she may be in. Given a fluent formula φ and a state s, a belief state Σ, and a set of belief states κ, we define: **(1)** $s \models \varphi$ for a state s if s is a model of φ; **(2)** $\Sigma \models \varphi$ for a belief state Σ if $s \models \varphi$ for each $s \in \Sigma$; **(3)** $\kappa \models \varphi$ for a set of belief states κ if $\Sigma \models \varphi$ for at least one $\Sigma \in \kappa$. Given a fluent formula φ, let us define $\Sigma_\varphi = \{s \mid s \text{ is a state}, s \models \varphi\}$. φ is said to be *consistent* if Σ_φ is not empty. The *direct effects* $e(a, s)$ of an action a in a state s are defined as $e(a, s) = \bigcup \{e(r) \mid r \in R_a, s \supseteq p(r)\}$.

The transition function for $\mathcal{B}_S$ maps pairs of action and belief state to sets of belief states. Let us start by defining the transition function Φ for the case of a single state. Let us write, for each fluent $f \in \mathbf{F}$, $\bar{f} = \neg f$, $\overline{\neg f} = f$, and $\bar{s} = \{\bar{l} \mid l \in s\}$ for a set of literals s. Let s be a state and a a non-sensing action executable in state s, $\Phi(a, s) = \{s' \mid s' \text{ is a state}, s' = Cl((s \cap s') \cup e(a, s))\}$.

Let Σ be a belief state and a is an action. If a is not executable in some $s' \in \Sigma$, we define $\Phi(a, \Sigma) = \emptyset$; otherwise,

- If a is a non-sensing action, $\Phi(a, \Sigma) = \{\bigcup_{s \in \Sigma} \Phi(a, s)\}$;
- If a is a sensing action a that determines the fluent f, $\Phi(a, \Sigma) = \{\Sigma_1, \Sigma_2\} \setminus \{\emptyset\}$ where $\Sigma_1 = \{s \in \Sigma \mid f \in s\}$ and $\Sigma_2 = \{s \in \Sigma \mid \neg f \in s\}$.

We are also interested in defining the transition function applied to a sequence of actions; let us define the function $\widehat{\Phi}$ which maps a sequence of actions and a set of belief states to a set of belief states: given a set of belief states κ and a sequence of actions α represented by a list of actions (using Prolog notation) $[a_1, \ldots, a_n] = [a_1 \mid \beta]$:

$$\widehat{\Phi}(\alpha, \kappa) = \begin{cases} \kappa & \text{if } n = 0 \\ \bigcup_{\Sigma \in \kappa} \Phi(a_1, \Sigma) & \text{if } n = 1 \wedge \Phi(a_1, \Sigma) \neq \emptyset \text{ for each } \Sigma \in \kappa \\ \widehat{\Phi}(\beta, \widehat{\Phi}(a_1, \kappa)) & \text{if } n > 1 \text{ and } \widehat{\Phi}(a_1, \kappa) \neq \emptyset \\ \emptyset & \text{otherwise} \end{cases} \tag{1}$$

We assume that for every action theory (D, Ψ_0), Ψ_0 is consistent. Since we are working with a history similar to that discussed in [9], we assume that the domains under consideration are deterministic.

3   Recovering from Inconsistent Histories

The transition function Φ provides a means for an agent to reason and plan in domains with sensing actions and incomplete knowledge about the initial state. It works well for hypothetical reasoning and planning but might be insufficient for an agent to use during the execution of a plan, as it might create discrepancies between the agent's hypothetical beliefs and the real-state of the world. Hence, it will not be help the agent to recover from false beliefs. Let us reconsider the problem in Example 1. We have that the initial belief state of the agent is $\Sigma = \{\{\neg on\}\}$ and the action *look* **determines** *on*. The state of the world is given by $\{on\}$. It is easy to see that the definition above yields $\Phi(look, \Sigma) = \{\{\neg on\}\}$ which indicates that the robot has false beliefs about the world. This is clearly not satisfactory; the robot, after observing that the light is on, should realize that the correct initial belief state is $\{\{on\}\}$ and change it accordingly. This issue becomes even more challenging if the realization of an incorrect initial belief state occurs after the execution of several actions. In this section, we propose a method for the robot to deal with this problem and to correct its initial beliefs.

Definition 1. *Let* $T = (D, \Psi_0)$ *be an action theory. A history of* T *is a sequence of pairs of actions and observations* $\alpha = [(a_1, \psi_1), \ldots, (a_n, \psi_n)]$ *where* a_i *is an action and* ψ_i *is a fluent formula. We assume that if* a_i *is a sensing action for the fluent* f, *then either* $\Psi_i \models f$ *or* $\Psi_i \models \neg f$. *We say that the history* α *is* inconsistent *with* T *if there exists some* k, $1 \leq k \leq n$, *such that* $\widehat{\Phi}([a_1, \ldots, a_k], \{\Sigma_{\Psi_0}\}) \not\models \psi_k$.

Intuitively, α indicates that the initial belief state Σ_0 of T is *incorrect*. We note that we overload the word "observation" in the definition of a history α. It does not imply that every action in α is a sensing action. We will assume that actions' effects are perfect (i.e., actions do not fail and do not produce wrong results). The case of uncertain effects will be left for future work. In this paper, we will focus on the following problem:

Given an action theory $T = (D, \Psi_0)$ *and a history* $\alpha = [(a_1, \psi_1), \ldots, (a_n, \psi_n)]$ *that is inconsistent with* T, *what is the correct initial belief state of* T? *I.e., what should the initial belief state of* T *be so that* α *is consistent with* T?

We note that this problem is similar to the problem discussed in the diagnosis literature, such as [3,4], which is concerned with identifying possible diagnosis given an action theory and a sequence of observations. The difference between this work and diagnosis lies in that this work focuses on the beliefs of agents along a history, whereas works in diagnosis concentrate in identifying defective components of the system represented by the action theory. Our work is closely related to the investigations of iterated belief revision in situation calculus, as in [9,16]. Our proposed approach combines regression and belief revision. We start with the definition of a regression function. This function is different for sensing and non-sensing actions. We start with the case of non-sensing actions (also known as *ontic actions*).

Regression by Non-sensing Actions. Let a be a non-sensing action and ψ and φ be conjunctions of fluent literals. We say φ is a *result* of the regression of a from ψ, denoted by $\varphi \xrightarrow{a} \psi$, if $\forall s \in \Sigma_\varphi.(\Phi(a, s) \models \psi)$.

Regression by Sensing Actions. Let a be a sensing action and ψ and φ be conjunctions of fluent literals. We say φ is a *result* of the regression of a from ψ, denoted by $\varphi \xrightarrow{a} \psi$, if there exists some $\Sigma \in \Phi(a, \Sigma_\varphi)$ such that $\Sigma \models \psi$.

Observe that the requirement on the regression function for sensing actions differs from its counterpart for non-sensing actions. This is because the result of the execution of a sensing action is not deterministically predictable as for a non-sensing action. We should only guarantee that it is possible to obtain ψ after the execution of a.

We define the *regression of action* a *from a conjunction of fluent literals* ψ, denoted by $\mathcal{R}(a, \psi)$, by $\mathcal{R}(a, \psi) = \bigvee_{\varphi \xrightarrow{a} \psi} \varphi$. $\mathcal{R}(a, \psi)$ is called the *result of the regression of a from* ψ. We say that $\mathcal{R}(a, \psi)$ is undefined and write $\mathcal{R}(a, \psi) = false$ if $\{\varphi \mid \varphi \xrightarrow{a} \psi\} = \emptyset$.

For an arbitrary formula ψ, we define $\mathcal{R}(a, \psi) = \bigvee_{i=1}^{k} \mathcal{R}(a, \psi_i)$. where $\bigvee_{i=1}^{k} \psi_i$ is the unique, full DNF representation of ψ.

Proposition 1. *For an arbitrary consistent formula* ψ *such that* $\mathcal{R}(a, \psi) \neq false$, *it holds that* $\Phi(a, \Sigma_{\mathcal{R}(a,\psi)}) \models \psi$.

Proof. All proofs are omitted for lack of space and detailed in [13][2].   □

We illustrate this definition using an example from [9].

Example 2 (Extended Litmus Test). Consider a domain with the fluents {*Acid, Litmus, Blue, Red*}, two dynamic laws for action *dip*, and two static causal laws:

dip **causes** Red **if** $Litmus, Acid$ $\neg Red$ **if** $Blue$

dip **causes** $Blue$ **if** $Litmus, \neg Acid$ $\neg Blue$ **if** Red

Consider $\psi = \neg Red \wedge \neg Blue$. Let us compute $\mathcal{R}(dip, \psi)$. Clearly, *Litmus* must be *false* before the execution of *dip*. For otherwise, the paper would change color. Similarly, both *Red* and *Blue* must be false for the execution of *dip*. As such, $\mathcal{R}(dip, \psi) = \neg Litmus \wedge \neg Red \wedge \neg Blue$.

We extend the regression function in order to deal with a history $\alpha = [(a_1, \psi_1), \ldots, (a_n, \psi_n)]$ for $n \geq 1$ as follows:

- For $n = 1$

$$\widehat{\mathcal{R}}([(a_1, \psi_1)]) = \begin{cases} \mathcal{R}^*(a_1, \psi_1) \text{ if } \mathcal{R}(a_1, \psi_1) \neq false \\ false \qquad\quad \text{otherwise} \end{cases} \quad (2)$$

- For $n > 1$

$$\widehat{\mathcal{R}}([(a_1, \psi_1), \ldots, (a_n, \psi_n)]) = \begin{cases} \widehat{\mathcal{R}}([(a_1, \psi_1), \ldots, (a_{n-1}, \psi_{n-1} \wedge \mathcal{R}^*(a_n, \psi_n)]) \\ \qquad\qquad \text{if } \psi_{n-1} \wedge \mathcal{R}^*(a_n, \psi_n) \not\equiv false \\ false \qquad\qquad\quad \text{otherwise} \end{cases}$$

$$(3)$$

In (2)–(3), $\mathcal{R}^*(a, \psi)$ denotes $\mathcal{R}(a, \psi)$ when a is a non-sensing action and $\mathcal{R}(a, \psi) \wedge \ell$ when a is a sensing action that senses f and $\ell = f$ if $\psi \models f$, $\ell = \neg f$ if $\psi \models \neg f$.

Given an action theory (D, Ψ_0). Let $\alpha = [(a_1, \psi_1), \ldots, (a_n, \psi_n)]$ be a history and $\widehat{\Phi}(\alpha, \{\Sigma_{\Psi_0}\}) \not\models \psi_n$. We can compute $\widehat{\mathcal{R}}(\alpha)$ and use it to correct the initial belief state. This can be done using a belief revision operator. Let us assume the existence of a belief revision operator $\star$, which maps pairs of formulas to formulas and satisfies the *AGM postulates* [1].

Definition 2. *Let* (D, Ψ_0) *be an action theory. Let* $\alpha = [(a_1, \psi_1), \ldots, (a_n, \psi_n)]$ *be a history and* $\widehat{\Phi}(\alpha, \{\Sigma_{\Psi_0}\}) \not\models \psi_n$. *The corrected initial belief state of* (D, Ψ_0) *is defined by* $\Psi_0 \star \widehat{\mathcal{R}}(\alpha)$.

---

[2] https://github.com/NMSU-KLAP/Repair-by-Regression.

There are several proposals for the operator $\star$ (e.g., [5, 6, 14, 19]). In this paper, we will consider two approaches for defining the $\star$ operator. We note that as pointed out in [2], only the operator proposed in [6] satisfies all AGM postulates. In this paper, we make use of the following two operators.

- **Satoh's revision operator** [14]: Let Δ be the symmetric difference of two sets. For formulae ψ and φ, we define

$$\Delta^{min}(\psi, \varphi) = min_{\subseteq}(\{s\Delta s' \mid s \in \Sigma_\psi, s' \in \Sigma_\varphi\}).$$

Furthermore, define $\Sigma_{\psi \star \varphi}$ as $\{s \in \Sigma_\varphi \mid \exists s' \in \Sigma_\psi$ such that $s'\Delta s \in \Delta^{min}(\psi, \varphi)\}$.

- **Dalal's belief revision operator** [6]: Let λ be a formula. Given s and s' be two states in Σ_λ, let us define $Diff(s, s') = |s\Delta s'|$. For a formula ψ and two arbitrary states s and s',

$$s \sqsubseteq_\psi s' \text{ iff } \exists r \in \Sigma_\psi \text{ s.t. } \forall r' \in \Sigma_\psi.[Diff(r, s) \leq Diff(r', s')]$$

Given two formulas ψ and φ, the revision of ψ by φ is defined by[3] $\psi \star \varphi = min(\Sigma_\varphi, \sqsubseteq_\psi)$.

Example 3 (Continuation of Example 2). Assume that the initial belief for the domain in Example 2 is specified by

$$\Psi_0 = Litmus \land \neg Red \land \neg Blue.$$

Consider the history $\alpha = [(dip, \psi)]$ where $\psi = \neg Red \land \neg Blue$. Let $s_1 = \{Litmus, Acid, \neg Red, \neg Blue\}$ and $s_2 = \{Litmus, \neg Acid, \neg Red, \neg Blue\}$. We have that $\Sigma_{\Psi_0} = \{s_1, s_2\}$ and $\Phi(dip, \Sigma_{\Psi_0}) = \{\{Litmus, Acid, Red, \neg Blue\}, \{Litmus, \neg Acid, \neg Red, Blue\}\}$ which indicates that the initial belief state is incorrect. We need to identify the correct initial belief in this situation.

The regression of dip from ψ gives us $\mathcal{R}(dip, \psi) = \neg Litmus \land \neg Red \land \neg Blue$. We want to compute $\Psi_0 \star \varphi$ where $\varphi = \mathcal{R}(dip, \psi)$.

- ***Using Satoh's operator***: $\Sigma_\varphi = \{s_3, s_4\}$ where $s_3 = \{\neg Litmus, Acid, \neg Red, \neg Blue\}$ and $s_4 = \{\neg Litmus, \neg Acid, \neg Red, \neg Blue\}$. We calculate[4]

$$\Delta^{min}(\Psi_0, \varphi) = min_{\subseteq}\{s_3\Delta s_1, s_3\Delta s_2, s_4\Delta s_1, s_4\Delta s_2\}$$
$$= min_{\subseteq}\{\{\neg Litmus, Litmus\}, \{Acid, \neg Litmus, Litmus, \neg Acit\}\}$$
$$= \{\{\neg Litmus, Litmus\}\}$$

which leads to $\Psi_0 \star \varphi = \{s_3, s_4\}$. In other words, $\neg Litmus$ is true in the initial belief state.

---

[3] The original definition by Dalal identifies the set of formulae which are true in $min(\Sigma_\varphi, \sqsubseteq_\psi)$.

[4] The results of the computation is the same if states are represented using only positive literals. In [14], $\{\{\neg Litmus, Litmus\}\}$ would be considered as $\{\{Litmus\}\}$.

- **Using Dalal's operator**: because Σ_{Ψ_0} has only two elements, s_1 and s_2, we have that $s_i \sqsubseteq s_i$ for $i = 3, 4$ and $s_3 \sqsubseteq_{\Psi_0} s_4$ and $s_4 \sqsubseteq_{\Psi_0} s_3$. Therefore, $\min(\Sigma_\varphi, \sqsubseteq_{\Psi_0}) = \{s_3, s_4\}$. In other words, we receive the same results as with Satoh's operator.

We revisit the story from the introduction and illustrate the definition with sensing actions.

Example 4. A simplified version of the story in the introduction, focused only on the sensing action *look*, can be described by the action theory consisting of the law "*look* **determines** *on*" and the initial belief state specified by the formula $\neg on$. Clearly, the history $[(look, on)]$ is inconsistent with the theory. To correct the initial belief state, we compute $\mathcal{R}(look, on) = True$ and $\mathcal{R}^*(look, on) = on$. $\neg on \star on$ results in on, which shows that our approach allows for the agent to correct its beliefs.

The correctness of our formalization is proved in the next proposition.

Proposition 2. *Given an action theory* (D, Ψ_0) *and an inconsistent history* $\alpha = [(a_1, \psi_1), \dots, (a_n, \psi_n)]$, *for every* $k = 1, \dots, n$, $\widehat{\Phi}([a_1, \dots, a_k], \Sigma_{\Psi_0'}) \models \psi_k$, *where* $\Psi_0' = \Psi_0 \star \varphi$ *and* $\varphi = \widehat{R}(\alpha)$.

4 A Logic Programming Implementation

We are interested in implementing a system that allows us to resolve situations where an agent encounters an inconsistent history. The proposed formalism in the previous section is general and both regression and $\star$ can be implemented in different ways. For example, regression has been mainly implemented by the planning community using an imperative language and $\star$ has been explored using answer set programming [8]. In this paper, we present an implementation using Prolog, as Prolog provides an elegant balance between declarative computational logic and procedural-style encoding. A detailed discussion on the choice of Prolog is included in the last subsection. Let D be an action domain. Consider a non-sensing action a and $R \subseteq R_a$, let us define $\mathit{eff}(R) = \bigcup_{r \in R}[e(r)]$ and $\mathit{pre}(R) = \bigcup_{r \in R}[p(r)]$ as the effects and the preconditions of R. We assume that a **executable_if** η_a belongs to D.

4.1 Regression of a Non-Sensing Action

Let us consider an action a and a consistent set of fluent literals ψ^5. We define

$$R_a^+(\psi) = \{r \in R_a \mid \psi \models p(r)\} \qquad R_a^-(\psi) = \{r \in R_a \mid \psi \models \neg p(r)\}$$

representing the set of dynamic laws that are applicable and not applicable, respectively, when a is executed and ψ is definitely true. We say that φ is a-*splittable* if $R_a = R_a^+(\varphi) \cup R_a^-(\varphi)$.

---

[5] Note we freely exchange between sets of literals and conjunctions of literals.

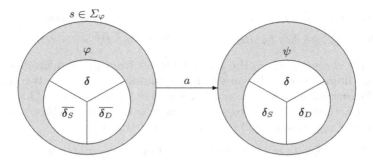

Fig. 1. Intuition for Regression

Proposition 3. *Consider two conjunctions φ and ψ and a non-sensing action a such that $\varphi \xrightarrow{a} \psi$. There exists a set of a-splittable conjunctions of literals $\{\varphi_1, \ldots, \varphi_k\}$ such that $\varphi \equiv \bigvee_{i=1}^{k} \varphi_i$ and $\varphi_i \xrightarrow{a} \psi$ for every $i = 1, \ldots, k$.*

For example, considering $\psi = (l_1 \wedge l_2) \vee (l_3 \wedge l_4)$ and $R_a = \{a \textbf{ causes } \{l_1\} \textbf{ if } \{l_2\}, a \textbf{ causes } \{l_3\} \textbf{ if } \{l_4\}\}$. Two a-splittable formulae are $\varphi_i = \neg l_2 \wedge l_2 \wedge \neg l_4$ and $\varphi_j = \neg l_3 \wedge l_4 \wedge \neg l_2$.

Due to Proposition 3, we will only need to identify a-splittable conjunctions in computing $\mathcal{R}(a, \psi)$. Clearly, if φ is the result of regression from ψ by a then a must be executable in any state $s \in \Sigma_\varphi$, i.e., $\forall_{s \in \Sigma_\varphi} [\eta_a \subseteq s]$.

Definition 3. *A consistent set of literals φ is a* potential regression result *from a conjunction of literals ψ with respect to a if $Cl(\varphi)$ is a-splittable, $\eta_a \subseteq Cl(\varphi)$, $pre(R_a^+(\varphi)) \subseteq Cl(\varphi)$; and $eff(R_a^+(\varphi)) \cup \psi$ is consistent.*

This definition guides the implementation during the nondeterministic computing of φ by reducing the number of guessed literals.

Given a potential regression result φ from ψ by a, we observe that the execution of a from any state $s \in \Sigma_\varphi$ would divide φ into three components as shown in Fig. 1 where

- δ: the set of inertial literals whose values do not change;
- $\overline{\delta_S}$: the set of literals whose values changed because of the application of *static causal laws* in the resulting state, i.e., the state containing ψ; and
- $\overline{\delta_D}$: the set of literals whose values changed because the effects of the *dynamic laws* in $R_a^+(\varphi)$.

This leads us to the following definition:

Definition 4. *A consistent set of literals φ is a* computed regression result *from ψ w.r.t. an ontic action a if*

- *φ is a potential regression result from ψ with respect to a*
- *for every γ such that $\gamma \cup \varphi$ is a state, there exists two consistent sets of literals δ, δ_S such that*

$$\delta \subseteq (\varphi \setminus \overline{\mathit{eff}(R_a^+(\varphi))}) \quad (4) \qquad\qquad Cl(\delta \cup \gamma \cup \delta_D) \text{ is a state} \quad (6)$$

$$(\varphi \setminus \overline{\mathit{eff}(R_a^+(\varphi))}) \setminus \delta = \delta_S \quad (5) \qquad\qquad \psi \cup \delta_S \subseteq Cl(\delta \cup \gamma \cup \delta_D) \quad (7)$$

Equation (4) characterizes δ, the inertial literals from φ; (5) identifies δ_S, the non-inertial literals from φ because of static causal laws; and the two equations (6) and (7) guarantee that the execution of a in $\delta \cup \varphi$ results in ψ. This allows to determine whether a potential regression result φ belongs to $\mathcal{R}(a, \psi)$. We prove that computed regression results are really what we need:

Proposition 4. *Let D be a deterministic action theory and a be a non-sensing action. If φ is a computed regression result from ψ with respect to a then $\varphi \overset{a}{\to} \psi$.*

The above proposition shows that if there exists no computed regression result from ψ with respect to a, then $\mathcal{R}(a, \psi) = \mathit{false}$. Using Propositions 3–4, we can compute the regression result of an arbitrary formula ψ by (i) computing a full DNF representation of ψ, $\bigvee_{i=1}^{k} \psi_i$; (ii) computing $\mathcal{R}(a, \psi_i)$; and (iii) returning $\mathcal{R}(a, \psi) = \bigvee_{i=1}^{k} \mathcal{R}(a, \psi_i)$ if $\mathcal{R}(a, \psi_i) \neq \mathit{false}$ for some i.

4.2   Regression of a Sensing Action

Assume that a is a sensing action with executability condition η_a and that a only senses one fluent f. Let ψ and φ be two conjunctions of literals such that $\varphi \overset{a}{\to} \psi$, then a must be executable in any state in Σ_φ. Furthermore, f is unknown in φ and, ψ differs from φ only by the observation f or $\neg f$.

Definition 5. *Let a be a sensing action that senses f. A consistent conjunction of literals φ is a computed regression result from ψ by a if $\eta_a \subseteq Cl(\varphi)$; $\{f, \neg f\} \cap Cl(\varphi) = \emptyset$; $\psi \setminus \{f, \neg f\} \subseteq Cl(\varphi)$; and if $f \in \psi$ then $\varphi \cup \{f\}$ is consistent and if $\neg f \in \psi$ then $\varphi \cup \{\neg f\}$ is consistent.*

Proposition 5. *Let φ be a computed regression result from ψ by a sensing action a. Then, $\varphi \overset{a}{\to} \psi$.*

The previous proposition and definition provides the basis for computing the regression with sensing actions. Intuitively, φ is the result of regression form $(\psi \setminus \{f, \neg f\}) \cup \eta_a$.

4.3   Implementation in Prolog

This section gives an overview of the implementation and some design decisions in it. The main purpose of the implementation is to guide the development of the definitions in the previous section and validate our ideas as we proceeded. Moreover it gives an overview of strengths and weakness of the theory from a pragmatic point of view.

We use Prolog for different reasons. The simplicity of Prolog in dealing with lists and formulae makes it a suitable platform for computing $\widehat{\mathcal{R}}$ and various belief revision operators. The computation of the regression function $\mathcal{R}$ is inherently non-deterministic, which matches well with Prolog's behavior. Last but not least, Prolog is declarative and modular, which provides a good platform for guaranteeing the correctness of the implementation and the ability to experiment with various belief revision operators. The implementation makes use of Prolog built-ins such as `foldl`, membership checking, union, set difference, etc. and has been tested with SWI-Prolog 8.0.3 and YAP 6.3.3 on Linux x86-64. The complete code is available on GitHub[6].

We represent a conjunction of literals as a list and a DNF formula as a list of lists of literals, respectively. Before we describe the main predicates, we discuss some auxiliary predicates. We use the conventional notation of Prolog with '+'/'−' param to indicate whether the parameter is an input/output parameter. In the following, ψ, ψ', and o are lists of lists of literals, representing formulae in DNF form; a is an action; γ is a list of literals.

- `forceObservation(`$+\psi$`, `$+o$`, `$-\psi'$`)`: returns ψ' that represents the conjunction $\psi \wedge o$; this is needed in the computation of $\widehat{\mathcal{R}}$ (Eq. 3); return ***False*** if $\psi \wedge o$ is inconsistent.
- `minimalPotentialRegressionResult(`$+\eta_a$`, `$+R_a$`, `$+\psi$`, `$-\varphi$`, `$-$Eav`)`: returns a minimal potential regression result φ and the effects of executing a in any state containing φ, Eav, given η_a, R_a, and ψ according to Definition 3;
- `minimalComputedRegressionResult(`$+$Eav`, `$+\psi$`, `$+\varphi'$`, `$-\varphi$`)`: returns a minimal (w.r.t. $\subseteq$) computed regression result φ containing φ', given φ', ψ, and Eav where φ' is a potential regression result.
- `revisionBySatoh(`$+\psi$`, `$+\varphi$`, `$-$Revision`)`: returns $\psi \star \varphi$ according to Satoh.
- `revisionByDalal(`$+\psi$`, `$+\varphi$`, `$-$Revision`)`: returns $\psi \star \varphi$ according to Dalal.

The main clauses used in the implementation of $\widehat{\mathcal{R}}$ are given below.

- `regression(`$+\alpha$`, `$-\varphi$`)`: This is the main predicate that returns $\widehat{\mathcal{R}}(\alpha)$ for a history α. It uses the predicate `foldl` to iteratively compute the regression over the suffixes of α.
- `regressionActionObservation(`$+(a,o)$`,`$+\psi$`, `$-\varphi$`)`: This clause returns $\varphi = \mathcal{R}(a, o \wedge \psi)$ if $o \wedge \psi$ is consistent and the regression of a from $o \wedge \psi$ is successful; and fails otherwise. It starts by computing $o \wedge \psi$ and then, depending on whether a is an ontic or a sensing action, computes $\mathcal{R}(a, o \wedge \psi)$ accordingly. Note that we assume that an action is either an ontic or a sensing action but not both.
- `regressionOnticAction(`$+a$`, `$+\psi$`, `$-\varphi$`)`: This clause computes $\varphi = \mathcal{R}(a, \psi)$ for an ontic action a and formula ψ. It uses the `minimalPotentialRegressionResult/5` and `minimalComputedRegressionResult/4` to identify all possible regression results by a from ψ. Observe that we only compute minimal (with respect to $\subseteq$) regression results since for consistent sets of literals $\varphi_1 \subseteq \varphi_2$, we have that $\Sigma_{\varphi_2} \subseteq \Sigma_{\varphi_1}$. Therefore, if $\Phi(a, \Sigma_{\varphi_1}) \models \psi$ then $\Phi(a, \Sigma_{\varphi_2}) \models \psi$.

---

[6] https://github.com/NMSU-KLAP/Repair-by-Regression.

- `regressionSensingAction(+a, +ψ, -φ)`: This clause computes $\varphi = \mathcal{R}(a, \psi)$ for a sensing action a and formula ψ.

We conclude the section with an example inspired by the example in [16].

Example 5. Consider an extension of Example 4 with $\mathbf{F} = \{in(k), on(k) \mid k = 1, \ldots, n\}$, and the laws with $x = 1, \ldots, n$, $y = x + 1$ if $x < n$ and $y = 1$ if $x = n$, $z = 1, \ldots, n$, and $z \neq x$:

leave(x) **causes** *in(y)* **if** *in(x)*	*look(k)* **determines** *on(k)*	$\neg in(y)$ **if** *in(x)*
turnOn(k) **causes** *on(k)* **if** *in(k)*	*look(k)* **executable_if** *in(k)*	

First, let us consider the case $n = 2$. Assume that the initial state is given by $in(2) \wedge \neg on(1)$. Consider the three histories: H_1 = `[(leave(2),[]),(look(1),[[on(1)]])]`, H_2 = `[(leave(2),[]),(turnOn(1),[]),(leave(1),[]), (look(2),[[on(2)]])]`, and H_3 = `[(leave(2),[]),(turnOn(2),[in(2)]), (look(1),[[on(1)]])]`.

The goal `regression(H_i, Regression_i)` returns `Regression_1` = `[[-in(1), in(2),on(1)]]`, `Regression_2` = `[[-in(1),in(2),on(2),on(1)], [-in(1), in(2),on(2),-on(1)]]`, and `Regression_3` = `[ ]`, respectively, where the empty list `[ ]` signifies that the regression fails. This is because `look(1)` is executable only if `in(1)` is true, but the observation immediately before the execution of `look(1)` indicates that `in(2)` is true.

With `I` = `[[-in(1),-on(1)]]`, `revisionByXxx(I,Regression_i,RISta te_i)`, where `Xxx` stands for Satoh or Dalal, returns `RIState_1=[[-in(1),in(2), on(1)]]`, `RIState_2=[[-in(1),in(2),on(2),-on(1)]]`, and `RI1State_3=[ ]`, respectively. We can easily verify that the results are correct.

To experiment with the system on larger problems, we consider the above domain with $n = 2, \ldots, 10$ and consider the initial belief state `I` = `[[in(n), on(n), on(n-1),...,on(1)]]` and the history `H` = `[(look(n),[[on(n)]]), (leave(n),[]),(look(1),[[on(1)]]),  (leave(1),[]),...,(leave(n-2), []),(look(n-1),[[-on(n-1)]])]`.

The problem can be stated as follows. Initially, the robot is in the room n and believes that all lights are on. It makes a tour, from room n to $1, \ldots, n - 1$. In each room, the robot looks at the light. At the end of the tour, it realizes that its initial belief is incorrect ($\neg on(n-1)$ is observed and it supposed to be $on(n-1)$). We tested with $n = 1, \ldots, 10$ and the system returns the result within 30 min. We observe that the size of the domain, in terms of the number of fluents and the number of actions, plays a significant role in the performance of the system. For $n = 10$, we have 20 fluents and the number of potential regression results for a non-sensing action (e.g., `leave(k)`) is small but checking whether or not a potential regression result is a computed regression result involves checking the number of possible states given a set of formulae, which could range from 2^1 to 2^{19}. We observe that the system spends most of the time doing just that.

We verify our observation by testing with a domain rich in static casual laws.

Example 6. Consider a pipe line with n sections[7] from [18]. This domain can be encoded by a domain with $\mathbf{F} = \{opened(k),\, pressured(k) \mid k = 1,\ldots,n\}$, and the following laws with $x = 1,\ldots,n;\, y = 2,\ldots,n$ and $k = 1,\ldots,n-1$:

$open(x)$ **causes** $opened(x)$ **if** $\top$ $sense(x)$ **determines** $pressured(x)$

$close(x)$ **causes** $\neg opened(x)$ **if** $\top$ $open(k)$ **executable_if** $\neg opended(k+1)$

   $\neg pressured(x)$ **if** $\neg opened(x)$ $pressured(y)$ **if** $opened(y), pressured(y\neg 1)$

  $\neg pressured(y)$ **if** $\neg pressured(y\neg 1)$ $pressured(1)$ **if** $opened(1)$

Assume that initially, the robot believes the first valve is opened and all other valves are closed. To start the burner, she will open the valves from 2 to n. After opening the n-the valve, she realizes that the burner does not start. It means that her initial belief is incorrect. Regression and revision is required, i.e., we need to compute the result $\widehat{\mathcal{R}}(H)$ where H = [(open(2),[]), (open(3),[]),..., (open(n),[-pressured(n)])]. We tested this problem with $n = 2,\ldots,8$. Again, the performance of the system degrades quickly and the problem of verifying the result of regression, as in Example 5, is also observed. For $n = 8$, the system took more than 1 h.

5 Related Work and Discussions

The present work is most closely related to studies in iterated belief change in a general setting of transition systems [9] or in situation calculus [16], i.e., iterated belief change in dynamic domains. It is therefore different from studies aimed at defining and/or characterizing a general iterated belief revision in the literature such as those summarized in [7,12].

The discussion in [9] has been extended to probabilistic setting in [10]. We will focus in comparing our work with the work in [9,16]. The key differences between our work and [9,16] are (*i*) we employ an action language with static causal laws to represent dynamic domains whereas [16] uses situation calculus and [9] uses the general notion of transition system; (*ii*) we focus on the implementation of the proposed operator and have a fully functional system for correcting the initial belief state; (*iii*) we consider sensing actions, which are also considered in [16] but not in [9]; and (*iv*) we do not consider nested beliefs as in [16].

Given an action theory (D, Ψ_0). D can be seen as a transition system whose transitions are defined by (s, a, s') iff $s' \in \Phi(a, s)$. Action histories, belief histories, and observation histories are defined in [9]. A pair (β, o) of an action history $\beta = [a_1,\ldots,a_n]$ and an observation history $o = [\psi_1,\ldots,\psi_n]$ in their definitions corresponds to a history $\alpha = [(a_1,\psi_1),\ldots,(a_n,\psi_n)]$ in our definition. We do not define belief histories explicitly but implicitly use $[\Phi(a_1,\Psi_0), \widehat{\Phi}([a_1,a_2],\Psi_0),\ldots,\widehat{\Phi}([a_1,\ldots,a_n],\Psi_0)]$ as the belief history corresponding to α. The idea of combining regression and a belief revision operator to correct the initial belief state is also present in [9]. Technically, regression from an

---

[7] We omit the precise description to save space.

observation φ by an action sequence β is defined as the set of states $\varphi^{-1}(\beta)$ that contains every state from which the execution of β results in a state satisfying φ. A revision is then used to identify the correct initial belief and the belief history is adjusted accordingly. The focus of the work in [9] is to define a belief evolution operator that combines belief change and belief revision and study properties of such operator. Therefore, the definitions in [9] are generic and no implementation is available.

Our proposed work could be viewed a concretization of the framework in [9], i.e., we developed and implemented the regression function and two belief revision operators. In addition, we use a language to specify dynamic systems while [9] assumes that the transition system is given. The work in [9] also considered situations when observations can be incorrect.

The work in [16] formalizes reasoning about beliefs in action domains with sensing actions using situation calculus. Unlike earlier approaches to reasoning with sensing actions (e.g., [15,17]), the formalism in [16] deals with incorrect beliefs. It introduced an explicit binary relation B, called an *accessibility relation*, between situations for modeling beliefs; and a function pl, called *plausibility function*, from situations to natural numbers for modeling the plausibility of situations. Successor states axioms are then defined for B and pl. This, together with the situation calculus foundational axioms, will allow agents for reasoning about beliefs, belief introspection, and awareness of mistakes. Roughly speaking, the plausibility function modifies the original definition of beliefs of an agent by Scherl and Levesque, $Bel(\psi, s) \overset{def}{=} \forall s'.[B(s', s) \supset \psi[s']]$, to $Bel(\psi, s) \overset{def}{=} \forall s'.[(B(s', s) \land (\forall s''.(B(s'', s) \supset pl(s') \leq pl(s''))) \supset \psi[s']]$, which basically states that the agent believes ψ is true in a situation s if ψ is true in any most plausible situations accessible to s. Under this framework, it is shown that sensing actions can be used to correct the incorrect beliefs of agents. Proposition 2 shows that our approach also allows agent to correct beliefs. We focus on the initial belief but the approach can easily be adapted to consider any states in a history. For example, assume that the agent believes that Σ is the current belief state, $\Sigma \models f$, and a is a sensing action that senses f and executable in Σ, then the following holds: if $\Phi(a, \Sigma) \models \neg f$ then the current belief state must be revised by $\neg f$, i.e., $\Sigma \star \neg f$. This result is similar to the Theorem 21 in [16]. Similar to [9], the work in [16] investigates properties of the belief operators while we focus on the development of a system that computes the correct initial belief state or, as indicated, the belief states along a history. We observe that the discussion in [16] does assume that all actions are always executable. A key difference between the framework of [16] and ours is how the approaches deal with static causal laws. Indeed, static causal laws could be compiled to effect axioms and dealt with in the framework of [16] while they are dealt with directly. For example, to work with Example 5, the approach of [16] requires that effects of actions, direct (e.g., $in(y)$ for the action $leave(x)$ or indirect ($\neg in(x)$), must be described as effects of the actions via successor state axioms. Indeed, there are certain advantages in dealing with static causal laws directly (see below).

The proposed work is considered in a setting similar to the one considered in the diagnosis literature such as those in [3,4]. We assumes that the history is complete and focus on repairing the initial beliefs of the reasoner if the history is consistent. On the other hand, approaches to diagnosis often assume an incomplete history and focus on identifying missing action occurrences that are the source of the history's inconsistency.

The proposed work is considered within the deterministic fragment of the action language $\mathcal{B}_S$ which is $\mathcal{A}_S$ extended with static causal laws. We focus on deterministic domains with static causal laws for two reasons. First, the use of static causal laws allows a natural and compact representation of many domains that would have otherwise required an exponential number of fluents. This covers the majority of benchmarks used in several planning competitions[8]. Furthermore, dealing directly with static causal laws in planning is advantageous and syntactical conditions guaranteeing determinism of domains with static causal laws can be found in [18]. Second, we employ the assumption sets forth in [9] that observations are correct. When domains are non-deterministic, this assumption must be lifted or the revision will need to be weaken as shown below.

Example 7. Consider a domain with the set of fluents $\{f, g, h\}$, an action a with a **causes** f **if** $\neg f$; a **causes** $\neg f$ **if** f and two laws g **if** $f, \neg h$; h **if** $f, \neg g$.

It is easy to see that this domain is non-deterministic. Assume that initially, the reasoner believe is $\bigvee_{s \in \Sigma} s$ where Σ is the set of all possible states. Consider the history $[(a, \psi)]$ with $\psi = f \wedge g \wedge \neg h$. It is easy to see that the regression of a from ψ, let us overload it with $\mathcal{R}(a, \psi)$, should be the set $\{\{\neg f, g, \neg h\}, \{\neg f, \neg g, \neg h\}\}$. Furthermore, the revision of the initial belief state by $\mathcal{R}(a, \psi)$ following either Satoh's or Dalal's approach yields $\mathcal{R}(a, \psi)$. However, the execution of a in $\{\neg f, \neg g, \neg h\}$ gives $\Phi(a, \{\neg f, \neg g, \neg h\}) = \{\{f, g, \neg h\}, \{f, \neg g, h\}\}$ which does not guarantee that the observation is true.

Example 7 shows that the non-determinism of actions leads to the non-determinism of regression, and therefore, would require a relaxed definition of regression or removal of the assumption that observations along the history are correct.

6 Conclusions

In this paper, we explore the problem of correcting the initial beliefs of an agent who, after executing a sequence of actions and making observations along the history, realizes that her initial beliefs are incorrect. Given an inconsistent history, the approach starts by regressing from the final to the first observation and revising the initial beliefs using the result of the regression. Unlike similar approaches explored in the literature, we consider sensing actions in the presence of static causal laws and propose algorithms for computing the correct initial beliefs. The

---

[8] E.g., all non-probabilistic domains in www.icaps-conference.org/competitions.

paper presents an implementation of the algorithms which takes advantage of the declarative nature of Prolog. Our current work aims at improving the performance using tabling, parallelism, and intermediate results minimization. These directions help increase the performance by removing unnecessary computations and utilizing the available hardware. In addition, we intend to explore also other directions as probabilistic settings and ASP implementations. At present, our approach assumes also that observations are correct and actions are perfect. We therefore plan to consider the problem of having observations which are uncertain and imperfect actions in the future.

References

1. Alchourrón, C.E., Gärdenfors, P., Makinson, D.: On the logic of theory change: partial meet contraction and revision functions. JSL **50**(2), 510–530 (1985)
2. Aravanis, T.I., Peppas, P., Williams, M.: Iterated belief revision and Dalal's operator. In: Hellenic Conference on Artificial Intelligence, pp. 26:1–26:4 (2018). https://doi.org/10.1145/3200947.3201038
3. Balduccini, M., Gelfond, M.: Diagnostic reasoning with a-prolog. Theory Pract. Logic Program. **3**(4,5), 425–461 (2003)
4. Baral, C., McIlraith, S., Son, T.C.: Formulating diagnostic problem solving using an action language with narratives and sensing. In: KRR, pp. 311–322 (2000)
5. Borgida, A.: Language features for flexible handling of exceptions in information systems. ACM Trans. Database Syst. **10**(4), 563–603 (1985)
6. Dalal, M.: Investigations into theory of knowledge base revision. In: Proceedings of the AAAI, pp. 449–479 (1988)
7. Delgrande, J.P., Peppas, P., Woltran, S.: General belief revision. J. ACM **65**(5), 29:1–29:34 (2018). https://doi.org/10.1145/3203409
8. Delgrande, J.P., Schaub, T., Tompits, H., Woltran, S.: Belief revision of logic programs under answer set semantics. In: KRR, pp. 411–421 (2008). http://www.aaai.org/Library/KR/2008/kr08-040.php
9. Hunter, A., Delgrande, J.P.: Iterated belief change due to actions and observations. J. Artif. Intell. Res. (JAIR) **40**, 269–304 (2011)
10. Hunter, A., Delgrande, J.P.: Belief change with uncertain action histories. J. Artif. Intell. Res. (JAIR) **53**, 779–824 (2015)
11. Lobo, J., Mendez, G., Taylor, S.: Adding knowledge to the action description language A. In: AAAI 1997, pp. 454–459 (1997)
12. Peppas, P.: A panorama of iterated revision. In: Hansson, S.O. (ed.) David Makinson on Classical Methods for Non-Classical Problems. OCL, vol. 3, pp. 71–94. Springer, Dordrecht (2014). https://doi.org/10.1007/978-94-007-7759-0_5
13. Pham, L., Pontelli, E., Tardivo, F., Son, T.C.: A logic programming approach to regression based repair of incorrect initial belief states. Technical report, NMSU (2020)
14. Satoh, K.: Nonmonotonic reasoning by minimal belief revision. In: Proceedings of the FGCS, pp. 455–462. Springer (1988)
15. Scherl, R., Levesque, H.: Knowledge, action, and the frame problem. Artif. Intel. **144**(1–2) (2003)
16. Shapiro, S., Pagnucco, M., Lespérance, Y., Levesque, H.J.: Iterated belief change in the situation calculus. Artif. Intell. **175**(1), 165–192 (2011)

17. Son, T.C., Baral, C.: Formalizing sensing actions - a transition function based approach. Artif. Intell. **125**(1–2), 19–91 (2001)
18. Tu, P., Son, T., Gelfond, M., Morales, R.: Approximation of action theories and its application to conformant planning. AIJ **175**(1), 79–119 (2011)
19. Winslett, M.: Reasoning about action using a possible models approach. In: AAAI, pp. 89–93 (1988)

Data Validation Meets Answer Set Programming

Mario Alviano$^{(\boxtimes)}$, Carmine Dodaro , and Arnel Zamayla

Department of Mathematics and Computer Science, University of Calabria,
Via P. Bucci, cubo 30B, 87036 Rende, CS, Italy
{alviano,dodaro,zamayla}@mat.unical.it

Abstract. Data validation may save the day of computer programmers, whatever programming language they use. In fact, processing invalid data is a waste of resources at best, and a drama at worst if the problem remains unnoticed and wrong results are used for business. Answer Set Programming is not an exception, but the quest for better and better performance resulted in systems that essentially do not validate data in any way. Even under the simplistic assumption that input and output data are eventually validated by external tools, invalid data may appear in other portions of the program, and go undetected until some other module of the designed software suddenly breaks. This paper formalizes the problem of data validation for ASP programs, introduces a declarative language to specify data validation, and presents a tool to inject data validation in ordinary programs. The proposed approach promotes fail-fast techniques at coding time without imposing any lag on the deployed system if data are pretended to be valid. Additionally, the proposed approach opens the possibility to take advantage of ASP declarativity for validating complex data of imperative programming languages.

Keywords: Answer Set Programming · Data validation · Secure coding · Fail-fast

1 Introduction

A popular Latin saying starts with *errare humanum est* (translated, to err is human), and clarifies how making mistakes is part of human nature. Computer programmers, being humans, are inclined and not indifferent to errors [22,23]. Whether a typo in notation, a misspelled word, or a wrong or fragile representation of data, errors in source code files may result in substantial delays in developing an application. Even worse, errors may stay unknown for a long time, until something happens that stimulates the error to cause a crash of the system or some other unwanted and unexpected behavior. In the worst scenario, unknown errors may lead to wrong results that are used to take some business decision, which in turn may ruin a company. (Refer to [28] for examples of typical errors in software systems.)

© Springer Nature Switzerland AG 2021
J. F. Morales and D. Orchard (Eds.): PADL 2021, LNCS 12548, pp. 90–106, 2021.
https://doi.org/10.1007/978-3-030-67438-0_6

Fail-fast systems are designed to break as soon as an unexpected condition is detected (refer to [31] for an example of fail-fast type checking in Java). As often it is the case, the idea is not limited to computer programming, and definitely not originated in software design. For example, many electrical devices have fail-fast mechanisms to provide overcurrent protection—it is better to melt an inexpensive fuse, than to burn a control board. Even if technically an electrical devise operating with a fuse replaced by a wire works as expected in most cases, no professional electrician would suggest to tamper with the system in this way. In fact, in case the replaced fuses melt again and again, it is usually evidence that the system has some malfunction that must be detected and fixed.

Computer programming should follow a similar fail-fast approach. Errors must be detected as soon as possible, and reported to the programmer in a non-skippable way, so that the malfunction can be quickly detected and fixed. Data validation is the process of ensuring that data conform to some specification, so that any process in which they are involved can safely work under all of the assumptions guaranteed by the specification. In particular, immutable objects are usually expected to be validated on creation, so that their consistency can be safely assumed anywhere in the system—this way, in fact, an invalid immutable object simply cannot exist because its construction would fail. Guaranteeing validity of mutable objects is usually more difficult and tedious, and almost impossible if there is no invariant on the validity of immutable objects. (Refer to [19] and [35] for details on how to tackle the complexity of a business domain in terms of domain primitives and entities.)

Answer Set Programming (ASP; [17, 27, 29]) should not be an exception when it comes at errors. However, the language offers very little in terms of protection mechanisms. No static or dynamic type checking are available, and programmers can rely on a very limited set of primitive types, namely integers, strings and alphanumeric constants, with no idiomatic way to enforce that the values of an argument must be of one of these types only—refer to [7] for details of the ASP-Core-2 format. More structured data types are usually represented by uninterpreted function symbols [3, 5, 6, 12, 25], but again there is no idiomatic way to really validate such structures. Similarly, there is no idiomatic way to specify that input relations satisfy some properties (often expressed in comments, to document the usage of ASP encodings). Even *integrity constraints* may be insufficient to achieve a reliable data validation, as they are cheerfully satisfied if at least one of their literals is false; in fact, integrity constraints are very convenient for discarding unwanted solutions, but not very effective in guaranteeing data integrity—invalid data in this case may lead to discard some wanted solution among thousands or more equally acceptable solutions, a very hard-to-spot unexpected outcome.

The lack of data validation in ASP is likely due to the quest for better and better performance. After a significant effort to optimize the search algorithms that are one of the main reasons of the success of ASP systems and solvers like CLINGO [14], DLV [24] and WASP [9], to sacrifice a few machine instructions just to validate data that are almost always valid sounds like a blasphemy.

Someone may argue that ASP is not intended to be a general purpose programming language, and therefore input and output are eventually validated by external tools. However, this is a very simplistic assumption, and invalid data may appear in other portions of the program, causing the loss of otherwise acceptable solutions. Everyone is free to follow their own path, but at some point in their life, perhaps after spending hours looking for a typo in the name of a function, any programmer will regret not having had an idiomatic way to specify the format of their data. Quoting the Latins, *errare humanum est, perseverare autem diabolicum*—to err is human, but to persist (in error) is diabolical.

This paper aims at rescuing ASP programmers from some problems due to data validation by proposing a framework called VALASP, written in Python and available at https://github.com/alviano/valasp. Specifically, a first contribution of this paper is the formalization of the problem of data validation for ASP programs by combining ASP rules with Python exceptions (Sect. 3.1). A second contribution of this paper is a declarative language based on the YAML serialization format to specify data validation for ASP programs (Sect. 3.2), and its compilation into Python code that can be processed by the ASP system CLINGO (Sect. 3.3). The proposed approach is to specify the format of some data of interest, leaving open the possibility to work with unspecified data types (Sect. 3). Moreover, the specification can be separated from the ASP program, and the fail-fast approach is achieved by injecting constraints that are guaranteed to be immediately satisfied when grounded, unless data are found to be invalid and some exception is raised. Such a behavior is obtained thanks to *interpreted functions*, briefly recalled in Sect. 2, where their use for data validation is also hinted. Finally, a few use cases are discussed in Sect. 4, among them the possibility to take advantage of ASP declarativity for validating complex Python data structures, and related work from the literature is discussed in Sect. 5—in particular, differences with sort typed systems like IDP [8] and SPARC [26].[1]

2   Background

ASP programs are usually evaluated by a two-steps procedure: first, object variables are eliminated by means of *intelligent grounding* techniques, and after that stable models of the resulting propositional program are searched by means of sophisticated non-chronological backtracking algorithms. Details of this procedure, as well as on the syntax and semantics of ASP, are out of the scope of this work. Therefore, this section only recalls the minimal background required to introduce the concepts presented in the next sections.

ASP is not particularly rich in terms of primitive types, and essentially allows for using integers and (double-quoted) strings. (We will use the syntax of CLINGO; [14].) More complex types, as for example dates or decimal numbers, can be represented by means of (non-interpreted) functions, or by the so called @-*terms*; in the latter case, the @-term must be associated with a Python

---

[1] An extended abstract of this work was presented at the International Conference on Logic Programming (ICLP) 2020 [2].

function mapping different objects to different symbols in a repeatable way—for example, by populating a table of symbols or by using a natural enumeration.

Example 1 (Primitive types and @-terms). Dates can be represented by strings, functions (tuples as a special case) or @-terms, among other possibilities. Hence, `"1983/09/12"`, `date(1983,9,12)` and `@date(1983,9,12)` can all represent the date 12 Sep. 1983, where the @-term is associated with the following Python code:

```
def date(year, month, day):
    res = datetime.datetime(year.number, month.number, day.number)
    return int(res.timestamp())
```

Each representation comes with pros and cons, discussed later in Sect. 3.   ■

Intelligent grounding may process rules in several orders, and literals within a rule can also be processed according to different ordering. A safe assumption made here is that all object variables of an @-term must be already bound to some ground term before the grounder can call the associated Python function.

Example 2 (@-term invocation). Consider the following program:

```
birthday(sofia, date(2019,6,25)).
birthday(bigel, date(1982,123)).  % Oops! I missed a comma, but where?!?
:- birthday(Person,Date), @is_triple_of_integer(Date) != 1.
```

The Python function associated with the @-term is called two times, with arguments `date(2019,6,25)` and `date(1982,123)`, so that some invariant can be enforced on the second argument of every instance of `birthday/2`.   ■

Data validation is the process of ensuring that data conform to some specification, so that any process in which they are involved can safely work under all of the assumptions guaranteed by the specification. Data can be found invalid because of an expected error-prone source (for example, user input from a terminal), or due to an unexpected misuse of some functionality of a system (this is usually the case with bugs). While in the first case it is natural to ask again for the data, in the second case failing fast may be the only reasonable choice, so that the problem can be noticed, traced, and eventually fixed. The fail-fast approach is particularly helpful at coding time, to avoid bug hunting at a later time, but it may also pay off after deploy if properly coupled with a recovery mechanism (for example, restart the process).

Example 3 (Data validation). The @-term from Example 2 can be associated with the following Python code:

```
def is_triple_of_integer(value):
    if value.type != Function: raise ValueError('wrong type')
    if value.name != 'date': raise ValueError('wrong name')
    if len(value.arguments) != 3: raise ValueError('not a triple')
    if any(arg for arg in value.arguments if arg.type != Number):
        raise ValueError('arguments must be integers')
    return 1
```

Indeed, the presence of `birthday(bigel, date(1982,123))` will be noticed because of abrupt termination of the grounding procedure. Adopting a fail-fast approach is the correct choice in this case, and any attempt of sanification is just a dangerous speculation on the invalid data—should it be `date(1982,1,23)`, or `date(1982,12,3)`?   ∎

3   A Data Validation Framework for ASP

Data validation can be used in ASP programs thanks to @-terms. However, the resulting code is likely to be less readable due to aspects that are not really the focus of the problem aimed to be addressed. We will illustrate our proposal to accomplish data validation without cluttering your ASP encoding in this section. First, the problem of data validation for ASP programs is formalized in Sect. 3.1, and a few minimal examples are provided. After that, a declarative language based on the YAML serialization format is introduced in Sect. 3.2 to specify data validation for ASP programs. Finally, Sect. 3.3 hints on how the YAML format is compiled into Python code that can be processed by the ASP system CLINGO.

3.1   Data Validation for ASP Programs

Let us fix a set S of *predicate and function names* (or *symbols*), a set $\mathcal{F}$ of *field names*, and a set $\mathcal{T} = \{$Integer, String, Alpha, Any$\}$ of *primitive types*. Each type is associated with a set of *facets*, or restrictions. The facets of Integer are enum to specify a list of acceptable values, min (by default -2^{31}) and max (by default $2^{31} - 1$) to specify (inclusive) bounds, and finally count, sum+ and sum- to specify bounds on the number of values, the sum of positive values and negative values. The facets of String and Alpha are enum and count as before, min and max to bound the length, and pattern to specify a regular expression. Other types have only the facet count.

A *user-defined symbol* s is any name in S. A *field declaration* is a tuple of the form (f, t, F), where f is a field name in $\mathcal{F}$, t is a type in $\mathcal{T}$ or a type defined by the user (i.e., a user-defined symbol), and F is a set of facets for t. A *field comparison* is an expression of the form $f \odot f'$, where $\odot$ is a comparison operator among ==, !=, <, <=, >=, and >.

A *user definition* is a tuple of the form (s, D, H, b, c, a), where s is a user-defined symbol, D is a set of field declarations, H is a set of field comparisons (also called *having properties*), and b, c, a are Python code blocks to be executed respectively before grounding, after the creation of an instance of the user-defined symbol, and after grounding. A *data validation specification* is a tuple of the form (P, A, U), where P is a Python program, A is an ASP program, and U is a set of user definitions.

Example 4 (Validation of dates). Let `date` be a ternary predicate representing a valid date, and `bday` be a binary predicate whose arguments represent a person and a date. A user definition u_{date} of `date` could be (date, {(year, Integer, ∅), (month, Integer, ∅), (day, Integer, ∅)}, ∅, ∅, c, ∅), where c is the following Python code block:

```
datetime.datetime(self.year, self.month, self.day).
```

A user definition u_{bday} of `bday` could be (bday, {(name, Alpha, ∅), (date, date, ∅)}, ∅, ∅, ∅, ∅). A data validation specification could be the triple (P, ∅, {u_{date}, u_{bday}}) where P is the Python code block

```
import datetime
```
■

Example 5 (Ordering of elements). Let `ordered_triple` be a ternary predicate representing a triple of integers in descendent order. A user definition could be (ordered_triple, {(first, Integer, ∅), (second, Integer, ∅), (third, Integer, ∅)}, {first < second, second < third}, ∅, ∅, ∅). ■

Example 6 (Overflow on integers). Let `income` be a binary predicate representing incomes of companies, which are summed up in an ASP program. A user definition of `income` could be $u_{income} :=$ (income, {(company, String, ∅), (amount, Integer, {min: 0, sum+: 2147483647})}, ∅, ∅, ∅, ∅), specifying that valid amounts are nonnegative and their sum must not overflow. A data validation specification could be (∅, ∅, {u_{income}}). ■

Example 7 (Validation of complex aggregates). Consider the constraint

```
:- bound(MAX), #sum{B-B',R : init_budget(R,B), budget_spent(R,B')} > MAX.
```

It bounds the total amount of residual budget, for example for researchers involved in a project. The above constraint can be part of a broader ASP program where `budget_spent/2` depends on some guess on resources and services to purchase. The aggregate above may overflow, and we are interested in detecting such cases and stopping the computation on such unreliable data. To this aim, we can introduce auxiliary predicates in the ASP program A of a data validation specification (∅, A, U):

```
residual_budget(B-B',R) :- init_budget(R,B), budget_spent(R,B').
```

Hence, we can provide a user definition (residual_budget, {(value, Integer, {min: 0, sum+: 2**31-1}), (id_res, Integer, {min: 0})}, ∅, ∅, ∅) in U. ■

Specification Application. Given an ASP program Π, and a data validation specification (P, A, U), the application of (P, A, U) to Π amounts to the following computational steps:

1. The Python program P is executed.
2. For all (s, D, H, b, c, a) ∈ U, the Python code block b is executed.
3. The ASP program $\Pi \cup A$ is grounded.
4. For all produced instances of a predicate s such that (s, D, H, b, c, a) ∈ U, all types and facets in D and all field comparisons in H are checked, and the Python block c is executed. If a check fails, an exception is raised.
5. For all (s, D, H, b, c, a) ∈ U, the Python code block a is executed.

Example 8. The application of the data validation specification from Example 4 to an ASP program whose intelligent grounding produces `bday(bigel, date(1982,123))` raises an exception due to the wrong type of the second argument, that is, function `date` is expected to have arity 3, but only 2 arguments are found.

The application of the data validation specification from Example 6 to an ASP program comprising facts `income("Acme ASP",1500000000)` and `income("Yoyodyne YAML",1500000000)` raises an exception due to the facet `sum+: 2147483647` of `amount`. This way, an overflow is prevented, for example in

```
total(T) :- T = #sum{A,C : income(C,A)}.
```

which would otherwise produce `total(-1294967296)` in CLINGO and DLV.   ∎

Computational Problem. Given an ASP program Π, and a data validation specification (P, A, U), we are interested in deciding whether the application of (P, A, U) to Π terminates without raising any exception.

Theorem 1. *Let Π be a program, and (P, A, U) be a data validation specification. Let $\mathcal{C}$ be the complexity class of deciding whether a given ground rule belongs to the intelligent grounding of the ASP program $\Pi \cup A$, and let $\mathcal{C}'$ be the complexity class of deciding whether a Python code block in (P, A, U) terminates without raising any exception. Hence, deciding whether the application of (P, A, U) to Π terminates without raising any exception belongs to the complexity class $\mathcal{C} \cup \mathcal{C}'$.*

The theorem above holds because Python code blocks and ASP grounding can be executed separately, and without interaction between them. If Python code blocks require polynomial execution time (for example, they comprise very simple `if` statements), $\mathcal{C} \cup \mathcal{C}'$ coincides with $\mathcal{C}$, that is, the complexity of our computational problem is dominated by the grounding procedure.

3.2   A YAML Language for Data Validation

YAML is a human friendly data serialization standard, whose syntax is well-suited for materializing the notion of data validation specification provided in Sect. 3.1. The YAML files processed by our framework are essentially dictionaries associating keys to other dictionaries, values, and lists. The key `valasp` is reserved, and cannot be used as a symbol or field name.

More in details, a data validation specification (P, A, U) is represented by a YAML file comprising the following lines:

```
valasp:
    python: |+
        <Python code block P>
    asp: |+
        <ASP program A>
```

and a block of lines for each user definition (s, D, H, b, c, a):

```
s:
    <field declarations D>
    valasp:
        having:
            - <field comparison h₁>
            - ...
            - <field comparison hₙ>
        before_grounding: |+
            <Python code block b>
        after_init: |+
            <Python code block c>
        after_grounding: |+
            <Python code block a>
```

Above, $h_1, \ldots, h_n$ are the field comparisons in H (for some $n \geq 0$), and a field declaration (f, t, F) is represented by

```
f:
    type: t
    <facets F>
```

where facets are written as key-value pairs.   .

Example 9. Below is a YAML file to validate predicate **bday** of Example 4.

```
valasp:
    python: |+
        import datetime

date:
    year: Integer
    month: Integer
    day: Integer

    valasp:
        after_init: |+
            datetime.datetime(self.year, self.month, self.day)

bday:
    name: Alpha
    date: date
```

The following, instead, is a YAML file to validate predicate **ordered_triple** of Example 5:

```
ordered_triple:
    first: Integer
    second: Integer
    third: Integer

    valasp:
        having:
            - first < second
```

```
      - second < third
```

Note that YAML lists can be written as multiple lines starting with a dash, or in square brackets. Regarding predicate `income` of Example 6, its YAML file is the following:

```
income:
    company: String
    amount:
        type: Integer
        min: 0
        sum+: Integer
```

Here, `sum+: Integer` is syntactic sugar for specifying that the sum of positive values must fit into a 32-bits integer—nicer than writing `max: 2147483647` or `max: 2**31-1` inside `sum+`.   ∎

3.3   The Python Compilation

The declarative specification for data validation expressed in YAML is compiled into Python code that can be processed by the ASP system CLINGO. The compilation injects data validation in the grounding process by introducing *constraint validators* of two kinds, namely *forward* and *implicit*, depending on the arity of the validated predicates and on how terms are passed to @-terms: for unary predicates, their unique terms are forwarded directly to the functions handling @-terms; for other predicates, instead, terms are grouped by functions with the same name of the validated predicate. Hence, for a predicate `pred` of arity 1, the (forward) constraint validator has the following form:

```
:- pred(X1), @valasp_validate_pred(X1) != 1.
```

Similarly, for a predicate `pred` of arity $n \geq 2$, the (implicit) constraint validator has the following form:

```
:- pred(X1,...,Xn), @valasp_validate_pred(pred(X1,...,Xn)) != 1.
```

In both cases, @-terms are associated with the Python function

```
def valasp_validate_pred(value):
    Pred(value)
    return 1
```

where `Pred` is a class whose name is obtained by capitalizing the first lowercase letter of `pred`, and whose constructor raises an exception if the provided data are invalid. In fact, class `Pred` is also an outcome of the compilation process, and materializes all validity conditions specified in the data validation specification in input.

In a nutshell, given a data validation specification (P, A, U) (represented in YAML), and an ASP program Π, the compilation produces a Python script with the following content:

1. The Python program P.
2. A Python class S for every $(s, D, H, b, c, a) \in U$ materializing all validity conditions: field declarations in D map to Python class annotations (and added as instance attributes on instance creation); field comparisons in H and the Python code block c are added to the `__post_init__` method (and executed after any instance creation); the Python code blocks b and a are respectively added to the class methods `before_grounding` and `after_grounding`.
3. Calls to any `before_grounding` method introduced in the previous steps.
4. Calls to CLINGO's API to ground the ASP program $\Pi \cup A \cup C$, where C is the set of constraint validators associated with U.
5. Calls to any `after_grounding` method introduced in the previous steps.

4   Use Cases and Assessment

This section reports a few use cases on two encodings from ASP competitions [15]. Each use case focuses on the validation of parts of an encoding, showing how the proposed framework can identify invalid data. (Tuning of the encoding is out of the scope of this paper.) Moreover, the overhead introduced by data validation is empirically assessed. Finally, an application of VALASP for validating complex Python data structures is shown.

4.1   Video Streaming—7th ASP Competition

Video streaming amounts to selecting an optimal set of video representations, in terms of resolution and bitrate, to satisfy user requirements. User requirements and solution are respectively encoded by `user(USERID, VIDEOTYPE, RESOLUTION, BANDWIDTH, MAXSAT, MAXBITRATE)` and `assign(USER_ID, VIDEO_TYPE, RESOLUTION, BITRATE, SAT)`. The overall satisfaction of users is maximized by the following weak constraint:

```
:~ assign(USER_ID,_,_,BITRATE,SAT_VALUE),
   user(USER_ID,_,_,_,BEST_SAT,_).
   [BEST_SAT-SAT_VALUE@1, USER_ID, assign]
```

According to the official description, available online at http://aspcomp2015. dibris.unige.it/Video_Streaming.pdf, instances of `user/6` can be validated with the following YAML specification:

```
user:
    userid:
        type: Integer
        min: 0
    videotype:
        type: String
        enum: [Documentary, Video, Cartoon, Sport]
    resolution:
        type: Integer
        enum: [224, 360, 720, 1080]
```

```
bandwidth:
    type: Integer
    min: 0
maxsat:
    type: Integer
    min: 0
maxbitrate:
    type: Integer
    min: 150
    max: 8650
valasp:
    after_init: |+
        if self.maxbitrate % 50 != 0: raise ValueError("unexpected
bitrate")
```

According to the above specification, the arguments `userid`, `bandwidth` and `maxsat` are non-negative integers; `videotype` is a string among `Documentary`, `Video`, `Cartoon`, and `Sport`; argument `resolution` is an integer among 224, 360, 720, and 1080; and `maxbitrate` is an integer between 150 and 8650, and it is divisible by 50.

The official encoding and instances do not have errors, as expected. However, the encoding is quite fragile and relies on several assumptions on the input data and on ASP internals—ASP systems use 32-bits integers for everything but the cost of a solution. To show how dangerous such assumptions are, consider a decision problem where a partial solution and a target satisfaction are given. Accordingly, the weak constraint is replaced by the following constraint:

```
:- target(T), #sum{BEST_SAT-SAT_VALUE, USER_ID :
    assign(USER_ID,_,_,BITRATE,SAT_VALUE),
    user(USER_ID,_,_,_,BEST_SAT,_)} > T.
```

In this case, the execution of CLINGO on the instances of the competition may lead to the error message `"Value too large to be stored in data type: Integer overflow!"`, produced while simplifying the sum. However, whether the message is shown or not depends on the partial solution provided in input. In fact, if the overflow is only due to the `assign/5` instances in input, the subsequent simplification step cannot notice the problem and a wrong answer is produced. The following YAML specification can help to detect these overflows:

```
target:
    value:
        type: Integer
        min: 0
sum_element:
    value:
        type: Integer
        min: 0
        sum+: Integer
    userid: Integer
valasp:
    asp: |+
```

```
    sum_element(BEST_SAT-SAT_VALUE,UID) :-
        assign(UID,_,_,BITRATE,SAT_VALUE),
user(UID,_,_,_,BEST_SAT,_).
```

4.2 Solitaire—4th ASP Competition

Solitaire represents a single-player game played on a 7×7 board where the 2×2 corners are omitted. We focus on the following rules defining the board:

```
range(1).
range(X+1) :- range(X), X < 7.
location(1,X) :- range(X), 3 <= X, X <= 5.
location(2,X) :- range(X), 3 <= X, X <= 5.
location(Y,X) :- range(Y), 3 <= Y, Y <= 5, range(X).
location(6,X) :- range(X), 3 <= X, X <= 5.
location(7,X) :- range(X), 3 <= X, X <= 5.
```

Those rules are interesting since an error in this point might be propagated all over the encoding. The YAML specification of `range` and `location` is the following:

```
range:
    value:
        type: Integer
        enum: [1, 2, 3, 4, 5, 6, 7]
location:
    x: range
    y: range
    valasp:
        after_grounding: |+
            pos = [1,2,6,7]
            if self.x.value in pos and self.y.value in pos:
                raise ValueError("Invalid position")
```

4.3 Empirical Assessment

The overhead introduced by VALASP to validate instances of the discussed problems was measured by running CLINGO with and without validation. The experiment was run on a 2.4 GHz Quad-Core Intel Core i5 with 16 GB of memory. VALASP was executed with the command-line option `--valid-only`, and CLINGO was executed with its Python interface; in both cases we disabled the computation of stable models since VALASP has no impact on the solving procedure. We remark here that the running time of VALASP includes grounding time. For each benchmark, we considered all available instances. Concerning video streaming, the average running time of CLINGO is 0.06 s, and the average running time of VALASP is 0.18 s. As for solitaire, the average running time of CLINGO and VALASP is respectively 0.07 and 0.13 s. We can conclude that no significative overhead is eventually introduced by VALASP on these testcases.

4.4 Application: VALASP to validate Python data

VALASP is not only a framework for the validation of ASP data, but also brings
the declarative power of ASP to validate complex Python data. For example,
consider a Python function F receiving in input a partially ordered set, that
is, a binary relation being reflexive, symmetric, and transitive. The binary relation is stored in a Python data structure, for example a list of pairs or a sparse
matrix. The Python function F works on the provided data under the assumption that it represents a partially ordered set. If input data is properly validated,
the Python function should verify that the binary relation is actually reflexive,
symmetric, and transitive. Usually, such a validation is achieved by implementing Python functions, with imperative and error-prone code. VALASP provides a
declarative alternative: the relation in input R can be mapped to ASP facts of
the form r(a,b), for all $(a, b) \in R$, for example with the help of a library like
CLORM (https://github.com/potassco/clorm), and the following data validation
specification can be used:

```
valasp:
    asp: |+
        element(X) :- r(X,Y).
        element(Y) :- r(X,Y).
        lost("reflexivity", X) :- element(X), not r(X,X).
        lost("symmetry", (X,Y)) :- r(X,Y), not r(Y,X).
        lost("transitivity", (X,Y,Z)) :- r(X,Y), r(Y,Z), not r(X,Z).

lost:
    property: String
    reason: Any
    valasp:
        after_init: |+
            raise ValueError(f"Lost {self.property} on {self.reason}")
```

(Note that the above example uses f-strings; https://www.python.org/dev/peps/
pep-0498/.) If relation R is not a partially ordered set, then it misses at least
one property among reflexivity, symmetry, and transitivity. Such a knowledge is
encoded in the ASP program above, which eventually produces an instance of
lost/2. According to the above data validation specification, VALASP will then
execute the Python code block given in the after_init, thus raising an exception
to inhibit the execution of function F on invalid data.

As another example of this kind, consider a Python function receiving in
input an undirected graph and working under the assumption that the graph
is connected. In order to validate such a precondition, the input graph can be
mapped to the ASP predicates vertex/1 and edge/2, and the following data
validation specification can be used:

```
valasp:
    asp: |+
        connected(FIRST) :- FIRST = #min{X : node(X)}.
        connected(Y) :- connected(X), edge(X,Y).
```

```
unconnected(X) :- node(X), not connected(X).
```

```
unconnected:
    node: Any
    valasp:
        after_init: |+
            raise ValueError(f"Unconnected node {self.node}")
```

If the input graph is not connected, an exception is raised, pointing to the unconnected node.

5 Related Work

The use of types in programming languages eases the representation of complex knowledge, favors the early detection of errors and provides an implicit documentation of source codes [32]. For example, by stating that the arguments of predicate bday are of types person_name and date, there is no need to document the way these elements are represented, and any attempt to instantiate this predicate with different types is blocked. ASP-Core-2 [7], on the other hand, is untyped: there is no way to state that arguments of a predicate must be of a specific type, the language offers a very limited set of primitive types, and there is no idiomatic way to declare user-defined types. This work targets ASP-Core-2, and its extensions implemented by CLINGO [14] and DLV2 [1], aiming at providing the missing idioms to specify types and to validate data.

Types are not new in logic-based languages, and in particular order-sorted logic has been formalized as first-order logic with sorted terms, where sorts are ordered to build a hierarchy [20]. IDP3 [8] and SPARC [26] are two systems with languages close to ASP-Core-2 and supporting sorted terms. There are many differences between these systems and the framework proposed in this work. First of all, VALASP is designed to be smoothly integrated with ASP-Core-2 projects: the programmer is free to choose what to validate and what to leave unchecked, and the original encoding can still be used as it is in case validation is not required in the deployed software. Sorted terms are also used to bound object variables in rules, while this is not possible with VALASP because it only deals with the aspect of data validation.

The framework uses @-terms to perform data validation by means of Python functions that are called during the grounding process. In the literature, @-terms and non-Herbrand functions [4] were used to enrich ASP with functionality that are otherwise not viable (if not in the Turing tarpit). External atoms in HEX [11] extend the notion of externally interpreted function to externally interpreted relations, and can be also used to achieve some form of data validation [34]. Hence, external atoms can be used as an alternative to @-terms for implementing the validation constraints defined in Sect. 3.3.

Finally, there are works in the literature that introduce data validation in Prolog systems [21] and that implement data validation for Constraint Logic Programming by means of Prolog systems [18,33]. The goal of those works is clearly related to this paper, but they differ on the way data validation is specified, on the target language and on the underlying implementation. Similarly, debugging techniques for ASP [10,13,16,30] share the goal to identify errors, but with a different approach. VALASP aims at blocking data validation errors in a very early stage, at coding time and by implementing fail-fast techniques to point to the source of the problem. Debugging techniques instead are useful to localize the origin of unattended behavior, and usually require interaction with the programmer. If VALASP is properly used, a debugger is still a useful software in the tool belt of an ASP programmer, but on the other hand it is likely that the number of debugging sessions will be reduced.

6   Conclusion

ASP programmers do mistakes, there is no shame in this. VALASP aims at early detection of data validity errors, and promotes a fail-fast approach so that the origin of the problem can be quickly identified and fixed. The proposed approach follows the separation of concerns design principle: validation rules are specified in YAML with Python and ASP snippets, and are separated from the business logic represented in ASP encodings. Such a design is useful to smoothly introduce data validation in ASP, as validation rules can be specified externally without the need to deeply change the way programs are written. If after deploy data can be safely assumed valid, VALASP can be easily discharged because the original encoding stays unchanged. Moreover, VALASP opens the possibility to take advantage of ASP declarativity for validating complex Python data structures, bringing the expression of data validation specifications at a higher level of abstraction.

References

1. Adrian, W.T., et al.: The ASP system DLV: advancements and applications. KI **32**(2–3), 177–179 (2018). https://doi.org/10.1007/s13218-018-0533-0
2. Alviano, M., Dodaro, C.: Data validation for answer set programming (extended abstract). In: Ricca, F., et al. (eds.) Proceedings 36th International Conference on Logic Programming (Technical Communications), Rende (CS), Italy, 18–24th September 2020. Electronic Proceedings in Theoretical Computer Science, EPTCS, vol. 325, pp. 93–95. Open Publishing Association (2020)
3. Alviano, M., Faber, W., Leone, N.: Disjunctive ASP with functions: decidable queries and effective computation. Theory Pract. Log. Program. **10**(4–6), 497–512 (2010). https://doi.org/10.1017/S1471068410000244
4. Balduccini, M.: ASP with non-Herbrand partial functions: a language and system for practical use. Theory Pract. Log. Program. **13**(4–5), 547–561 (2013). https://doi.org/10.1017/S1471068413000343
5. Baselice, S., Bonatti, P.A.: A decidable subclass of finitary programs. Theory Pract. Log. Program. **10**(4–6), 481–496 (2010). https://doi.org/10.1017/S1471068410000232

6. Calimeri, F., Cozza, S., Ianni, G., Leone, N.: Finitely recursive programs: decidability and bottom-up computation. AI Commun. **24**(4), 311–334 (2011). https://doi.org/10.3233/AIC-2011-0509
7. Calimeri, F., et al.: ASP-Core-2 input language format. Theory Pract. Log. Program. **20**(2), 294–309 (2020). https://doi.org/10.1017/S1471068419000450
8. Cat, B.D., Bogaerts, B., Bruynooghe, M., Janssens, G., Denecker, M.: Predicate logic as a modeling language: the IDP system. In: Kifer, M., Liu, Y.A. (eds.) Declarative Logic Programming: Theory, Systems, and Applications, pp. 279–323. ACM/Morgan & Claypool (2018). https://doi.org/10.1145/3191315.3191321
9. Dodaro, C., Alviano, M., Faber, W., Leone, N., Ricca, F., Sirianni, M.: The birth of a WASP: preliminary report on a new ASP solver. In: Fioravanti, F. (ed.) Proceedings of the 26th Italian Conference on Computational Logic, Pescara, Italy, 31 August–2 September 2011. CEUR Workshop Proceedings, vol. 810, pp. 99–113. CEUR-WS.org (2011). http://ceur-ws.org/Vol-810/paper-l06.pdf
10. Dodaro, C., Gasteiger, P., Reale, K., Ricca, F., Schekotihin, K.: Debugging nonground ASP programs: technique and graphical tools. Theory Pract. Log. Program. **19**(2), 290–316 (2019). https://doi.org/10.1017/S1471068418000492
11. Eiter, T., et al.: The DLVHEX system. KI **32**(2–3), 187–189 (2018). https://doi.org/10.1007/s13218-018-0535-y
12. Eiter, T., Simkus, M.: Bidirectional answer set programs with function symbols. In: Boutilier, C. (ed.) Proceedings of IJCAI, pp. 765–771 (2009). http://ijcai.org/Proceedings/09/Papers/132.pdf
13. Fandinno, J., Schulz, C.: Answering the "why" in answer set programming - a survey of explanation approaches. Theory Pract. Log. Program. **19**(2), 114–203 (2019). https://doi.org/10.1017/S1471068418000534
14. Gebser, M., et al.: The Potsdam answer set solving collection 5.0. KI **32**(2–3), 181–182 (2018). https://doi.org/10.1007/s13218-018-0528-x
15. Gebser, M., Maratea, M., Ricca, F.: The seventh answer set programming competition: design and results. Theory Pract. Log. Program. **20**(2), 176–204 (2020)
16. Gebser, M., Pührer, J., Schaub, T., Tompits, H.: A meta-programming technique for debugging answer-set programs. In: Fox, D., Gomes, C.P. (eds.) Proceedings of AAAI, pp. 448–453. AAAI Press (2008). http://www.aaai.org/Library/AAAI/2008/aaai08-071.php
17. Gelfond, M., Lifschitz, V.: Classical negation in logic programs and disjunctive databases. New Gener. Comput. **9**(3/4), 365–386 (1991). https://doi.org/10.1007/BF03037169
18. Hermenegildo, M., Puebla, G., Bueno, F., López-García, P.: Program debugging and validation using semantic approximations and partial specifications. In: Widmayer, P., Eidenbenz, S., Triguero, F., Morales, R., Conejo, R., Hennessy, M. (eds.) ICALP 2002. LNCS, vol. 2380, pp. 69–72. Springer, Heidelberg (2002). https://doi.org/10.1007/3-540-45465-9_7
19. Johnsson, D.B., Deogun, D., Sawano, D.: Secure by Design. Manning Publications, Shelter Island (2019)
20. Kaneiwa, K.: Order-sorted logic programming with predicate hierarchy. Artif. Intell. **158**(2), 155–188 (2004). https://doi.org/10.1016/j.artint.2004.05.001
21. Kiel, R., Schader, M.: A tool for validating PROLOG programs. In: Bock, H.H., Ihm, P. (eds) Classification, Data Analysis, and Knowledge Organization. STUDIES CLASS. Springer, Heidelberg (1991). https://doi.org/10.1007/978-3-642-76307-6_24

22. Ko, A.J., Myers, B.A.: Development and evaluation of a model of programming errors. In: Proceedings of HCC, pp. 7–14. IEEE Computer Society (2003). https://doi.org/10.1109/HCC.2003.1260196

23. Ko, A.J., Myers, B.A.: A framework and methodology for studying the causes of software errors in programming systems. J. Vis. Lang. Comput. 16(1–2), 41–84 (2005). https://doi.org/10.1016/j.jvlc.2004.08.003

24. Leone, N., et al.: Enhancing DLV for large-scale reasoning. In: Balduccini, M., Lierler, Y., Woltran, S. (eds.) LPNMR 2019. LNCS, vol. 11481, pp. 312–325. Springer, Cham (2019). https://doi.org/10.1007/978-3-030-20528-7_23

25. Lierler, Y., Lifschitz, V.: One more decidable class of finitely ground programs. In: Hill, P.M., Warren, D.S. (eds.) ICLP 2009. LNCS, vol. 5649, pp. 489–493. Springer, Heidelberg (2009). https://doi.org/10.1007/978-3-642-02846-5_40

26. Marcopoulos, E., Zhang, Y.: OnlineSPARC: a programming environment for answer set programming. Theory Pract. Log. Program. 19(2), 262–289 (2019). https://doi.org/10.1017/S1471068418000509

27. Marek, V.W., Truszczyński, M.: Stable models and an alternative logic programming paradigm. In: Apt, K.R., Marek, V.W., Truszczynski, M., Warren, D.S. (eds.) The Logic Programming Paradigm. AI, pp. 375–398. Springer, Heidelberg (1999). https://doi.org/10.1007/978-3-642-60085-2_17

28. Natella, R., Winter, S., Cotroneo, D., Suri, N.: Analyzing the effects of bugs on software interfaces. IEEE Trans. Softw. Eng. 46(3), 280–301 (2020). https://doi.org/10.1109/TSE.2018.2850755

29. Niemelä, I.: Logic programming with stable model semantics as constraint programming paradigm. Ann. Math. Artif. Intell. 25(3–4), 241–273 (1999). https://doi.org/10.1023/A:1018930122475

30. Oetsch, J., Pührer, J., Tompits, H.: Catching the ouroboros: on debugging nonground answer-set programs. Theory Pract. Log. Program. 10(4–6), 513–529 (2010). https://doi.org/10.1017/S1471068410000256

31. Padhye, R., Sen, K.: Efficient fail-fast dynamic subtype checking. In: Bonetta, D., Liu, Y.D. (eds.) Proceedings of VMIL@SPLASH, pp. 32–37. ACM (2019). https://doi.org/10.1145/3358504.3361229

32. Pierce, B.C.: Types and Programming Languages. MIT Press, Cambridge (2002)

33. Puebla, G., Bueno, F., Hermenegildo, M.: A generic preprocessor for program validation and debugging. In: Deransart, P., Hermenegildo, M.V., Małuszynski, J. (eds.) Analysis and Visualization Tools for Constraint Programming. LNCS, vol. 1870, pp. 63–107. Springer, Heidelberg (2000). https://doi.org/10.1007/10722311_3

34. Redl, C.: Extending answer set programs with interpreted functions as first-class citizens. In: Lierler, Y., Taha, W. (eds.) PADL 2017. LNCS, vol. 10137, pp. 68–85. Springer, Cham (2017). https://doi.org/10.1007/978-3-319-51676-9_5

35. Vernon, V.: Domain-Driven Design Distilled. Addison-Wesley, Boston (2016)

Lightweight Declarative Server-Side Web Programming

Michael Hanus$^{(\boxtimes)}$ ⓘ

Institut für Informatik, CAU Kiel, 24098 Kiel, Germany
mh@informatik.uni-kiel.de

Abstract. Web interfaces are an important part of many applications but their implementation is full of pitfalls due to the client/server nature of web programming. This paper presents a lightweight approach to web programming based on a standard infrastructure, in particular, the common CGI protocol between client and server. No specific additions are necessary on the server side. Our approach exploits declarative programming features to provide a high-level API for server-side web scripting. This API allows to check many programming errors at compile time by using functional (static typing, higher-order functions) as well as logic (free variables) programming features. Together with further abstractions, like session handling, persistence, and typeful database access, it is used for non-trivial web applications.

1 Introduction

A web interface provides an easy access to software systems, since it does not require local software installations (one can assume that desktop computers as well as mobile devices are equipped with some web browser). Implementing a web interface for some application program can be challenging due to the client/server nature of web programming. The application program, running on a web server, has to generate an HTML page containing form elements. The client, using a web browser, fills the form with data and submits a request back to the server which creates and sends an answer to the client. Since the standard protocols, HTTP and the Common Gateway Interface (CGI), are stateless without a permanent connection between the server and the client, additional programming infrastructure is required for the application program.

There are various proposals to abstract from these raw protocols. Some approaches use specialized languages, like MAWL [16], DynDoc [20], or Links [4]. If the application is implemented in another language, the use of such languages causes a gap during software development. Therefore, many specific libraries have been developed for existing programming languages (e.g., [3,17,19,23,26]). Such libraries often support a convenient construction of web pages but provide only limited static checks for programming errors. For instance, web forms use string constants to identify input fields. If these string constants are used in the application program, typos in the strings are not detected at compile time and

© Springer Nature Switzerland AG 2021
J. F. Morales and D. Orchard (Eds.): PADL 2021, LNCS 12548, pp. 107–123, 2021.
https://doi.org/10.1007/978-3-030-67438-0_7

might lead to dynamic execution errors. Furthermore, a web form has two parts: a program generating the form (or a static web page containing form elements) and a program executed when the form is submitted (specified by some URL in the form). Obviously, this is more complex and error-prone than implementing a graphical user interface (GUI) with event handlers for a desktop application.

To hide this complexity, one can try to support a continuation-based programming model for web forms, i.e., one can try to associate handlers to submit buttons (and similar interaction elements) which are responsible to process the event, e.g., to return a new web page with the computed result. These handlers can be implemented by processes running on the web server (servlets) and by encoding some required data as hidden fields in the web form [6,22]. This seems necessary due to the stateless nature of CGI. Since a CGI program running on a server is terminated after delivering a web page containing form elements, some resources must be kept on the server to answer form submissions. This programming model requires specific extensions on the web server (e.g., servlets) and/or permanent processes created by invoking a CGI script.[1]

In this paper we present a new approach to server-side web programming with a continuation-based programming model. It is lightweight from a programming point of view: the programmer implements the web form together with the event handlers in a single program rather than separating the application into different programs or scripts. The program runs on a standard web server without specific extensions. We show an implementation of our approach in the functional logic programming language Curry [13]. The combined features of Curry enable the implementation as a library and supports the checking of inconsistencies in web forms, like missing identifiers, at compile time. Thus, any application implemented in Curry (i.e., also functional or logic programming applications) can easily be equipped with a web interface by using our library.

Some characteristic features of our approach are:

- We use standard CGI without additional requirements on the web browser or web server extensions.
- The web server is not loaded with permanent processes for CGI interactions.
- Our model for web programming is continuation-based, i.e., a web form can contain any number of interaction elements with associated event handlers that are invoked when a client starts an activity.
- The API for our programming model is implemented as a Curry library without any language extension. The API supports compositionality (combine several forms in one web page) and ensures the consistency of web forms and their handlers at compile time.
- Our event handler model abstracts from the raw CGI protocol and interaction (which is implemented by environment variables and value decoding on the server side).

---

[1] Actually, this was the approach taken in a very early continuation-based library for web programming in Curry [6]. The practical problems caused by the web-server processes motivated the current approach.

Note that our approach is oriented towards server-side web programming where the application data is stored on the server and accessed and manipulated via web browsers. Client-side web programming, where computations take place in the web browser, is an independent aspect not covered by our approach.

This paper is structured as follows. The next section provides a short overview of the main features of Curry as relevant for this paper. Sections 3 and 4 discuss our approach to model basic HTML documents and interactive web forms. Section 5 introduces a type model for web forms that allows to detect some inconsistencies at compile time. Section 6 shows the implementation of stateful web interactions via a session concept. The implementation of our library is sketched in Sect. 7. Useful extensions of our approach and related work are discussed in the final sections before we conclude.

2 Functional Logic Programming with Curry

As mentioned above, the combined features of the declarative multi-paradigm language Curry [13] are important to provide the high-level approach to web programming described below. Since Curry is basically an extension of Haskell, we assume familiarity with functional programming and Haskell and review only those additional aspects of Curry which are necessary to understand our concept. More details about functional logic programming can be found in the surveys [2,9].

Curry amalgamates features from functional programming (demand-driven evaluation, strong typing, higher-order functions) and logic programming (computing with partial information, unification, constraints). The syntax of Curry is close to Haskell[2] [18]. In addition, Curry allows free (logic) variables in conditions and right-hand sides of defining rules. The operational semantics is based on an optimal evaluation strategy [1]—a conservative extension of lazy functional programming and logic programming.

A Curry program consists of data type definitions (introducing *constructors* for the data types) and *functions* or *operations* on these types. As an example, we show the definition of two operations on lists: the well-known list concatenation and an operation `last` which exploits logic programming features to compute the last element of a list:

```
(++) :: [a]  →  [a]  →  [a]         last :: [a]  →  a
[]      ++ ys = ys                  last xs | _ ++ [e] == xs
(x:xs) ++ ys = x : (xs ++ ys)              = e   where e free
```

Note that, in contrast to Prolog, variables not occurring in the left-hand side of a rule must be declared as `free` (apart from anonymous variables, like "_"). Since "++" can be called with free variables in arguments, the condition in the rule of `last` is solved by instantiating `e` and the anonymous free variable "_"

---

[2] Variables and function names usually start with lowercase letters and the names of type and data constructors start with an uppercase letter. The application of f to e is denoted by juxtaposition ("$f\ e$").

to appropriate values before reducing the call to "++". Free variables are also essential for our approach to web programming.

Curry has more features than described so far.[3] In this work, we exploit two of them. *Type classes* allow to express ad-hoc polymorphism in a structured manner [25]. We will use them to enforce structural constraints when using web forms. *Monadic I/O* [24] is a declarative concept to structure interactive programs by enforcing sequential evaluation by monadic operations. We will use it to access a possible state used in web forms. Since we assume familiarity with Haskell, we skip a detailed discussion of these concepts.

3   Modeling Basic HTML

Before describing our approach to implement dynamic web pages, we start by modeling basic HTML documents in Curry.

Since HTML documents have a tree-like structure, they can be represented in logic or functional languages in a straightforward manner [3,17]. Here, we define the type of basic HTML expressions in Curry as follows:

```
data BaseHtml = BaseText   String
              | BaseStruct String Attrs [BaseHtml]
type Attrs = [(String,String)]
```

Thus, a basic HTML expression is either a plain string (`BaseText`) or a structure consisting of a tag, a list of attributes (name/value pairs), and a list of HTML expressions contained in this structure.

Since writing HTML documents in a program could be tedious with this definition, one can define operations as useful abbreviations (`htmlQuote` transforms characters with a special meaning in HTML, like <, >, &, ", into their HTML quoted form):

```
htxt s = BaseText (htmlQuote s)       -- plain text
h1     = BaseStruct "h1"     []       -- level 1 header
strong = BaseStruct "strong" []       -- important content
hrule  = BaseStruct "hr"     [] []    -- line break
...
```

A complete web page contains a title, optional parameters (e.g., cookies, style sheets), and a content (the actual library supports more alteratives, e.g., plain text documents):

```
data HtmlPage = HtmlPage String [PageParam] [BaseHtml]
```

As before, we add some useful abbreviations:

```
page title hexps = HtmlPage title [] hexps

headerPage title hexps = page title (h1 [htxt title] : hexps)
```

As an example, we define a web page with a simple multiplication table. The function

---

[3] Actually, Curry is intended as an extension of Haskell although not all of the numerous features of Haskell are actually supported.

```
mult2html :: (Int,Int,Int)  →  [BaseHtml]
mult2html (x,y,z) = [htxt $ show x ++ " * " ++ show y ++ " = ",
                     strong [htxt $ show z], hrule]
```

maps a triple of integers into a line showing their multiplication in HTML format.
Then the operation

```
multPage :: HtmlPage
multPage = headerPage "Multiplication of Digits" $
  concatMap mult2html [ (x,y,x*y) | x <- [1..10], y <- [1..x] ]
```

exploits standard operations and list comprehensions to define our main web
page. One can easily define a pretty-printing operation

```
showHtmlPage :: HtmlPage  →  String
```

which transforms an `HtmlPage` term into the corresponding HTML string. If we
install a Curry program with the main operation

```
main = putStrLn $ showHtmlPage multPage
```

as a CGI executable on a web server, we get a simple dynamically generated
web page. Since web server programs written with our library are always pages
that are dynamically generated, we assume in the following that a dynamic web
page is of type "IO HtmlPage".[4]

A CGI program generates a web page when a client accesses it. Hence, we
can make it more dynamic by accessing data from its execution environment.
For instance, the following page shows the current server time:

```
timePage :: IO HtmlPage
timePage = do time <- getLocalTime
              return $ headerPage "Current Server Time"
                       [htxt $ calendarTimeToString time]
```

4   HTML Forms

HTML forms are basic elements to interact with applications running on some
server via a client's web browser. HTML forms are embedded in HTML pages and
contain input elements to be filled out by the user and interaction elements (e.g.,
buttons) to submit the form data to a web server. When a form is submitted,
the data contained in the input elements is encoded and sent to the server which
starts a program, also called *form handler*, to react to the submission. The
activated program decodes the input data, runs the application with the data,
and returns an HTML page which is then sent back to the client.

The following HTML page contains a form with an input field to enter string:

```
<html>
  <head><title>String input form</title></head>
  <body>
    <form method="post" action="http://.../handler.cgi">
      Enter a string: <input type="text" name="FIELD1"/>
```

---

[4] Actually, there is a simple script to wrap such web page definitions with
`showHtmlPage` before compiling and installing it.

```
    <input type="submit" value="Submit"/>
   </form>
  </body>
 </html>
```

In a typical scenario, such a document is generated by some program. When the client presses the Submit button, the identifier FIELD1 together with the contents of this text field is transmitted to the web browser which executes the program identified by the URL in the action attribute of the form.

In contrast to GUI programming for desktop applications, web interfaces are split into two independent parts accessible via different URLs: the first part generates the document containing the form, and the second part processes it and returns an answer document. Although there are many libraries and web frameworks to integrate these parts in one program from which these two parts are generated, there is the problem to ensure the consistency of both parts. Since input fields are part of the HTML structure and not program entities, their values are identified by strings, like FIELD1, so that the form handler has to access the actual input values via these strings. Thus, undefined input fields or typos in names of input fields are not detected at compile time but lead to execution errors or unintended behaviors.

The objective of our approach is to simplify the programming of web interfaces and make them more reliable by providing static consistency checks. As we will see, the functional and logic features of Curry are useful to support such a programming interface. In the following, we present our approach from a programmer's perspective before we discuss its implementation in Sect. 7.

Our programming model is based on two ideas:

1. Input elements are referenced by program variables rather than strings. Thus, typos in element names lead to accesses to undefined variables which will be reported at compile time.
2. Interaction elements, like submit buttons, are equipped with event handlers which process user inputs and return HTML documents. In order to access the actual form input, an event handler is invoked with an environment to look up the input data.

To refer to input elements, there is a type

```
data HtmlRef = HtmlRef String
```

This type is abstract, i.e., the constructor is not exported so that it cannot be used in an application program. Thus, the only way to use references in forms is via free variables. This is intended, as we will see later.

Input elements are constructed with references. For instance, a text input field is constructed by "textField ref cont" where ref is a reference of type HtmlRef and cont an initial contents. Since an interaction element, like a submit button, has an event handler, we have the following type synonyms:

```
type HtmlEnv = HtmlRef  →  String
type HtmlHandler = HtmlEnv  →  IO HtmlPage
```

Fig. 1. An HTML page with a form to compute the length or reverse a string

An environment is just a mapping from references to strings and a handler maps an environment into an action which manipulates the server environment (e.g., database updates) and returns a new page. Then "`button s hdlr`" constructs a button with label `s` and associated handler `hdlr` (of type `HtmlHandler`). With these elements, we can define a form, as shown in Fig. 1, with a text input field and two submit buttons: one to compute the length of the string and another one to reverse the string.

```
lengthRevForm =
  [htxt "Enter a string: ", textField tref "",
   button "Length" lengthHandler, button "Reverse" revHandler]
  where
   tref free

   lengthHandler env = return $ page "Answer"
    [h1 [htxt $ "String length: " ++ show (length (env tref))]]

   revHandler env = return $ page "Answer"
    [h1 [htxt $ "Reversed input: " ++ reverse (env tref)]]
```

Since references to input elements are of type `HtmlRef` and there are no visible constructors of this type, only free variables can be used for this purpose. If these variables are in the scope of the event handler, one can easily access the actual input available when the handler is invoked by applying the environment to the reference (as with (`env tref`) above).

How can we invoke an event handler when a form is submitted? Note that the event handler is introduced with the form but the form submission takes place at some later point of time. One possibility is to start, together with the created form, a process which contains the code of the event handlers in this form. When a form is submitted, the input data is passed to this process. This has some similarity with servlets and was the basis of an early approach to HTML programming in Curry [6]. A disadvantage of that approach is the creation of many processes whose lifetime is not easy to determine, since form submissions might never take place. This could be improved by sharing processes, introducing timeouts etc, but it turned out to be a source of practical run-time problems in larger applications.

Another possibility is to submit the same program again but in a different mode: instead of producing the form elements, the event handler of the corresponding submit button is executed. In order to execute this handler, its code must be accessible from a top-level operation in the program. Therefore, we require that forms must be declared as top-level entities. In order to use forms in arbitrary HTML documents, we distinguish between a *form definition* and its actual use. To define a form as a top-level entity, there is a constructor `simpleFormDef` (later, we will see its concrete type and more complex form definitions) which wraps a form layout together with its event handlers into a form definition. For instance, we turn our form above into a form definition by

```
lengthRevFormDef = simpleFormDef lengthRevForm
```

We can *use a form* in an HTML document by wrapping the form definition with operation `formElem`. For instance, the following code defines an HTML page containing our form:

```
stringInputPage = return $
  headerPage "String input" [formElem lengthRevFormDef]
```

The advantage of distinguishing a form definition from its actual use is that we can use a form in any HTML document, in particular, recursively in the answer computed by an event handler. For instance, a form to compute the length of an input string and showing the form again in the answer can be defined as:

```
lengthForm = simpleFormDef
  [htxt "Enter a string: ", textField tref "",
   button "Length"
    (\env → return $ page "Answer"
              [h1 [htxt $ "Length: " ++ show (length (env tref))],
               hrule, formElem lengthForm])]
  where tref free
```

Note that this compact definition is enabled by the combined logic and functional features of Curry: free variables, like `tref`, as "unknown" references instead of concrete strings, and event handlers, i.e., functions, in data structures. Next we show how to exploit advanced typing features from functional programming to make form programming more reliable.

5   Stronger Form Typing

Our modeling of forms assumes that input elements and submit buttons are used inside a form definition so that the corresponding event handlers can be invoked when the form is used. However, it seems that elements like `textField` or `button` can be mixed with basic HTML elements, like `htxt` or `strong`, so that they can also occur in basic HTML documents without an associated form. In order to avoid such problems, we exploit type classes to enforce more structure.

Basic HTML elements, like `htxt` or `h1`, can be used inside and outside forms, but input elements and submit buttons should be used only inside forms. This demands for some kind of overloading which is supported via type classes in a structured way [25]. Hence, we introduce a type class `HTML` which supports operations to construct HTML documents with textual and structured elements:[5]

```
class HTML a where
  htmlText   :: String  →  a
  htmlStruct :: String  →  Attrs  →  [a]  →  a
```

The type of basic HTML expressions is an instance of this class:

```
instance HTML BaseHtml where
  htmlText   = BaseText
  htmlStruct = BaseStruct
```

To model form elements, we introduce an extended data type for general HTML expressions which also contains alternatives for elements with references (input elements) and elements with event handlers (e.g., buttons).

```
data HtmlExp = HtmlText    String
             | HtmlStruct  String Attrs [HtmlExp]
             | HtmlInput   HtmlRef HtmlExp
             | HtmlEvent   HtmlRef HtmlHandler HtmlExp
```

The actual use of the additional constructors to model input and interaction elements is not relevant here. For the moment it is only important that input and interaction elements are of type `HtmlExp` rather than `BaseHtml`, e.g., the types of text input fields and buttons are

```
textField :: HtmlRef  →  String  →  HtmlExp
button    :: String   →  HtmlHandler  →  HtmlExp
```

Now we can show the actual types of the operations to define simple forms and to use them (the type constructor `HtmlFormDef` will be discussed later):

```
simpleFormDef :: [HtmlExp]  →  HtmlFormDef ()
formElem      :: HtmlFormDef a  →  BaseHtml
```

Thanks to these type signatures, input and interaction elements (of type `HtmlExp`) can be used inside a form definition but not in basic HTML documents outside form elements. Moreover, forms cannot be nested, as required by the HTML standard,[6] since the result type of `formElem` is `BaseHtml` rather than `HtmlExp`.

In order to use other basic HTML elements inside and outside forms, we define the type of general HTML expressions also as an instance of class `HTML`:

```
instance HTML HtmlExp where
  htmlText   = HtmlText
  htmlStruct = HtmlStruct
```

Finally, we redefine the abbreviations for basic HTML elements introduced in Sect. 3 by overloading them with type class `HTML`:

---

[5] The actual definition in our library contains more operations which are not relevant here.

[6] https://html.spec.whatwg.org/multipage/forms.html#the-form-element.

```
htxt :: HTML h => String  →  h
htxt s = htmlText (htmlQuote s)
h1 :: HTML h => [h]  →  h
h1 = htmlStruct "h1" []
...
```

Hence, we can use these elements inside and outside HTML forms, but the definition of an HTML page with buttons outside forms, like

```
page "Illegal" [..., button "Submit" ...]
```

leads to a static type error.

6 Stateful Forms

The HTML forms presented so far are quite limited. Form definitions are top-level entities. Therefore, data from the context of the form (e.g., database entities, authentication data) cannot be used in the form. Hence, we need to extend forms with the possibility to access some state. To show such *stateful forms*, it is only necessary to read data, whereas the manipulation of data is usually performed by the event handlers (therefore, event handlers are of type IO). For this purpose, there is a monad `FormReader` with operations to read data (see below), i.e., the `FormReader` monad is a restriction of the IO monad where only read operations are supported.

To define a stateful form, one has to provide a `FormReader` action to read data of some type a and an operation which maps values of this type into an HTML form. Hence, a stateful form can be defined by the operation

```
formDef :: FormReader a  →  (a  →  [HtmlExp])  →  HtmlFormDef a
```

Since the data might be read several times (to construct the form layout, to start an event handler, or if the form has multiple occurrences in a web page), it is important to use the restricted `FormReader` monad for data access instead of general IO actions. Therefore, an operation of type `HtmlFormDef a` defines a form which reads some data of type a and use this data to generate the actual HTML form.

Although HTTP is a stateless protocol, typical web applications require a session concept to pass information between different web pages, like the login name of a user or the contents of a virtual shopping basket. A session concept can be implemented via cookies to identify a client in a session. The session information itself should be stored in the server for security reasons [14]. In order to hide the details of session handling, there is a library (more details can be found in [11]) which provides the following operations (the type variable a denotes the type of session data):

```
getSessionData    :: Global (SessionStore a)  →  a  →  FormReader a
putSessionData    :: Global (SessionStore a)  →  a  →  IO ()
removeSessionData :: Global (SessionStore a)  →  IO ()
```

Here, "`Global (SessionStore a)`" is the type of a top-level entity referring to some cell with session information of type a. `getSessionData` retrieves information of the current session (and returns the second argument if there is no information, e.g., in case of a new session), `putSessionData` stores information in the current session, and `removeSessionData` removes such information.

In order to see an application of this concept, we implement a number guessing game: the client has to guess a number known by the server, and the server responds whether the client's number is smaller, larger, or correct. In the latter case, the number of trials is shown.[7] Hence, the session state contains the number of trials and has the following type:

```
trials :: Global (SessionStore Int)
```

The form definition consists of an action that reads the current session data and the HTML form for this data:

```
guessForm = formDef (getSessionData trials 1) guessFormHtml

guessFormHtml t = [htxt "Guess a number: ", textField nref "",
                   button "Check" guessHandler]
  where
   nref free

   guessHandler env = do
     let g = read (env nref)
     if g == 42
       then do removeSessionData trials
               return $ headerPage
                 ("Correct! " ++ show t ++ " guesses!") []
       else do putSessionData trials (t+1)
               return $ headerPage
                 ("Too " ++ if g<42 then "small" else "large")
                 [formElem guessForm]
```

The form handler reads the user input from the environment (one could add an additional check whether the input is a number string) and compares it with the "secret" number. If it is equal, the session data is removed before returning the answer, otherwise the session data is updated so that the next form invocation gets the updated data.

7 Implementation

The main objective of this work is to provide an approach to server-side web programming that is easy to use. We have already seen that event handlers for interaction elements, free variables to identify input elements, and advanced typing leads to a compact and reliable programming model. Now we discuss the implementation of our approach. In order to keep it also lightweight and easy to use, we base it on existing interfaces provided by any common web server. For this purpose, we show how to compile a Curry program containing the definition of a web page and various forms into a single executable to be installed as a CGI program on a web server.

---

[7] Of course, this game can be implemented on the client side, but a realistic example with database access needs too much space.

As an example, consider the compilation of `stringInputPage` of Sect. 4. When the generated CGI program is invoked, it has to write the HTML text of the page described by this operation on the standard output. In order to avoid installing various CGI programs or forking processes on the server, the same executable is invoked when the form is submitted by one of the two submit buttons. Thus, the executable has to check the context of its invocation in order to choose the right behavior. For this purpose, form elements are translated at run time as follows:

1. Each form contains a hidden field `FORMID` with the unique name of the form (the qualified name of the defining operation).
2. All input and interaction elements have unique identifiers. These identifiers are generated at run time (when the form is computed) by instantiating free `HtmlRef` variables with unique strings.
3. When the CGI program is invoked, it checks whether the field `FORMID` is set. If not, the main page is generated, otherwise the corresponding form is executed.

For instance, the HTML element "`formElem lengthRevFormDef`" is translated into

```
<form method="post" action="?">
  <input type="hidden" name="FORMID" value="LR.lengthRevFormDef"/>
  Enter a string: <input type="text" name="FIELD_0" value=""/>
  <input type="submit" name="FIELD_1" value="Length"/>
  <input type="submit" name="FIELD_2" value="Reverse"/>
</form>
```

The actual implementation combines a standard Curry compiler with a simple preprocessor[8] (`curry2cgi`) that wraps the operation defining the main page and all form definitions with a dispatcher of type

```
printMainPage :: [(String, [(String,String)] → IO ())]
                 → IO HtmlPage → IO ()
```

The first argument is a list of pairs consisting of a form identifier and a form implementation. The latter is an operation which takes a list of name/value pairs (the actual form inputs passed by CGI). For instance, if the operation `stringInputPage` is defined in program `LR`, this operation is compiled into

```
main = printMainPage
         [("LR.lengthRevFormDef", execFormDef lengthRevFormDef)]
         stringInputPage
```

which is finally compiled by the Curry compiler into a CGI executable.

The operation `execFormDef` translates a form definition into an operation which takes the CGI name/value pairs and write the HTML text produced by the corresponding event handler on the standard output. For this purpose, `execFormDef` executes the `FormReader` action of the form definition to read the required data, constructs the HTML form of the form definition to find the corresponding event handler and executes this handler by transforming the CGI name/value pairs into a `HtmlEnv` mapping.

The actual implementation of our library and the `curry2cgi` preprocessor is available as a Curry package (`html2`) which also contains the examples shown

---

[8] The preprocessor is used since contemporary Curry implementations do not provide access to entities of the program at run time.

in this paper. The library and the preprocessor exploit only standard features of Curry. The preprocessor uses libraries for meta-programming to read and represent source programs as abstract syntax trees in order to collect the forms defined in a program, and also performs some checks to ensure the correct use of the library at compile time, e.g., whether the operation formElem is applied to top-level entities.

8 Extensions

The programming interface for HTML forms is a basis on which further abstractions can be added. Some abstractions have been proposed for an earlier (less reliable) approach to HTML programming [6]. Since they have been adapted to this new approach, we sketch them in the following.

As apparent from the definition of HtmlEnv, the input elements have always string values so that other kinds of values, like numbers, emails, URLs, or structured data, must be extracted from strings. Since this requires some (tedious) code for checking the validity of values in input fields, providing appropriate error messages, etc, a more abstract layer to construct *web user interfaces* (*WUIs*) in a type-oriented manner is proposed in [7]. Using WUIs, one can construct for each type of an application program a WUI which implements a web-based interface to manipulate values of this type. For instance, the corresponding library contains predefined WUIs to manipulate strings (wString) or to select a value (wSelect) from a given list of values (where the first argument shows a value as a string), where "WuiSpec a" denotes the type of a WUI to modify values of type a:

```
wString :: WuiSpec String
wSelect :: (a → String) → [a] → WuiSpec a
```

To construct WUIs for complex data types, there are *WUI combinators* that map simpler WUIs to WUIs for structured types. For instance, there is a family of WUI combinators for tuple types:

```
wPair   :: WuiSpec a → WuiSpec b → WuiSpec (a,b)
wTriple :: WuiSpec a → WuiSpec b → WuiSpec c → WuiSpec (a,b,c)
...
```

Thus, "wPair wString (wSelect show [1..31])" defines a WUI to manipulate a pair of a string and a number between 1 and 31. WUIs can easily be adapted to specific requirements. For instance, one can attach a predicate so that the resulting WUI accepts only values satisfying this predicate. Thus,

```
wString 'withCondition' (not . null)
```

specifies a WUI that accepts only non-empty strings. There are further combinators to change the default rendering or error messages and to transform a WUI into an HTML form to be embedded in web pages.

Based on WUIs and abstractions for typeful database programming [12], there is a web framework to generate a complete web-based system to manipulate data stored in relational databases from an entity-relationship (ER) model of the data [11]. The generated system supports authentication, authorization, session handling, and ensures the consistency of the database w.r.t. the data dependencies specified in the ER model. Since the framework generates high-level Curry code, it can easily be adapted to individual customer requirements.

To support domain-specific syntax in Curry programs, there is a preprocessor for Curry programs which replaces domain-specific syntax by standard Curry syntax. For instance, one can embed HTML fragments in Curry programs (instead of expressions constructed by `htxt`, `h1`, `strong`, etc.) and one can also write database queries in SQL syntax which is checked for type consistency against a given ER model [12].

Our model for web programming and the extensions described above have been used for non-trivial web applications, like the curricula and module information system of our department[9] or Smap,[10] a web-based system to write, store, and execute programs in various programming languages.

9   Related Work

Due to the importance of web programming, there exist for almost any programming language various approaches to implement dynamic web pages. In the following, we discuss approaches related to declarative languages.

There are many approaches to hide low-level details of HTML and CGI programming in purely functional languages. For instance, Meijer [17] presents a Haskell library to free the programmer fom parsing and printing CGI-based interactions. Thiemann [21,22] proposes typed representations of HTML (and XML) documents by exploiting the type class system of Haskell. This can be considered as a further refinement of our representation of basic HTML documents and could also be added to our library. WASH [23] adds a session concept as a further abstraction in order to support server-side web applications. It is based on CGI and uses hidden input fields in HTML documents in order to add session-based stateful computations to CGI, similarly (but technically a bit different) from the early HTML library of Curry [6]. Since storing information in hidden input fields could be a source to attack web systems [14], we avoid them in our approach by taking the price into account that all data must be stored as session data kept on the server side.

The iData toolkit [19] supports the construction of web forms in a type-safe and declarative programming style based on purely functional programming. This toolkit follows the model-view-controller pattern and provides specific abstractions to manipulate data in web forms, similarly to the type-oriented web user interfaces library for Curry [7].

The Haskell library Haste.App [5] supports an approach to write web applications as a single program where type annotations are used to determine which parts are executed on the client (web browser) or on the server. Thus, separate server executables and JavaScript code is generated from a single program using this library and two compilers. This library exploits Haskell's type system to

---

[9] https://mdb.ps.informatik.uni-kiel.de/.

[10] https://smap.informatik.uni-kiel.de/.

implement server and client code in a single program and ensures a type-safe communication between the client and server side. Since this approach concentrates on an elegant model for the communication aspects of web applications, the integration into web documents is done in the traditional way, i.e., by using raw strings to identify input elements.

There are also proposals for specific programming languages for web applications. For instance, Links [4] supports the implementation of a web application in a single program from which server and client side code (O'Caml and JavaScript programs) as well as database code (SQL) is generated. Being a specialized language, Links has some support to attach program variables to input fields so that their correct use is checked by the Links compiler. However, this input field checking is done by the compiler so that general form abstraction and composition is not supported.

The PLT Scheme Web Server [15] is an approach to write web applications in PLT Scheme. Since the complete web server is implemented in PLT Scheme and supports servlets running on the web server, one can implement web pages and form interactions in a single program. Due to the dynamic nature of PLT Scheme, the consistency of input fields and their use in form handlers is not checked at compile time.

Related to logic programming, there are less advanced approaches. There are libraries for converting HTML documents to data terms so that convenient Prolog notation can be used to describe HTML documents [26]. The PiLLoW library [3] also supports dynamic web pages by providing abstractions for HTML forms and CGI communication. Due to the dynamically typed nature of Prolog, static checks on the form of HTML documents are not supported so that this library provides rather basic abstractions for web programming.

10   Conclusions

We presented a new approach to server-side web programming in the declarative language Curry. The approach is lightweight since its implementation is based on a library together with a wrapper for the main operation, and the execution of applications using this library does not require specific extensions for a web server rather than the ability to execute CGI programs. Our interface for web programming exploits the combined functional and logic features provided by Curry: free variables as references to input elements, functions in data structures as event handlers for interaction elements, and strong typing to check the consistent use of these elements at compile time. As a result, we obtain a more reliable and declarative approach to web programming compared to other alternatives.

Our approach is focused on the server side, i.e., it is intended to implement web interfaces to an application keeping their data on a server. Our model returns for each user request a new web page containing the answer information. Nevertheless, it could also be combined with client-side programming by generating JavaScript. Conceptually, this was tried for Curry with web user interfaces that perform immediate checks by compiling parts of the Curry program to JavaScript

[8] or by a generic concept for declarative user interfaces that can be compiled as a desktop or as a web application [10]. For future work, we want to extend our implementation so that event handlers do not return complete HTML pages but only updates to be performed on the current page via DOM and Ajax.

Another line for future work is the integration of our programming model in a web browser so that the program is not started for every interaction in order to reduce the startup time. Nevertheless, our current implementation is sufficient for systems with a limited load, as demonstrated by existing applications mentioned in this paper.

References

1. Antoy, S., Echahed, R., Hanus, M.: A needed narrowing strategy. J. ACM **47**(4), 776–822 (2000)
2. Antoy, S., Hanus, M.: Functional logic programming. Commun. ACM **53**(4), 74–85 (2010)
3. Cabeza, D., Hermenegildo, M.: Distributed WWW programming using (CIAO-)Prolog and the PiLLoW library. Theory Pract. Log. Program. **1**(3), 251–282 (2001)
4. Cooper, E., Lindley, S., Wadler, P., Yallop, J.: Links: web programming without tiers. In: de Boer, F.S., Bonsangue, M.M., Graf, S., de Roever, W.-P. (eds.) FMCO 2006. LNCS, vol. 4709, pp. 266–296. Springer, Heidelberg (2007). https://doi.org/10.1007/978-3-540-74792-5_12
5. Ekblad, A., Claessen, K.: A seamless, client-centric programming model for type safe web applications. In: Proceedings of the 2014 ACM SIGPLAN Symposium on Haskell, pp. 79–89. ACM Press (2014)
6. Hanus, M.: High-level server side web scripting in curry. In: Ramakrishnan, I.V. (ed.) PADL 2001. LNCS, vol. 1990, pp. 76–92. Springer, Heidelberg (2001). https://doi.org/10.1007/3-540-45241-9_6
7. Hanus, M.: Type-oriented construction of web user interfaces. In: Proceedings of the 8th ACM SIGPLAN International Conference on Principles and Practice of Declarative Programming (PPDP 2006), pp. 27–38. ACM Press (2006)
8. Hanus, M.: Putting declarative programming into the web: translating curry to JavaScript. In: Proceedings of the 9th ACM SIGPLAN International Conference on Principles and Practice of Declarative Programming (PPDP 2007), pp. 155–166. ACM Press (2007)
9. Hanus, M.: Functional logic programming: from theory to curry. In: Voronkov, A., Weidenbach, C. (eds.) Programming Logics. LNCS, vol. 7797, pp. 123–168. Springer, Heidelberg (2013). https://doi.org/10.1007/978-3-642-37651-1_6
10. Hanus, M., Kluß, C.: Declarative programming of user interfaces. In: Gill, A., Swift, T. (eds.) PADL 2009. LNCS, vol. 5418, pp. 16–30. Springer, Heidelberg (2008). https://doi.org/10.1007/978-3-540-92995-6_2
11. Hanus, M., Koschnicke, S.: An ER-based framework for declarative web programming. Theory Pract. Log. Program. **14**(3), 269–291 (2014)
12. Hanus, M., Krone, J.: A typeful integration of SQL into curry. In: Proceedings of the 24th International Workshop on Functional and (Constraint) Logic Programming, volume 234 of Electronic Proceedings in Theoretical Computer Science, pp. 104–119. Open Publishing Association (2017)

13. Hanus, M. (eds.): Curry: an integrated functional logic language (vers. 0.9.0) (2016). http://www.curry-lang.org
14. Huseby, S.H.: Innocent Code: A Security Wake-Up Call for Web Programmers. Wiley (2003)
15. Krishnamurthi, S., McCarthy, J.A., Graunke, P.T., Pettyjohn, G., Felleisen, M.: Implementation and use of the PLT scheme web server. High. Order Symbol. Comput. **20**(4), 431–460 (2007)
16. Ladd, D.A., Ramming, J.C.: Programming the web: an application-oriented language for hypermedia service programming. World Wide Web J. **1**(1) (1996)
17. Meijer, E.: Server side web scripting in Haskell. J. Funct. Program. **10**(1), 1–18 (2000)
18. Peyton Jones, S. (ed.) Haskell 98 Language and Libraries-The Revised Report. Cambridge University Press (2003)
19. Plasmeijer, R., Achten, P.: iData for the world wide web – programming interconnected web forms. In: Hagiya, M., Wadler, P. (eds.) FLOPS 2006. LNCS, vol. 3945, pp. 242–258. Springer, Heidelberg (2006). https://doi.org/10.1007/11737414_17
20. Sandholm, A., Schwartzbach, M.I.: A type system for dynamic web documents. In: Proceedings of the 27th ACM Symposium on Principles of Programming Languages, pp. 290–301 (2000)
21. Thiemann, P.: A typed representation for HTML and XML documents in Haskell. J. Funct. Program. **12**(4–5), 435–468 (2002)
22. Thiemann, P.: WASH/CGI: server-side web scripting with sessions and typed, compositional forms. In: Krishnamurthi, S., Ramakrishnan, C.R. (eds.) PADL 2002. LNCS, vol. 2257, pp. 192–208. Springer, Heidelberg (2002). https://doi.org/10.1007/3-540-45587-6_13
23. Thiemann, P.: WASH server pages. In: Hagiya, M., Wadler, P. (eds.) FLOPS 2006. LNCS, vol. 3945, pp. 277–293. Springer, Heidelberg (2006). https://doi.org/10.1007/11737414_19
24. Wadler, P.: How to declare an imperative. ACM Comput. Surv. **29**(3), 240–263 (1997)
25. Wadler, P., Blott, S.: How to make ad-hoc polymorphism less ad hoc. In: Proceedings of POPL 1989, pp. 60–76 (1989)
26. Wielemaker, J., Huang, Z., van der Meij, L.: SWI-Prolog and the web. Theory Pract. Log. Program. **8**(3), 363–392 (2008)

Declarative Approaches to Testing and Debugging

ConFuzz: Coverage-Guided Property Fuzzing for Event-Driven Programs

Sumit Padhiyar[✉] and K. C. Sivaramakrishnan

IIT Madras, Chennai, India
{sumitpad,kcsrk}@cse.iitm.ac.in

Abstract. Bug-free concurrent programs are hard to write due to non-determinism arising out of concurrency and program inputs. Since concurrency bugs typically manifest under specific inputs and thread schedules, conventional testing methodologies for concurrent programs like stress testing and random testing, which explore random schedules, have a strong chance of missing buggy schedules.

In this paper, we introduce a novel technique that combines property-based testing with mutation-based, grey box fuzzer, applied to event-driven OCaml programs. We have implemented this technique in ConFuzz, a *directed* concurrency bug-finding tool for event-driven OCaml programs. Using ConFuzz, programmers specify high-level program properties as *assertions* in the concurrent program. ConFuzz uses the popular greybox fuzzer AFL to generate inputs as well as concurrent schedules to maximise the likelihood of finding new schedules and paths in the program so as to make the assertion fail. ConFuzz does not require any modification to the concurrent program, which is free to perform arbitrary I/O operations. Our experimental results show that ConFuzz is easy-to-use, effective, detects concurrency bugs faster than Node.Fz - a random fuzzer for event-driven JavaScript programs, and is able to reproduce known concurrency bugs in widely used OCaml libraries.

Keywords: Concurrency testing · Fuzzing

1 Introduction

Event-driven concurrent programming is used in I/O heavy applications such as web browsers, network servers, web applications and file synchronizers. On the client-side, JavaScript natively supports event-driven programming through promises and async/await [3] in order to be able to retrieve multiple resources concurrently from the Web, without blocking the user-interface rendering. On the server-side, several popular and widely used frameworks such as Node.js (JavsScript) [27], Lwt (OCaml) [23,37], Async (OCaml) [2], Twisted (Python) [35], use event-driven concurrent programming model for building scalable network services.

© The Author(s) 2021
J. F. Morales and D. Orchard (Eds.): PADL 2021, LNCS 12548, pp. 127–144, 2021.
https://doi.org/10.1007/978-3-030-67438-0_8

Event-driven programs are typically single-threaded, with the idea that rather than performing I/O actions synchronously, which may block the execution of the program, all the I/O is performed asynchronously, by attaching a *callback function* that gets invoked when the I/O operation is completed. An *event loop* sits at the heart of the programming model that concurrently performs the I/O operations, and schedules the callback functions to be resumed when the corresponding I/O is completed. The concurrent I/O is typically offloaded to a library such as libuv [21] and libev [20], which in turn discharge concurrent I/O through efficient operating system dependent mechanisms such as epoll [11] on Linux, kqueue [18] on FreeBSD, OpenBSD and macOS, and IOCP [16] on Windows.

Single-threaded event-driven programs avoid concurrency bugs arising from multi-threaded execution such as data races and race conditions. Despite this, event-driven programs suffer from concurrency bugs due to the non-deterministic order in which the events may be resolved. For example, callbacks attached to a timer event and DNS resolution request may execute in different orders based on the order in which the events arrive. As event-driven programs are single-threaded, they do not contain data races related bugs which makes it unsuitable to apply data race detectors developed for detecting multi-threading bugs [12, 39].

Moreover, the erroneous condition in a concurrent program may not be the mere presence of a race, but a complex assertion expressed over the current program state. For example, in the case of a timer event and DNS resolution request, the timer may be intended for timing out the DNS resolution request. On successful resolution, the timer event is cancelled. Then, the safety property is that if the timer callback is running, then the DNS resolution request is still pending. It is unclear how to express this complex property as races.

To help uncover such complex concurrency bugs that may arise in event-driven concurrent programs, we present a novel technique that combines property-based testing on the lines of QuickCheck [6] with AFL fuzzer [1], the state-of-the-art, mutation-based, grey box fuzzer, and apply it to generate not only inputs that may cause the property to fail, but also to drive the various scheduling decisions in the event-driven program. AFL works by instrumenting the program under test to observe the control-flow edges, mutates the input such that new paths are uncovered. In addition to different paths, a concurrent program also has to contend with the exponential number of schedules available, many of which may lead to the same behaviour. Our key observation is that we can use AFL's grey box fuzzing capability to direct the search towards new schedules, and thus lead to property failure.

We have implemented this technique in ConFuzz, a concurrent property fuzz testing tool for concurrent OCaml programs using the popular Lwt [23, 37] library(asynchronous I/O library). Properties are expressed as assertions in the source code, and ConFuzz aims to identify the input and the schedule that will cause the assertion to fail. ConFuzz supports record and replay to reproduce the failure. Once a bug is identified, ConFuzz can *deterministically reproduce* the concurrency bug. ConFuzz is developed as a drop-in replacement for the Lwt library and does not require any change to the code other than writing the assertion and the wrapper code to drive the tool.

The main contributions of this paper are as follows:

- We present a novel technique that combines property-based testing with mutation-based, grey box fuzzer applied to test the schedules of event-driven OCaml programs.
- We implement the technique in ConFuzz, a drop-in replacement for testing event-driven OCaml programs written using the Lwt library.
- We show by experimental evaluation that ConFuzz is more effective and efficient than the state-of-the-art random fuzzing tool Node.Fz and stress testing in finding concurrency bugs. We reproduce known concurrency bugs by testing ConFuzz on 8 real-world concurrent OCaml programs and 3 benchmark programs.

2   Motivating Example

We describe a simple, adversarial example to illustrate the effectiveness of ConFuzz over Node.Fz and stress testing. Figure 1 shows an OCaml concurrent program written using the Lwt library [37]. The program contains a single function linear_eq that takes an integer argument i. linear_eq creates three concurrent tasks p1,

```
let linear_eq i =
  let x = ref i in
  let p1 = pause () >>= fun () ->
    x := !x - 2; return_unit in
  let p2 = pause () >>= fun () ->
    x := !x * 4; return_unit in
  let p3 = pause () >>= fun () ->
    x := !x + 70; return_unit in
  Lwt_main.run (join[p1;p2;p3]);
  assert (!x <> 0)
```

Fig. 1. A program with a concurrency bug

p2, and p3, each modifying the shared mutable reference x. The pause operation pauses the concurrent task, registering the function fun ()-> ... following the >>= operator as a callback to be executed in the future. Importantly, the tasks p1, p2, and p3 may be executed in any order.

This program has a concurrency bug; there exists a particular combination of input value i and interleaving between the tasks that will cause the value of x to become 0, causing the assertion to fail. There are 2^{63}[1] possibilities for the value of i and 6 (3!) possible schedules for the 3 tasks. Out of these, there are only 3 possible combinations of input and schedule for which the assertion fails.

- $i = -17$ and schedule = [p2; p1; p3] : $((-17 * 4) - 2) + 70 = 0$.
- $i = -68$ and schedule = [p1; p3; p2] : $((-68 - 2) + 70) * 4 = 0$.
- $i = -68$ and schedule = [p3; p1; p2] : $((-68 + 70) - 2) * 4 = 0$.

---

[1] OCaml uses tagged integer representation [19].

As the bug in example program depends on input and interleaving, concurrency testing techniques focusing only on generating different interleavings will fail to find this bug. This is evident when the program is executed under different testing techniques. Table 2 shows a comparison of ConFuzz with the random concurrency fuzzing tool Node.Fz [7] and stress testing for the example program.

Node.Fz is a concurrency fuzzing tool similar to ConFuzz, which generates random interleavings rather than being guided by AFL. Node.Fz focuses only on finding buggy interleavings. As Node.Fz is implemented in JavaScript, we port the underlying technique in OCaml. We refer to

Testing Technique	Executions (millions)	Time (minutes)	Bug Found
ConFuzz	3.26	18	**Yes**
Node.Fz[7]	110	60	**No**
Stress	131	60	**No**

Fig. 2. Comparing different testing techniques

the OCaml port of Node.Fz technique when referring to Node.Fz. Stress testing runs a program repeatedly with random input values. We test the example program with each technique until a bug is found or a timeout of 1 h is reached. We report the number of executions and time taken if the bug was found. Only ConFuzz was able to find the bug. Although this example is synthetic, we observe similar patterns in real world programs where the bug depends on the combination of the input value and the schedule, and cannot be discovered with a tool that only focuses on one of the sources of non-determinism.

Real world event-driven programs also involve file and network I/O, timer completions, etc. ConFuzz can test *unmodified* programs that involve complex I/O behaviour. Figure 3 shows a function `pipe_chars` that takes three character arguments. The function creates a shared `pipe` as a pair of input (`ic`) and output (`oc`) file descriptors. The `sender` task sends the characters over `oc`. The three `recvr` tasks each receive a single character, convert that to the corresponding upper

```
let pipe_chars a b c =
  let res = ref [] in
  let ic, oc = pipe () in
  let sender =
    write_char oc a >>= fun () ->
    write_char oc b >>= fun () ->
    write_char oc c >>= fun () ->
    return_unit
  in
  let recvr () =
    read_char ic >>= fun c ->
    res := Char.uppercase_ascii c::!res;
    return_unit
  in
  Lwt_main.run (join [recvr(); recvr();
                      recvr(); sender]);
  assert (!res <> ['B';'U';'G'])
```

Fig. 3. A program with a concurrency bug

case character, and append it to a global list reference `res`. The assertion checks that the final result in `res` is not `['B';'U';'G']`. Due to input and scheduling non-determinism, there are plenty of schedules. However, the assertion failure is triggered with only 6 distinct inputs, each of which is a permutation of 'b', 'u', 'g' for the input arguments to the function, and a corresponding permutation of the recvr tasks. ConFuzz was able to find a buggy input and schedule in under a minute. This illustrates that ConFuzz is applicable to real world event-driven concurrent programs.

3   Lwt: Event-Driven Model

In this section, we discuss the event-driven model in Lwt. Lwt [37] is the most widely used asynchronous I/O library in the OCaml ecosystem. Lwt lies at the heart of the stack in the MirageOS [24], a library operating system for constructing Unikernels. MirageOS is embedded in Docker for Mac and Windows apps [8] and hence, runs on millions of developer machines across the world. Hence, our choice of Lwt is timely and practical. That said, the ideas presented in this paper can be applied to other event-driven libraries such as Node.js [27]. Lwt event model is shown in Fig. 4.

Under cooperative threading, each task voluntarily yields control to other tasks when it is no longer able to make progress. Lwt event model consists of an event loop engine and a worker pool. The event loop engine manages timers, read and write I/O events on regis-

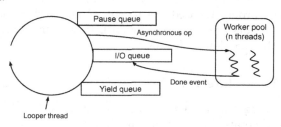

Fig. 4. Lwt event model

tered file descriptors and executes the callbacks registered with the events. Lwt event loop engine can be configured to use various engines such as libev [20], Unix's select [33] and poll [30].

Lwt event loop consists of three event queues, each holding a different class of events with their attached callbacks. The three queues are yield, pause and I/O queue. All yielded and paused callbacks are inserted in yield and pause queue respectively. The I/O queue comprises of the timer and I/O events and is handled by libev engine. The *looper thread* examines each of the queues and executes the pending callbacks without interruption until they give up control. Lwt does not guarantee the relative execution order between two events in the same or different queues. The computationally intensive tasks and blocking system calls are offloaded to the *worker pool* of threads which execute the tasks so that they do not block the event loop. The non-determinism in the execution order of the events gives rise to concurrency bugs.

4   ConFuzz

In this section, we present the architecture of the ConFuzz tool, starting with a background of the technique ConFuzz builds upon.

4.1 Background

Fuzzing is an effective technique for testing software by feeding random input to induce the program to crash. American Fuzzy Lop (AFL) [1] is a coverage-guided fuzzer [28], which inserts lightweight instrumentation in the program under test to collect code coverage information such as program execution paths. AFL starts with a seed test case, which it mutates with a combination of random and deterministic techniques that aims to find new execution paths in the program. On detecting a new execution path, the corresponding input test case is saved for further mutation. During fuzzing, the input test cases that results in a crash are saved, thus finding the exact test case that results in a crash.

Property-based testing, introduced by QuickCheck [6], works by testing an executable (predicate) on a stream of randomly generated inputs. Property-based testing is typically equipped with a generator that randomly generates inputs for the executable predicate. While property based testing works well in many cases, random generation of inputs may not cover large parts of the programs where the bugs may lie. Crowbar [9] is a testing tool for OCaml that combines property-based testing with AFL. Rather than generating random inputs, the inputs are generated by AFL to maximise the discovery of execution paths in the function under test.

4.2 Architecture

ConFuzz extends Crowbar in order to generate inputs that maximize the coverage of the state space introduced by non-deterministic execution of concurrent event-driven programs. ConFuzz is built on top of Crowbar by forking it. Figure 5 shows ConFuzz's architecture. Con-Fuzz controls Lwt's scheduler by capturing the non-determinism present

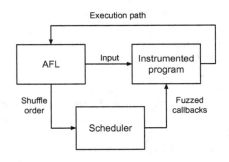

Fig. 5. ConFuzz architecture

in the Lwt programs. To explore properties on a wide range of different schedules, ConFuzz generates various legal event schedules by alternating the order of event callback execution with the help of AFL. AFL generates execution order (*shuffle order*) for the captured concurrent events, which is then enforced by controlled scheduler (*fuzzed callbacks*). The properties are tested repeatedly with different test inputs and event schedules. The test input and the event schedules that result in property failures are detected as a crash by AFL, resulting in the detection of concurrency bug. Although example programs in the paper use simple inputs, ConFuzz does support generators for complex inputs like QuickCheck [6].

Unlike other concurrency testing tools [7,26], which fuzz the schedules for a specific input, ConFuzz can fuzz both input and the schedule, which improves both the ease-of-use and effectiveness of the tool. Similar to other concurrency testing tools, ConFuzz also supports record and replay feature, which records the event schedule that leads to a concurrency bug. The input and the buggy schedule are saved in a separate file, which when executed with test binary, deterministically reproduces the bug. Thus, ConFuzz helps to debug concurrency bug by reliably reproducing the bug.

5   Fuzzing Under Non-determinism

In this section, we discuss the non-determinism present in Lwt concurrent programs. We then show how ConFuzz captures and fuzzes this non-determinism.

5.1   Non-determinism in Lwt

I/O and Timer Non-determinism. Lwt permits asynchronous network and file I/O by registering callbacks against I/O operations. Since the completion of I/O operations is non-deterministic, the callbacks may be triggered in a non-deterministic order. Moreover, there is also the possibility of races between callbacks in order to access shared resources such as sockets and file descriptors. Lwt also supports registering callbacks to timer events which are triggered at *some time* after the expiration of the timer. Any assumption about the precise time at which the callbacks will run may lead to concurrency bugs. As described in Sect. 3, both the timer and the I/O events are processed in the I/O event queue. For example, a user code expecting a network request to complete within a certain time period may go wrong if the network callback is executed after the timer callback. This bug can be caught by fuzzing the I/O event queue that reorders the timer and the network callbacks.

Worker Pool Non-determinism. Lwt offloads blocking system calls and long running tasks to the worker pool. Lwt uses a worker pool comprising of a fixed number of kernel threads. The kernel threads are scheduled by the operating system and makes the execution of offloaded tasks non-deterministic.

Callback Non-determinism. Lwtyield and pause primitives enable long running computation to give up execution to another callback voluntarily. In Lwt, the yielded and paused callbacks may be evaluated in any order. Any assumption on the order in which the yielded and paused callbacks are executed may lead to concurrency bugs. These bugs can be identified by fuzzing the yield and pause queues.

5.2   Capturing Non-determinism

In this section, we discuss how ConFuzz controls the non-determinism described in Sect. 5.1.

Event Loop Queues. Lwt event loop queues – yield, pause and I/O – are the primary sources of non-determinism in an Lwt program. To capture and control the non-determinism arising out of these queues, we insert calls to ConFuzz scheduler in the event loop before executing the callbacks of yield and pause queues. ConFuzz scheduler then fuzzes the order of callbacks in the queues to generate alternative schedules.

Worker Pools. Non-determinism in the worker pool is influenced by multiple factors such as the number of threads, the thread scheduling by the operating system and the order in which the tasks are offloaded. For deterministic processing and completion order of tasks, we reduce the worker pool size to one. This change serializes the tasks handled by the worker pool. The worker pool tasks are executed one after another. By reducing the worker pool to one thread, ConFuzz can deterministically replay the order of worker pool task execution.

In Lwt to signal task completion, the worker pool thread writes to a common file descriptor which is intercepted by the event loop and processed as an I/O event. The single file descriptor is shared by all the tasks for indicating task completion. Thus, Lwt multiplexes a single file descriptor for many worker pool tasks. Multiplexing prevents changing the order of task completion relative to I/O and as a result, miss some of the bugs.

To overcome this, ConFuzz eliminates multiplexing by assigning a file descriptor per task. During the event loop I/O phase, task completion I/O events are fuzzed along with other I/O events and timers. De-multiplexing enables ConFuzz to shuffle the order of task completion relative to other tasks as well as timer and I/O events.

To change the processing order of worker pool tasks, we delay the execution of offloaded tasks. During each iteration of the event loop, the offloaded tasks are collected in a list. At the start of the next iteration of the event loop, ConFuzz scheduler shuffles the processing order of the tasks. The tasks are then executed synchronously. By delaying the task execution by one iteration, ConFuzz collects enough tasks to shuffle. We believe that delaying tasks by one iteration would suffice to generate the task processing orders that would occur in production environments. It is highly unlikely that a task from the second iteration is started and completed before tasks from the first iteration, given that Lwt tasks are started off in a FIFO manner.

Synchronous task execution also helps in deterministically generating a buggy schedule. As the number of completed tasks remains the same in every schedule, ConFuzz has to just reorder tasks to reproduce a bug. This design choice lets ConFuzz generate task processing and completion order independently. However, delaying and synchronous task execution can prevent ConFuzz from missing schedules containing bugs arising from the worker pool related races. In ConFuzz, we trade-off schedule space generation to reliably reproducing concurrency bug by deterministic schedule generation. ConFuzz does not guarantee the absence of bugs but reliably reproduces discovered concurrency bugs.

Promise Callbacks. As promise callbacks are executed non-deterministically, promise callback ordering is also fuzzed by ConFuzz. Before execution, the order of callbacks attached to a promise is changed by ConFuzz scheduler. By fuzzing promise callbacks, ConFuzz generates alternative ordering of callback execution.

5.3   ConFuzz Scheduler

To generate a varied event schedules, ConFuzz scheduler controls the Lwt event loop and the worker pool as shown in Fig. 6. To change the order of events, ConFuzz scheduler exposes `fuzz_list` : `'a list -> 'a list` function, which takes a list and returns a shuffled list. The

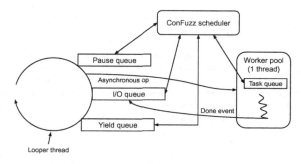

Fig. 6. ConFuzz scheduler

changes to the Lwt scheduler that require changing the order of events (Sect. 5.2) call this function to shuffle the callback list. On executing the shuffled list, the program is executed under a particular schedule.

To reorder callbacks, ConFuzz scheduler asks AFL to generate random numbers. The random numbers then determine the ordering of the callbacks. On detecting a concurrency bug, the generated random numbers are saved in a separate file as a schedule trace. With the schedule trace, the scheduler can reproduce a schedule. Using this capability of the scheduler, ConFuzz can replay a schedule to reliably expose the detected concurrency bugs. Deterministic replay helps programmers find the exact cause of concurrency bugs.

The order of callback execution affects the program's execution path. Due to the program instrumentation, AFL recognises the program execution path in every program run. AFL being a coverage guided fuzzer, tries to increase coverage (execution paths). AFL thus generates random numbers that produce alternative callback orderings. Alternative callback orderings result in new schedules that exercise new program execution paths. ConFuzz scheduler keeps on generating new schedules until AFL is able to find new execution paths. ConFuzz thus uses AFL fuzzing to execute program under different execution schedules.

6   Evaluation

In this section, we evaluate the effectiveness of ConFuzz in finding concurrency bugs in real-world OCaml applications and benchmark programs. Additionally, we check the efficiency of ConFuzz in terms of time required to detect concurrency bugs in comparison to Node.Fz and stress testing. Node.Fz[7] is a concurrency bug finding fuzzing tool for event-driven JavaScript programs. As Node.Fz randomly perturbs the execution of a JavaScript program, we use ConFuzz's random testing mode (Sect. 4.2) to simulate Node.Fz technique. Stress testing runs

Table 1. Experimental subjects

Type	Name (abbreviation)	Description	GitHub Stars	Size (LoC)	Issue #
Real world applications	irmin(IR)	Distributed database	1,284	18.6K	270
	lwt (LWT)	Concurrent programming library	448	12.2k	583
	mirage-tcpip (TCP)	Networking stack for Mirage OS	253	4.9K	86
	ghost (GHO)	Blogging engine	35,000	50K	1834
	porybox (PB)	Pokémon platform	29	7.9K	157
	node-mkdirp (NKD)	Recursive mkdir	2,200	0.5K	2
	node-logger-file (CLF)	Logging module	2	0.9K	1
	fiware-pep-steelskin (FPS)	Policy enforcement point proxy	11	8.2K	269
Benchmark programs	Motivating example (MX)	Linear equation with concurrency	–	–	–
	Benchmark 1 (B1)	Bank transactions	–	–	–
	Benchmark 2 (B2)	Schedule coverage	–	–	–

a program repeatedly with random input values. Stress testing does not generate program interleavings as done by ConFuzz and executes programs directly under OS scheduler. We design and conduct experiments to answer the following questions:

1. **RQ1: Effectiveness** – How frequently is ConFuzz able to find bugs?
2. **RQ2: Efficiency** – How many executions are required to detect bugs by ConFuzz as compared to Node.Fz and stress testing?
3. **RQ3: Practicality** – Can ConFuzz detect and reproduce known concurrency bugs in real-world OCaml applications?

6.1   Experimental Subjects and Setup

We evaluated ConFuzz on both real-world OCaml applications and benchmark programs. Table 1 summarises the applications and benchmark programs used for the evaluation. We have used eight real-world applications and three benchmark programs as experimental subjects for evaluating ConFuzz. All of the programs contain at least one known concurrency bug.

To identify known concurrency bugs, we searched across GitHub bug reports for closed bugs in Lwt based OCaml projects. We select a bug only if the bug report contains a clear description or has an automated test case to reproduce the bug. We found three Lwt based OCaml bugs - IR, LWT and TCP as shown in Table 1. Apart from OCaml bugs, we have build a dataset of 15 known concurrency real-world JavaScript bugs mentioned in the related work [5,7,38]. We abstracted the buggy concurrent code of JavaScript bugs and ported it to standalone OCaml programs. We excluded those bugs from the JavaScript dataset which could not be ported to OCaml or have an incomplete bug report. We were able to port 5 JavaScript bugs from the dataset. The five JavaScript bugs used in the evaluation are GHO, PB, NKD, CLF and FPS. MX is the motivating example from Sect. 2. Benchmark B1 simulates concurrent bank transactions, adapted from the VeriFIT repository of concurrency bugs [36]. Concurrent bank transactions in B1 causes the bank account log to get corrupted. Benchmark B2 simulates a bug depending on a particular concurrent interleaving and gets exposed only when B2 is executed under that buggy interleaving. B2 is explained in detail in section RQ2.

We design our experiments to compare ConFuzz's bug detection capability with Node.Fz and stress testing (hereby referred to as the testing techniques). We perform 30 testing runs for each experimental subject (Table 1) and testing technique. A *testing run* is a single invocation of the testing technique. The performance metric we focus on is mean time to failure (MTTF), which measures how quickly a concurrency bug is found in terms of time. A single *test execution* indicates one execution of the respective application's test case. For each subject and testing technique, we execute respective subject application until the first concurrency bug is found or a timeout of 1 h occurs. For each such run, we note the time taken to find the first concurrency

Table 2. Bug detection capability of the techniques. Each entry is the fraction of the testing runs that manifested the concurrency bug.

	Stress	Node.Fz	ConFuzz
IR	1.00	0.00	1.00
LWT	0.00	1.00	1.00
TCP	0.00	1.00	1.00
GHO	0.00	0.00	1.00
PB	0.00	0.00	1.00
NKD	0.4	0.53	1.00
CLF	0.43	0.56	1.00
FPS	0.00	0.96	1.00
MX	0.00	0.00	1.00
B1	0.87	0.6	1.00
B2	0.00	0.00	1.00
Avg	0.24	0.42	1.00

bug and whether a bug was found or not. We ran all of our experiments on a machine with 6-Core Intel i5-8500 processor, 16 GB RAM, running Linux 4.15.0-1034.

6.2 Experimental Results

RQ1: Effectiveness. Table 2 shows the bug detection capabilities of the three testing techniques. The first column shows the abbreviation of the experimental subjects. The second to fourth column shows the bug detection results of Stress, Node.Fz and ConFuzz testing, respectively. Each cell in the table shows the fraction of the testing runs that detected a concurrency bug out of the total 30 testing runs per experimental subject and testing technique.

As shown in Table 2, ConFuzz detected concurrency bugs in every testing run for all experimental subjects (all cells are 1.00). In the case of GHO, PB, MX and B2, only ConFuzz was able to detect a bug. Despite capturing the non-determinism, Node.Fz could not detect a bug in IR, GHO, PB,

Table 3. Mean time to find the concurrency bug (seconds)

	Stress	Node.Fz	ConFuzz
IR	37.7	–	1.03
LWT	–	295.73	243.3
TCP	–	315.03	94.16
GHO	–	–	0.33
PB	–	–	0.3
NKD	1738.83	1104.62	42.23
CLF	685.1	1086.2	231.96
FPS	–	696.55	103.13
MX	–	–	981.17
B1	918.8	1333.89	384.6
B2	–	–	59.26

MX and B2. This confirms that ConFuzz was able to generate concurrent schedules along with inputs more effectively. Stress testing was more effective in the case of IR and B1 than Node.Fz with a ratio of 1.00 and 0.87 respectively. Both IR and B1 comprises a lot of files I/O. We suspect that due to OS-level nondeterminism, stress testing is more effective than Node.Fz, as Node.Fz finds it difficult to generate the exact buggy schedule for file I/O. This provides a helpful insight that ConFuzz is good at generating a prefix or exact schedule that can cause concurrency errors. In addition, ConFuzz does not produce *false positives*, as schedules explored by ConFuzz are all legal schedules in Lwt. Thus, the results confirm that ConFuzz is effective at detecting concurrency bugs.

RQ2: Efficiency. Table 3 shows the efficiency results of the three testing techniques. The second to fourth column shows the efficiency results of stress, Node.Fz and ConFuzz testing respectively. Each cell represents the average time (in seconds) taken to detect the first concurrency bug per experimental subject and testing technique over 30 testing runs. '-' in the cell indicates that none of the 30 testing runs detected a concurrency bug within the timeout of 1 h.

As shown in Table 3, for every experimental subject, ConFuzz took significantly less time (column 4) to find bug than other techniques. ConFuzz is 26×, 6× and 4.7× faster than Node.Fz for NKD, FPS and CLF bugs respectively. For NKD and IR bugs, ConFuzz is 41× and 36× faster than stress testing respectively. Except for LWT, ConFuzz is at least 2× faster than second fastest technique.

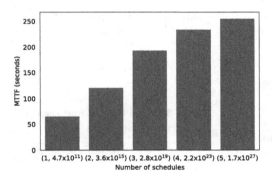

Fig. 7. Efficiency of ConFuzz as schedule space increases. The total number of schedules is given by $f(n) = (3!)^{(10*n+20)/2}$. The labels on the x-axis show $(n, f(n))$.

Note that for NKD, CLF, FPS and B1 bugs, the average time of Node.Fz and stress testing does not include testing runs which failed to detect concurrency bug. Due to its efficiency, ConFuzz enables a developer to explore a broader schedule space of the concurrent program than Node.Fz and other techniques with the same test time budget. Thereby increasing the chances of finding bug in the same limited test time budget. Thus, these results illustrate that ConFuzz is efficient in detecting concurrency bugs.

To evaluate the efficiency of ConFuzz on a program containing a large schedule space, we modify the motivating example in Fig. 1 to have a large number of concurrent schedules. We define a concurrent schedule as the order in which the callbacks attached to the events are executed. The total number of concurrent schedules of the modified program is given by the following formula parameterised over n:

$$Total\ number\ of\ schedules = (3!)^{(10*n+20)/2} \qquad (1)$$

where n controls the degree of concurrency in the program. Only one concurrent schedule out of the many schedules results in a concurrency bug. Figure 7 shows the efficiency of ConFuzz over large schedule spaces. We increase n from 1 to 5 to generate a large schedule space. Note that benchmark B2 used as an experimental subject in evaluation is modified program with n equals to 1. Figure 7 graph shows mean time to failure (MMTF) as the schedule space is increased. As evident from the graph, even for the program with a large schedule space, ConFuzz was able to detect the bug within minutes. Note that Node.Fz and stress testing fails to detect the bug for the modified program. Despite the number of schedules increasing exponentially, MTTF increased linearly. This shows the efficiency of ConFuzz to find bugs even in programs with large schedule spaces.

RQ3: Practicality. As shown in Table 2, ConFuzz is able to reliably reproduce concurrency bugs in real-world applications and widely used software. Table 1 includes links to the original bug reports. We have made available an replication package comprising of the ConFuzz tool and the experimental subjects online[2]. In the sequel, we discuss the details of the irmin(IR) bug from Table 1.

Irmin #270[3]. Irmin is a distributed database built on the principles of Git. Similar to Git, the objects in Irmin are organised into directories. Irmin allows users to install *watchers* on directories which are callback functions that get triggered once when for every change in the directory. The bug had to do with the callbacks begin invoked multiple times if multiple watchers were registered to the same directory in quick succession. The patch is shown in Fig. 8. When there are

```
let start_watchdog ~delay dir =
  match watchdog dir with
  | Some _ ->
    assert (nb_listeners dir <> 0);
    Lwt.return_unit
  | None    ->
-   Log.debug "Start watchdog for %s" dir;
+   (* Note: multiple threads can wait here
    *)
    listen dir ~delay ~callback >|=
        fun u ->
-   Hashtbl.add watchdogs dir u
+   match watchdog dir with
+   | Some _ -> u ()
+   | None ->
+   Log.debug "Start watchdog for %s" dir;
+   Hashtbl.add watchdogs dir u
```

Fig. 8. Irmin bug #270

concurrent calls to `start_watchdog` in succession, it might turn out that all of them are blocked at `listen`. When the callback is triggered, each of these callbacks now adds an entry to the `watchdogs` hash table. The fix is to only add one entry to the hash table and for the rest, directly call the callback function. The property that we tested was that the callback function is invoked only once.

---

[2] See https://github.com/SumitPadhiyar/ConFuzz_PADL_2021.

[3] https://github.com/mirage/irmin/issues/270.

Observe that the bug is input dependent; the bug is triggered only if concurrent calls to `start_watchdog` work on the same directory `dir` and the `delay` is such that they are all released in the same round.

7 Limitations

While our experimental evaluation shows that ConFuzz is highly effective in finding bugs, we discuss some of the limitations in our approach. While ConFuzz captures most of the non-determinism present in event-driven concurrent programs, it cannot capture and control external non-determinism such as file read/write or network response. External non-determinism arises when interacting with external resources like file system, database, etc. which are outside the scope of ConFuzz.

To be completely certain about the order in which the asynchronous tasks are executed, ConFuzz serializes the worker pool tasks which might result in missing some of the concurrency bugs arising out of the worker pool-related races (although the concurrency bug study by Davis et al. [7] did not identify any such races). Serializing worker pool tasks help ConFuzz to *deterministically reproduce* detected bugs. We trade-off missing some of the worker pool related concurrency bugs with the deterministic reproducibility of the detected bugs. Being a property-based testing framework, ConFuzz aims to generate failing tests cases that falsify the property. Hence, ConFuzz does not aim to detect traditional concurrency bugs such as data races and race conditions.

8 Related Work

To the best of our knowledge, ConFuzz is the first tool to apply coverage-guided fuzzing, not just to maximize the coverage of the source code of program, but also to maximize the schedule space coverage introduced by a non-deterministic event-driven program. In this section, we compare ConFuzz to related work.

Concurrency Fuzzing: AFL has been used previously to detect concurrency vulnerabilities in a Heuristic Framework [22] for multi-threaded programs. Unlike ConFuzz, Heuristic Framework generates interleavings by changing thread priorities instead of controlling the scheduler directly, thereby losing the bug replay capability. Due to its approach, Heuristic Framework can only find specific type of concurrency bugs and has false positives. Heuristic Framework is applied to multi-threaded programs whereas ConFuzz is applied to event-driven programs. The most similar work to ConFuzz is the concurrency fuzzing tool Node.Fz [7]. Node.Fz fuzzes the order of events and callbacks randomly to explore different schedules. Node.Fz can only find bugs that manifest purely as a result of particular scheduling, not as a property of program inputs. As Sect. 6 illustrates, the coverage-guided fuzzing of ConFuzz is much more effective than Node.Fz at finding the same concurrency bugs.

Multithreaded Programs: Many approaches and tools have been developed to identify concurrency bugs in multi-threaded programs. FastTrack [13], Eraser [32], CalFuzzer [17] aims to detect multi-threaded concurrency bugs like data races, deadlock. ConTest [10], RaceFuzzer [34] uses random fuzzing to generate varied thread schedules. These approaches apply to multi-threaded programs for detecting concurrency bugs such as atomicity violations and race conditions on shared memory and are not directly applicable to event-driven programs interacting with the external world by performing I/O. Systematic exploration techniques such as model checking attempt to explore the schedule space of a given program exhaustively to find concurrency bugs. CHESS [26] is a state-less model checker exploring the schedule space in a systematic manner. While exhaustive state space exploration is expensive and given a limited test time budget, ConFuzz explores broader input and schedule space, which is more likely to detect bugs.

Application Domains: There are bug detection techniques to identify concurrency errors in client-side JavaScript web applications. WAVE [14], WebRacer [29] and EventRacer [31] propose to find concurrency bugs in client-side elements like browser's DOM and webpage loading through static analysis or dynamic analysis. Though client-side web apps are event-driven, these techniques are tuned for client-side key elements like DOM and web page loading which are not present in server-side like OCaml concurrent programs. Thus, the above approaches cannot be directly applied to event-driven OCaml applications. Android is another event-driven programming environment in combination with multi-threaded programming model. Several dynamic data race detectors [4, 15, 25] have been proposed for Android apps. These tools are tightly coupled with the Android system and target mainly shared memory races rather than violations due to I/O events.

9   Conclusions and Future Work

In this paper, we have presented a novel technique that combines QuickCheck-style property-based testing with coverage-guided fuzzing for finding concurrency bugs in event-driven programs. We implemented the technique in a tool called ConFuzz using AFL for coverage-guided fuzzing for event-driven OCaml programs written using the Lwt library. Our performance evaluation shows that coverage-guided fuzzing of ConFuzz is more effective and efficient than the random fuzzing tool Node.Fz in finding the bugs. We also show that ConFuzz can detect bugs in large and widely used real-world OCaml applications without having to modify the code under test. As future work, we are keen to extend ConFuzz to test shared memory multi-threaded applications.

References

1. American fuzzy lop (2020). https://lcamtuf.coredump.cx/afl
2. Async: Typeful concurrent programming (2020). https://opensource.janestreet.com/async/
3. Asynchronous Javascript (2020). https://developer.mozilla.org/en-US/docs/Learn/JavaScript/Asynchronous
4. Bielik, P., Raychev, V., Vechev, M.: Scalable race detection for android applications. SIGPLAN Not. **50**(10), 332–348 (2015). https://doi.org/10.1145/2858965.2814303
5. Chang, X., Dou, W., Gao, Y., Wang, J., Wei, J., Huang, T.: Detecting atomicity violations for event-driven node.js applications. In: Proceedings of the 41st International Conference on Software Engineering, ICSE 2019, pp. 631–642. IEEE Press (2019). https://doi.org/10.1109/ICSE.2019.00073
6. Claessen, K., Hughes, J.: QuickCheck: a lightweight tool for random testing of Haskell programs. In: Proceedings of the Fifth ACM SIGPLAN International Conference on Functional Programming, ICFP 2000, pp. 268–279. Association for Computing Machinery, New York (2000). https://doi.org/10.1145/351240.351266
7. Davis, J., Thekumparampil, A., Lee, D.: Node.fz: fuzzing the server-side event-driven architecture. In: Proceedings of the Twelfth European Conference on Computer Systems, EuroSys 2017, pp. 145–160. Association for Computing Machinery, New York (2017). https://doi.org/10.1145/3064176.3064188
8. Improving docker with unikernels: Introducing HyperKit, VPNKit and DataKit (2020). https://www.docker.com/blog/docker-unikernels-open-source/
9. Dolan, S., Preston, M.: Testing with Crowbar. In: OCaml Workshop (2017)
10. Edelstein, O., Farchi, E., Goldin, E., Nir-Buchbinder, Y., Ratsaby, G., Ur, S.: Framework for testing multi-threaded Java programs. Concurr. Comput.: Pract. Exp. **15**, 485-499 (2003)
11. epoll: I/O event notification facility (2020). http://man7.org/linux/man-pages/man7/epoll.7.html
12. Flanagan, C., Freund, S.N.: FastTrack: efficient and precise dynamic race detection. In: Proceedings of the 30th ACM SIGPLAN Conference on Programming Language Design and Implementation, PLDI 2009, pp. 121–133. Association for Computing Machinery, New York (2009). https://doi.org/10.1145/1542476.1542490
13. Flanagan, C., Freund, S.N.: FastTrack: efficient and precise dynamic race detection. SIGPLAN Not. **44**(6), 121–133 (2009). https://doi.org/10.1145/1543135.1542490
14. Hong, S., Park, Y., Kim, M.: Detecting concurrency errors in client-side java script web applications. In: Proceedings of the 2014 IEEE International Conference on Software Testing, Verification, and Validation, ICST 2014, pp. 61–70. IEEE Computer Society, USA (2014). https://doi.org/10.1109/ICST.2014.17
15. Hsiao, C.H., et al.: Race detection for event-driven mobile applications. In: Proceedings of the 35th ACM SIGPLAN Conference on Programming Language Design and Implementation, PLDI 2014, pp. 326–336. Association for Computing Machinery, New York (2014). https://doi.org/10.1145/2594291.2594330
16. I/O completion ports (2020). https://docs.microsoft.com/en-us/windows/win32/fileio/i-o-completion-ports
17. Joshi, P., Naik, M., Park, C.-S., Sen, K.: CALFUZZER: an extensible active testing framework for concurrent programs. In: Bouajjani, A., Maler, O. (eds.) CAV 2009. LNCS, vol. 5643, pp. 675–681. Springer, Heidelberg (2009). https://doi.org/10.1007/978-3-642-02658-4_54

18. kqueue, kevent - kernel event notification mechanism (2020). https://www.freebsd.org/cgi/man.cgi?kqueue
19. Leroy, X.: The ZINC Experiment: An Economical Implementation of the ML Language. Technical report RT-0117, INRIA, February 1990. https://hal.inria.fr/inria-00070049
20. Libev event loop (2019). http://software.schmorp.de/pkg/libev.html
21. Libuv: Cross-platform asynchronous I/O (2020). https://libuv.org/
22. Liu, C., Zou, D., Luo, P., Zhu, B.B., Jin, H.: A heuristic framework to detect concurrency vulnerabilities. In: Proceedings of the 34th Annual Computer Security Applications Conference, ACSAC 2018, pp. 529–541. Association for Computing Machinery, New York (2018). https://doi.org/10.1145/3274694.3274718
23. Lwt: OCaml promises and concurrent I/O (2020). https://ocsigen.org/lwt/5.2.0/manual/manual
24. Madhavapeddy, A., et al.: Unikernels: library operating systems for the cloud. In: Proceedings of the Eighteenth International Conference on Architectural Support for Programming Languages and Operating Systems, ASPLOS 2013, pp. 461–472. Association for Computing Machinery, New York (2013). https://doi.org/10.1145/2451116.2451167
25. Maiya, P., Kanade, A., Majumdar, R.: Race detection for android applications. SIGPLAN Not. **49**(6), 316–325 (2014). https://doi.org/10.1145/2666356.2594311
26. Musuvathi, M., Qadeer, S.: CHESS: systematic stress testing of concurrent software. In: Puebla, G. (ed.) LOPSTR 2006. LNCS, vol. 4407, pp. 15–16. Springer, Heidelberg (2007). https://doi.org/10.1007/978-3-540-71410-1_2
27. Node.js is a Javascript runtime built on chrome's v8 Javascript engine (2020). https://nodejs.org/en/
28. Padhye, R., Lemieux, C., Sen, K.: JQF: coverage-guided property-based testing in Java. In: Proceedings of the 28th ACM SIGSOFT International Symposium on Software Testing and Analysis, ISSTA 2019, pp. 398–401. Association for Computing Machinery, New York (2019). https://doi.org/10.1145/3293882.3339002
29. Petrov, B., Vechev, M., Sridharan, M., Dolby, J.: Race detection for web applications. In: Proceedings of the 33rd ACM SIGPLAN Conference on Programming Language Design and Implementation, PLDI 2012, pp. 251–262. Association for Computing Machinery, New York (2012). https://doi.org/10.1145/2254064.2254095
30. Poll system call (2019). http://man7.org/linux/man-pages/man2/poll.2.html
31. Raychev, V., Vechev, M., Sridharan, M.: Effective race detection for event-driven programs. In: Proceedings of the 2013 ACM SIGPLAN International Conference on Object Oriented Programming Systems Languages & Applications, OOPSLA 2013, pp. 151–166. Association for Computing Machinery, New York (2013). https://doi.org/10.1145/2509136.2509538
32. Savage, S., Burrows, M., Nelson, G., Sobalvarro, P., Anderson, T.: Eraser: a dynamic data race detector for multithreaded programs. ACM Trans. Comput. Syst. **15**(4), 391–411 (1997). https://doi.org/10.1145/265924.265927
33. Select system call (2019). http://man7.org/linux/man-pages/man2/select.2.html
34. Sen, K.: Race directed random testing of concurrent programs. In: Proceedings of the 29th ACM SIGPLAN Conference on Programming Language Design and Implementation, PLDI 2008, pp. 11–21. Association for Computing Machinery, New York (2008). https://doi.org/10.1145/1375581.1375584
35. Twisted: an event-driven networking engine written in Python (2020). https://twistedmatrix.com/trac/

36. Verifit repository of test cases for concurrency testing (2020). http://www.fit.vutbr.cz/research/groups/verifit/benchmarks/
37. Vouillon, J.: Lwt: a cooperative thread library. In: Proceedings of the 2008 ACM SIGPLAN Workshop on ML, ML 2008, pp. 3–12. Association for Computing Machinery, New York (2008). https://doi.org/10.1145/1411304.1411307
38. Wang, J., et al.: A comprehensive study on real world concurrency bugs in node.js. In: Proceedings of the 32nd IEEE/ACM International Conference on Automated Software Engineering, ASE 2017, pp. 520–531. IEEE Press (2017)
39. Yu, Y., Rodeheffer, T., Chen, W.: RaceTrack: efficient detection of data race conditions via adaptive tracking. In: Proceedings of the Twentieth ACM Symposium on Operating Systems Principles, SOSP 2005, pp. 221–234. Association for Computing Machinery, New York (2005). https://doi.org/10.1145/1095810.1095832

Causal-Consistent Reversible Debugging: Improving CauDEr

Juan José González-Abril and Germán Vidal[✉]

MiST, VRAIN, Universitat Politècnica de València, Valencia, Spain
juagona6@posgrado.upv.es, gvidal@dsic.upv.es

Abstract. Causal-consistent reversible debugging allows one to explore concurrent computations back and forth in order to locate the source of an error. In this setting, backward steps can be chosen freely as long as they are *causal consistent*, i.e., as long as all the actions that depend on the action we want to undo have been already undone. Here, we consider a framework for causal-consistent reversible debugging in the functional and concurrent language Erlang. This framework considered programs translated to an intermediate representation, called Core Erlang. Although using such an intermediate representation simplified both the formal definitions and their implementation in a debugging tool, the choice of Core Erlang also complicated the use of the debugger. In this paper, we extend the framework in order to deal with *source* Erlang programs, also including some features that were not considered before. Moreover, we integrate the two existing approaches (user-driven debugging and replay debugging) into a single, more general framework, and develop a new version of the debugging tool CauDEr including all the mentioned extensions as well as a renovated user interface.

1 Introduction

Reversible debugging is a well established technique [4,18] which advocates that, in order to find the location of an error, it is often more natural to explore a computation *backwards* from the observable misbehavior. Therefore, reversible debuggers allow one to explore a computation back and forth. There are already a number of software debuggers that follow this idea (e.g., Undo [17]). Typically, one can undo the steps of a computation in exactly the inverse order of the original forward computation. However, in the context of a concurrent language like Erlang, reversible debugging becomes much more complex. On the one hand, in these languages, there is no clear (total) order for the actions of the concurrent processes, since the semantics is often nondeterministic. On the other hand, one is typically interested in a particular process, e.g., the one that exhibited a

---

This work has been partially supported by EU (FEDER) and Spanish MCI/AEI under grants TIN2016-76843-C4-1-R and PID2019-104735RB-C41, by the *Generalitat Valenciana* under grant Prometeo/2019/098 (DeepTrust), and by French ANR project DCore ANR-18-CE25-0007.

© Springer Nature Switzerland AG 2021
J. F. Morales and D. Orchard (Eds.): PADL 2021, LNCS 12548, pp. 145–160, 2021.
https://doi.org/10.1007/978-3-030-67438-0_9

misbehavior. Thus, undoing the steps of *all* processes in the very same order of the forward computation is very inconvenient, since we had to go through many actions that are completely unrelated to the process of interest.

Recently, *causal-consistent* reversible debugging [2] has been introduced in order to overcome these problems. In this setting, concurrent actions can be undone freely as long as they are causal-consistent, i.e., no action is undone until all the actions that depend on this one have been already undone. For instance, one cannot undo the spawning of a process until all the actions of this process have been undone.

A reversible semantics for (Core) Erlang was first introduced in [13] and, then, extended and improved in [9]. A causal-consistent reversible debugger, CauDEr, that follows these ideas was then presented in [8].[1] In the original approach, both the forward and the backward computations were driven by the user (i.e., the user selects the process of interest as well as the message to be received when there are several possibilities), so we refer to this approach as *user-driven* debugging. However, when a computation fails, it is often very difficult, even impossible, to replicate the same computation in the debugger. This is a well-known problem in the debugging of concurrent programs. Therefore, [11] introduces a novel approach, called *replay* debugging, that is based on a light program instrumentation so that the execution of the instrumented program produces an associated *log*. This log can then be used for the debugger to replay the same computation or a *causally equivalent* one (i.e., one that at least respects the same order between dependent actions).

Unfortunately, all these works consider the intermediate language Core Erlang [1]. Dealing with (a subset of) Core Erlang made the theoretical developments easier (without loss of generality, since programs are automatically transformed from source Erlang to Core Erlang during the compilation process). The reversible debugger CauDEr considers Core Erlang too, which greatly simplified the implementation task. Unfortunately, as a result, the debugger is rather difficult to use since the programmer is often not familiar with the Core Erlang representation of her program. Compare, for instance, the following Erlang code defining the factorial function:

```
fact(0)            -> 1;
fact(N) when N>0 -> N * fact(N-1).
```

and the corresponding representation in Core Erlang:

```
'fact'/1 =
  fun (_0) ->
    case _0 of
      <0> when 'true' -> 1
```

---

[1] To the best of our knowledge, CauDEr is the first *causal-consistent* reversible debugger for a realistic programming language. Previous approaches did not consider concurrency, only allowed a *deterministic* replay—e.g., the case of rr [15] and ocamldebug [12]—or considered a very simple language, as in [2]. The reader is referred to [11] for a detailed comparison of CauDEr with other, related approaches.

```
<N> when call 'erlang':'>'(N, 0) ->
    let <_1> = call 'erlang':'-'(N, 1)
    in let <_2> = apply 'fact'/1(_1)
    in call 'erlang':'*'(N, _2)
<_3> when 'true' ->
    primop 'match_fail'({'function_clause',_3})
  end
end
```

On the other hand, while Erlang remains relatively stable, the Core Erlang specification changes (often undocumented) with some releases of the Erlang/OTP compiler, which makes maintaining the debugger quite a difficult task.

In this paper, we extend the causal-consistent approach to reversible debugging of Erlang in order to deal with (a significant subset of) the source language. The main contributions are the following:

- We redefine both the standard and the reversible semantics in order to deal with source Erlang expressions.
- Moreover, we integrate the two previous approaches, the *user-driven* reversible debugger of [9] and the *replay* debugger of [11], intro a single, more general framework.
- Finally, we have implemented a new version of the CauDEr reversible debugger [8] which implements the above contributions, also redesigning the user interface.

2 The Source Language

In this section, we informally introduce the syntax and semantics of the considered language, a significant subset of Erlang. A complete, more formal definition can be found in [3]. We also discuss the main differences with previous work that considered Core Erlang instead.

Erlang is a typical higher-order, eager functional language extended with some additional features for message-passing concurrency. Let us first consider the sequential component of the language, which includes the following elements:

- *Variables*, denoted with identifiers that start with an uppercase letter.
- *Atoms*, denoted with identifiers that start with a lowercase letter. Atoms are used, e.g., to denote constants and function names.
- *Data constructors*. Erlang only considers lists (using Prolog notation, i.e., $[e_1|e_2]$ denotes a list with first element e_1 and tail e_2) and tuples, denoted by an expression of the form $\{e_1, \ldots, e_n\}$, where $e_1, \ldots, e_n$ are expressions, $n \geq 0$. However, Erlang does not allow user-defined constructors as in, e.g., Haskell.
- *Values*, which are built from literals (e.g., numbers), atoms and data constructors.
- *Patterns*, which are similar to values but might also include variables.

- *Expressions.* Besides variables, values and patterns, we consider the following types of expressions:

  - *Sequences* of the form $e_1, \ldots, e_n$ where e_i is a single expression (i.e., it cannot be a sequence), $i = 1, \ldots, n$. Evaluation proceeds from left to right: first, we evaluate e_1 to some value v_1 thus producing $v_1, e_2, \ldots, e_n$. If $n > 1$, the sequence is then reduced to $e_2, \ldots, e_n$, and so forth. Therefore, sequences are eventually evaluated to a (single) value. The use of sequences of expressions in the right-hand sides of functions is a distinctive feature of Erlang. In the following, we assume that all expressions are single expressions except otherwise stated.
  - *Pattern matching* equations of the form $p = e$, where p is a pattern and e is an expression. Here, we evaluate e to a value v and, then, try to find a substitution σ such that $p\sigma = v$. If so, the equation is reduced to v and σ is applied to the complete expression. E.g., the expression "$\{X, Y\} = \{ok, 40 + 2\}, X$" is reduced to "$\{ok, 42\}, ok$" and, then, to ok.
  - *Case* expressions like case e of $cl_1; \ldots; cl_n$ end, where each clause cl_i has the form "p_i [when g_i] $\rightarrow e_i$" with p_i a pattern, g_i a *guard* and e_i an expression (possibly a sequence), $i = 1, \ldots, n$. *Guards* are optional, and can only contain calls to built-in functions (typically, arithmetic and relational operators). A case expression then selects the first clause such that the pattern matching equation $p_i = e$ holds for some substitution σ and $g_i\sigma$ reduces to true. Then, the case expression reduces to $e_i\sigma$.
  - *If* expressions have the form if $g_1 \rightarrow e_1; \ldots; g_n \rightarrow e_n$ end, where g_i is a guard and e_i is an expression (possibly a sequence), $i = 1, \ldots, n$. It proceeds in the obvious way by returning the first expression e_i such that the corresponding guard g_i holds.
  - *Anonymous functions* (often called *funs* in the language Erlang) have the form "fun $(p_1, \ldots, p_n)$ [when g] $\rightarrow e$ end," where $p_1, \ldots, p_n$ are patterns, g is a guard (optional), and e is an expression (possibly a sequence).
  - *Function calls* have the usual form, $f(e_1, \ldots, e_n)$, where f is either an atom (denoting a function name) or a fun, and $e_1, \ldots, e_n$ are expressions.

Concurrency in Erlang mainly follows the *actor model*, where processes (actors) interact through message sending and receiving. Here, we use the term *system* to refer to the complete runtime application. In this scheme, each process has an associated *pid* (for process *id*entifier) that is unique in the system. Moreover, processes are supposed to have a local mailbox (a queue) where messages are stored when they are received, and until they are *consumed*. In order to model concurrency, the following elements are introduced:

- The built-in function spawn is used to create a new process. Here, for simplicity, we assume that the arguments are a function name and a list of arguments. E.g., the expression spawn(foo, $[e_1, e_2]$) evaluates e_1, e_2 to some values v_1, v_2, spawns a new process with a fresh pid p that evaluates $foo(v_1, v_2)$ as a side-effect, and returns the pid p.

```
main() ->
  spawn(customer1, [self()]),        customer1(S) ->
  spawn(customer2, [self()]),          S ! {add,3},
  server(0).                           S ! {del,10,self()},
                                       receive
server(N) ->                             N -> io:format("Stock: ~p~n",[N])
  receive                              end,
    {add,M}                            S ! stop.
        -> server(N+M);
    {del,M,C} when N>=M              customer2(S) ->
        -> K = N-M, C ! K, server(K);  S ! {add,5},
    stop                               S ! {add,1},
        -> ok                          S ! {add,4}.
  end.
```

Fig. 1. A simple Erlang program.

- Message sending is denoted with an expression of the form $e_1 \ ! \ e_2$. Here, expressions e_1, e_2 are first evaluated to some values v_1, v_2 and v_2 is returned. Moreover, as a side effect, v_2 (the *message*) is eventually stored in the mailbox of the process with pid v_1 (if any).
- Messages are consumed with a statement of the form receive $cl_1; \ldots; cl_n$ end. The evaluation of a receive statement is similar to a case expression of the form case v of $cl_1; \ldots; cl_n$ end, where v is the first message in the process' mailbox that matches some clause. When no message in the mailbox matches any clause (or the mailbox is empty), computation *suspends* until a matching message arrives. Then, as a side effect, the selected message is removed from the process' mailbox.
- Finally, the (0-ary) *built-in* function self evaluates to the pid of the current process.

An Erlang program is given by a set of function definitions, where each function definition has the form

$$f(p_{11}, \ldots, p_{1n}) \ [\text{when } g_1] \ \rightarrow e_1;$$
$$f(p_{21}, \ldots, p_{2n}) \ [\text{when } g_2] \ \rightarrow e_2;$$
$$\ldots$$
$$f(p_{m1}, \ldots, p_{mn}) \ [\text{when } g_m] \ \rightarrow e_m.$$

Where p_{ij} is a pattern, g_i is a guard (optional), and e_i is an expression (possibly a sequence), $i = 1, \ldots, m$. Let us illustrate the main ingredients of the language with a simple example:

Example 1. Consider the program shown in Fig. 1. Here, we consider that the execution starts with the call main(). Function main then spawns two new processes that will evaluate customer1(S) and customer2(S), respectively, where S is the pid of the current process (the *server*). Finally, it calls server(0), where function server implements a simple server to update the current stock (initialized to 0). It accepts three types of requests:

- $\{\mathtt{add}, \mathtt{M}\}$: in this case, it simply calls the server with the updated argument $\mathtt{N} + \mathtt{M}$.[2]
- $\{\mathtt{del}, \mathtt{M}, \mathtt{C}\}$: assuming that $\mathtt{N} >= \mathtt{M}$ holds, the server computes the new stock $(\mathtt{N} - \mathtt{M})$, sends it back to the customer and, then, calls the server with the updated value.
- Finally, $\mathtt{stop}$ simply terminates the execution of the server.

Each customer performs a number of requests to the server, also waiting for a reply when the message is $\{\mathtt{del}, 10, \mathtt{self}()\}$ since the server replies with the updated stock in this case. Here, $\mathtt{format}$ is a *built-in* function with the usual meaning, that belongs to module $\mathtt{io}$.[3]

Note that we cannot make any assumption regarding the order in which the messages from these two customers reach the server. In particular, if message $\{\mathtt{del}, 10, \mathtt{self}()\}$ arrives when the stock is smaller than 10, it will stay in the process' mailbox until all the messages from $\mathtt{customer2}$ are received (i.e., $\{\mathtt{add}, 5\}$, $\{\mathtt{add}, 1\}$, and $\{\mathtt{add}, 4\}$).

Let us now consider the semantics of the language. In some previous formalization [9], a system included both a *global mailbox*, common to all processes, and a *local mailbox* associated to each process. Here, when a message is sent, it is first stored in the global mailbox (which is called the *ether* in [16]). Then, eventually, the message is delivered to the target process and stored in its local mailbox, so that it can be consumed with a receive statement. In this paper, similarly to [11], we abstract away the local mailboxes and just consider a single global mailbox. There is no loss of generality in this decision, since one can just define an appropriate structure of queues in the global mailbox so that it includes all local mailboxes of the system. Nevertheless, for simplicity, we will assume in the following that our global mailbox is just a set of messages of the form $\{p, p', v\}$, where p is the pid of the sender, p' is the pid of the target, and v is the message. We note that this abstraction has no impact for *replay* debugging since one follows the steps of an actual execution anyway. For user-driven debugging it might involve exploring some computations that are not feasible though.

In the following, a *process* is denoted by a configuration of the form $\langle p, e, \theta, S \rangle$, where p is the process' pid, e is an expression (to be evaluated), θ is a substitution (the current environment), and S is a stack (initially empty, see below). A *system* is then denoted by $\Gamma; \Pi$, where Γ is a global mailbox and Π is a pool of processes, denoted as $\langle p_1, \theta_1, e_1, S_1 \rangle \mid \cdots \mid \langle p_n, \theta_n, e_n, S_n \rangle$; here "$\mid$" represents an associative and commutative operator. We often denote a system as $\Gamma; \langle p, \theta, e, S \rangle \mid \Pi$ to point out that $\langle p, \theta, e, S \rangle$ is an arbitrary process of the pool (thanks to the fact that "$\mid$" is associative and commutative).

An *initial system* has the form $\{\ \}; \langle p, id, e, [\ ] \rangle$, where $\{\ \}$ is an empty global mailbox, p is a pid, id is the identity substitution, e is an expression (typically a function application that starts the execution), and $[\ ]$ is an empty stack.

---

[2] Note that the *state* of the process is represented by the argument of the call to function $\mathtt{server}$.

[3] In Erlang, function calls are often prefixed by the module where the function is defined.

Our (reduction) semantics is defined at two levels: first, we have a (labelled) transition relation on expressions. Here, we define a typical higher-order, eager small-step semantics for sequential expressions. In contrast to previous approaches (e.g., [9,11]), we introduce the use of stacks in order to avoid producing illegal expressions in some cases. Consider, for instance, the following function definition:

$$\texttt{foo}(\texttt{X}) \rightarrow \texttt{Y} = 1, \texttt{X} + \texttt{Y}.$$

and the expression "case foo(41) of R → R end." Here, by unfolding the call to function foo we might get "case Y = 1, 42 + Y of R → R end," which is not legal since sequences of expressions are not allowed in the argument of a case expression. A similar situation might occur when evaluating a case or an if expression, since they can also return a sequence of expressions. We avoid all these illegal intermediate expressions by moving the current environment to a stack and starting a subcomputation. When the subcomputation ends, we recover the environment from the stack and continue with the original computation. E.g., the following rules define the evaluation of a function call:

$$(Call1)\ \frac{\mathsf{match\_fun}((v_1,\ldots,v_n),\mathsf{def}(f/n,\mathsf{P})) = (\sigma,e)}{\theta, C[f(v_1,\ldots,v_n)], S \xrightarrow{\tau} \sigma, e, (\theta, C[\_]):S}$$

$$(Return)\ \frac{}{\sigma, v, (\theta, C[\_]):S \xrightarrow{\tau} \theta, C[v], S}$$

Here, $C[e]$ denotes an arbitrary (possibly empty) evaluation *context* where e is the next expression to be reduced according to an eager semantics. The auxiliary functions def and match_fun are used to look for the definition of a function f/n in a program P and for computing the corresponding matching substitution, respectively; here, e is the body of the selected clause and σ is the matching substitution. If a value is eventually obtained, rule *Return* applies and recovers the old environment $(\theta, C[\_])$ from the stack.

Regarding the semantics of expressions with side effects (spawn, sending and receiving messages, and self), we label the step with enough information for the next level—the system semantics—to perform the side effect. For instance, For spawning a process, we have these two rules:

$$(SpawnExp)\ \frac{}{\theta, C[\mathsf{spawn}(f, [\overline{v_n}])], S \xrightarrow{\mathsf{spawn}(\kappa,f,[v_1,\ldots,v_n])} \theta, C[\kappa], S}$$

$$(Spawn)\ \frac{\theta, e, S \xrightarrow{\mathsf{spawn}(\kappa,f,[v_1,\ldots,v_n])} \theta', e', S'\ \text{and}\ p'\ \text{is a fresh pid}}{\varGamma; \langle p, \theta, e, S\rangle \mid \varPi \hookrightarrow \varGamma; \langle p, \theta', e'\{\kappa \mapsto p'\}, S'\rangle \mid \langle p', id, f(v_1,\ldots,v_n), [\ ]\rangle \mid \varPi}$$

Here, the first rule just reduces a call to spawn to a fresh variable κ, a sort of "future", since the pid of the new process is not visible at the expression level. The step is labelled with $\mathsf{spawn}(\kappa, f, [v_1, \ldots, v_n])$. Then, the system rule *Spawn* completes the step by adding a new process initialized to $\langle p', id, f(v_1, \ldots, v_n), [\ ]\rangle$; moreover, κ is bound to the (fresh) pid of the new process. We have similar rules for evaluating the sending and receiving of messages, for sequential expressions, etc. The complete transition rules of both the semantics of expressions ($\rightarrow$) and the semantics of systems ($\hookrightarrow$) can be found in [3].

The main advantage of this hierarchical definition of the semantics is that one can produce different *non-standard* versions of the semantics by only replacing the transition rules for systems. For instance, a *tracing semantics* can be simply obtained by instrumenting the standard semantics as follows:

- First, we tag messages with a fresh label, so that we can easily relate messages sent and received. Without the labels, messages with the same value could not be distinguished. In particular, messages in the global mailbox have now the form $\{p, p', \{v, \ell\}\}$ instead of $\{p, p', v\}$, where ℓ is a label that must be unique in the system.
- Then, each step $s_1 \hookrightarrow_{p,r} s_2$ is labeled with a pair p, r where p is the pid of the selected process and r is either seq for sequential steps, send(ℓ) for sending a message labeled with ℓ, rec(ℓ) for receiving a message labeled with ℓ, spawn(p) for spawning a process with pid p, and self for evaluating a call of the form self().

The complete *tracing semantics* can also be found in [3].

As in [11], we can instantiate to our setting the well-known *happened-before* relation [5]. In the following, we refer to one-step reductions $s \hookrightarrow_{p,r} s'$ as *transitions*, and to longer reductions as *derivations*.

Definition 1 (happened-before, independence). *Given a derivation d and two transitions $t_1 = (s_1 \hookrightarrow_{p_1,r_1} s'_1)$ and $t_2 = (s_2 \hookrightarrow_{p_2,r_2} s'_2)$ in d, we say that t_1 happened before t_2, in symbols $t_1 \rightsquigarrow t_2$, if one of the following conditions holds:*

- *they consider the same process, i.e., $p_1 = p_2$, and t_1 comes before t_2;*
- *t_1 spawns a process p, i.e., $r_1 = $ spawn(p), and t_2 is performed by process p, i.e., $p_2 = p$;*
- *t_1 sends a message ℓ, i.e., $r_1 = $ send(ℓ), and t_2 receives the same message ℓ, i.e., $r_2 = $ rec(ℓ).*

Furthermore, if $t_1 \rightsquigarrow t_2$ and $t_2 \rightsquigarrow t_3$, then $t_1 \rightsquigarrow t_3$ (transitivity). Two transitions t_1 and t_2 are independent *if $t_1 \not\rightsquigarrow t_2$ and $t_2 \not\rightsquigarrow t_1$.*

An interesting property of our semantics is that consecutive independent transitions can be switched without changing the final state.

The happened-before relation gives rise to an equivalence relation equating all derivations that only differ in the switch of independent transitions. Formally,

Definition 2 (causally equivalent derivations). *Let d_1 and d_2 be derivations under the tracing semantics. We say that d_1 and d_2 are causally equivalent, in symbols $d_1 \approx d_2$, if d_1 can be obtained from d_2 by a finite number of switches of pairs of consecutive independent transitions.*

The tracing semantics can be used as a model to instrument a program so that it produces a log of the computation as a side-effect. This log can then be used to *replay* this computation (or a causally equivalent one) in the debugger. Formally, a *process log* ω is a (finite) sequence of events $(r_1, r_2, \ldots)$ where each r_i is either spawn(p), send(ℓ) or rec(ℓ), with p a pid and ℓ a message identifier. A *system log* $\mathcal{W}$ is defined as a partial mapping from pids to processes' logs (an empty log is denoted by $[\,]$). Here, the notation $\mathcal{W}[p \mapsto \omega]$ is used to denote that ω is the log of the process with pid p; as usual, we use this notation either as a condition on a system log $\mathcal{W}$ or as a modification of $\mathcal{W}$.

Besides defining a tracing semantics that produces a system log of a computation as a side effect, we can also define a reversible semantics by instrumenting the rules of the system semantics as shown in the next section.

3 A Causal-Consistent Reversible Semantics

In this section, we first present an instrumented semantics which is reversible, i.e., we define an appropriate *Landauer embedding* [6] for the standard semantics. Then, we introduce a backward semantics that proceeds in the opposite direction. Both the forward and backward semantics are *uncontrolled*, i.e., they have several sources of nondeterminism:

1. *Direction*: they can proceed both forward and backward.
2. *Choice of process*: in general, several processes may perform a reduction step, and an arbitrary one is chosen.
3. *Message delivery*: when there are several (matching) messages targeted to the same process, any of them can be received.
4. Finally, (fresh) pids and message labels are chosen in a random way.

We note that, when we proceed in *replay* mode, the last choices (3–4) are made deterministic. Nevertheless, the calculus is still highly nondeterministic. Therefore, we will finally introduce a *controlled* version of the semantics where reductions are driven by the user requests (e.g., "go ahead until the sending of a message labeled with ℓ", "go backwards up to the step immediately before process p was spawned", etc). The controlled semantics is formalized as a third layer (on top of the rules for expressions and systems).

3.1 A Reversible Semantics

In the following, a *system* is denoted by a triple $\mathcal{W}; \Gamma; \Pi$, where $\mathcal{W}$ is a (possibly empty) *system log*, Γ is a global mailbox, and Π is a pool of processes. Furthermore, a *process* is now represented by a configuration of the form $\langle p, h, \theta, e, S \rangle$, where p is the pid of the process, h is a process *history*, θ is an environment, e is an expression to be evaluated, and S is an stack. In this context, a history h records the intermediate states of a process using terms headed by constructors seq, send, rec, spawn, and self, and whose arguments are the information required to (deterministically) undo the step, following a typical Landauer embedding [6].

(Seq)
$$\dfrac{\theta, e, S \xrightarrow{\tau} \theta', e', S'}{\mathcal{W}; \Gamma; \langle p, h, \theta, e, S \rangle \mid \Pi \to_{p,\text{seq},\{\text{s}\}} \mathcal{W}; \Gamma; \langle p, \text{seq}(\theta, e, S) + h, \theta', e', S' \rangle \mid \Pi}$$

$(Send)$
$$\dfrac{\theta, e, S \xrightarrow{\text{send}(p',v)} \theta', e', S' \text{ and } \ell \text{ is a fresh identifier}}{\mathcal{W}[p \mapsto [\,]]; \Gamma; \langle p, h, \theta, e, S \rangle \mid \Pi \to_{p,\text{send}(\ell),\{\text{s},\ell\Uparrow\}} \begin{array}{l}\mathcal{W}; \Gamma \cup \{(p, p', \{v, \ell\})\}; \\ \langle p, \text{send}(\theta, e, S, p', \{v, \ell\}) + h, \theta', e', S' \rangle \mid \Pi\end{array}}$$

$$\dfrac{\theta, e, S \xrightarrow{\text{send}(p',v)} \theta', e', S'}{\mathcal{W}[p \mapsto \text{send}(\ell) + \omega]; \Gamma; \langle p, h, \theta, e, S \rangle \mid \Pi \to_{p,\text{send}(\ell),\{\text{s},\ell\Uparrow\}} \begin{array}{l}\mathcal{W}[p \mapsto \omega]; \Gamma \cup \{(p, p', \{v, \ell\})\}; \\ \langle p, \text{send}(\theta, e, S, p', \{v, \ell\}) + h, \theta', e', S' \rangle \mid \Pi\end{array}}$$

$(Receive)$
$$\dfrac{\theta, e, S \xrightarrow{\text{rec}(\kappa, \overline{cl_n})} \theta', e', S' \text{ and } \text{match\_rec}(\overline{cl_n}\theta, v) = (\theta_i, e_i)}{\begin{array}{l}\mathcal{W}[p \mapsto [\,]]; \Gamma \cup \{(p', p, \{v, \ell\})\}\langle p, h, \theta, e, S \rangle \mid \Pi \\ \to_{p,\text{rec}(\ell),\{\text{s},\ell\Downarrow\}} \mathcal{W}; \Gamma; \langle p, \text{rec}(\theta, e, S, p', \{v, \ell\}) + h, \theta'\theta_i, e'\{\kappa \mapsto e_i\}, S' \rangle \mid \Pi\end{array}}$$

$$\dfrac{\theta, e, S \xrightarrow{\text{rec}(\kappa, \overline{cl_n})} \theta', e', S' \text{ and } \text{matchrec}(\theta, \overline{cl_n}, v) = (\theta_i, e_i)}{\begin{array}{l}\mathcal{W}[p \mapsto \text{rec}(\ell) + \omega]; \Gamma \cup \{(p', p, \{v, \ell\})\}\langle p, h, \theta, e, S \rangle \mid \Pi \\ \to_{p,\text{rec}(\ell),\{\text{s},\ell\Downarrow\}} \mathcal{W}[p \mapsto \omega]; \Gamma; \langle p, \text{rec}(\theta, e, S, p', \{v, \ell\}) + h, \theta'\theta_i, e'\{\kappa \mapsto e_i\}, S' \rangle \mid \Pi\end{array}}$$

$(Spawn)$
$$\dfrac{\theta, e, S \xrightarrow{\text{spawn}(\kappa, mod, f, [\overline{v_n}])} \theta', e', S' \text{ and } p' \text{ is a fresh identifier}}{\begin{array}{l}\mathcal{W}[p \mapsto [\,]]; \Gamma; \langle p, h, \theta, e, S \rangle \mid \Pi \to_{p,\text{spawn}(p'),\{\text{s},\text{sp}_{p'}\}} \mathcal{W}; \Gamma; \langle p, \text{spawn}(\theta, e, S, p') + h, \theta', e'\{\kappa \mapsto p'\}, S' \rangle \\ \mid \langle p', [\,], id, mod: f(\overline{v_n}), [\,] \rangle \mid \Pi\end{array}}$$

$$\dfrac{\theta, e, S \xrightarrow{\text{spawn}(\kappa, mod, f, [\overline{v_n}])} \theta', e', S'}{\begin{array}{l}\mathcal{W}[p \mapsto \text{spawn}(p') + \omega]; \Gamma; \langle p, h, \theta, e, S \rangle \mid \Pi \\ \to_{p,\text{spawn}(p'),\{\text{s},\text{sp}_{p'}\}} \mathcal{W}[p \mapsto \omega]; \Gamma; \langle p, \text{spawn}(\theta, e, S, p') + h, \theta', e'\{\kappa \mapsto p'\}, S' \rangle \\ \mid \langle p', [\,], id, mod: f(\overline{v_n}), [\,] \rangle \mid \Pi\end{array}}$$

$(Self)$
$$\dfrac{\theta, e, S \xrightarrow{\text{self}(\kappa)} \theta', e', S'}{\mathcal{W}; \Gamma; \langle p, h, \theta, e, S \rangle \mid \Pi \to_{p,\text{self},\{\text{s}\}} \mathcal{W}; \Gamma; \langle p, \text{self}(\theta, e, S) + h, \theta', e'\{\kappa \mapsto p\}, S' \rangle \mid \Pi}$$

Fig. 2. Uncontrolled forward semantics

$(\overline{Seq})$
$$\mathcal{W}; \Gamma; \langle p, \text{seq}(\theta, e, S) + h, \theta', e', S' \rangle \mid \Pi \leftharpoonup_{p,\text{seq},\{\text{s}\}\cup\mathcal{V}} \mathcal{W}; \Gamma; \langle p, h, \theta, e, S \rangle \mid \Pi$$
$$\text{where } \mathcal{V} = \mathcal{D}om(\theta')\backslash\mathcal{D}om(\theta)$$

$(\overline{Send})$
$$\mathcal{W}[p \mapsto \omega]; \Gamma \cup \{(p, p', \{v, \ell\})\}; \langle p, \text{send}(\theta, e, S, p', \{v, \ell\}) + h, \theta', e', S' \rangle \mid \Pi$$
$$\leftharpoonup_{p,\text{send}(\ell),\{\text{s},\ell\Uparrow\}} \mathcal{W}[p \mapsto \text{send}(\ell) + \omega]; \Gamma; \langle p, h, \theta, e, S \rangle \mid \Pi$$

$(\overline{Receive})$
$$\mathcal{W}[p \mapsto \omega]; \Gamma; \langle p, \omega, \text{rec}(\theta, e, S, p', \{v, \ell\}) + h, \theta', e', S' \rangle \mid \Pi$$
$$\leftharpoonup_{p,\text{rec}(\ell),\{\text{s},\ell\Downarrow\}\cup\mathcal{V}} \mathcal{W}[p \mapsto \text{rec}(\ell) + \omega]; \Gamma \cup \{(p', p, \{v, \ell\})\}; \langle p, h, \theta, e, S \rangle \mid \Pi$$
$$\text{where } \mathcal{V} = \mathcal{D}om(\theta')\backslash\mathcal{D}om(\theta)$$

$(\overline{Spawn})$
$$\mathcal{W}[p \mapsto \omega]; \Gamma; \langle p, \text{spawn}(\theta, e, S, p') + h, \theta', e', S' \rangle \mid \langle p', \omega', [\,], id, e'' \rangle \mid \Pi$$
$$\leftharpoonup_{p,\text{spawn}(p'),\{\text{s},\text{sp}_{p'}\}} \mathcal{W}[p \mapsto \text{spawn}(p') + \omega]; \Gamma; \langle p, \text{spawn}(p') +, h, \theta, e, S \rangle \mid \Pi$$

$(\overline{Self})$
$$\mathcal{W}; \Gamma; \langle p, \text{self}(\theta, e, S) + h, \theta', e', S' \rangle \mid \Pi \leftharpoonup_{p,\text{self},\{\text{s}\}} \mathcal{W}; \Gamma; \langle p, h, \theta, e, S \rangle \mid \Pi$$

Fig. 3. Uncontrolled backward semantics

The rules of the (forward) reversible semantics are shown in Fig. 2. The subscripts of the arrows can be ignored for now. They will become relevant for the controlled semantics. The premises of the rules consider the reduction of an expression, $\theta, e, S \xrightarrow{label} \theta', e', S'$, where the *label* includes enough information to perform the corresponding side-effects (if any). Let us briefly explain the transition rules:

- Rule *Seq* considers the reduction of a sequential expression, which is denoted by a transition labelled with τ at the expression level. In this case, no side-effect is required. Therefore, the rule only updates the process configuration with the new values, θ', e', S', and adds a new item $\mathsf{seq}(\theta, e, S)$ to the history, so that a backward step becomes trivially deterministic. Although this is orthogonal to the topic of this paper, the stored information can be optimized, e.g., along the lines of [14].
- As for sending a message, we distinguish two cases. When the process log is empty, we tag the message with a fresh identifier; when the log is not empty, the tag is obtained from an element $\mathsf{send}(\ell)$ in the log (which is then removed). In both cases, besides adding the new message to the global mailbox, a new item of the form $\mathsf{send}(\theta, e, S, p', \{v, \ell\})$ is added to the history so that the step becomes reversible.
- Receiving a message proceeds much in a similar way. We also have two rules depending on whether the process log is empty or not.[4] If there is no log, an arbitrary message is received. Otherwise, if we have an item $\mathsf{rec}(\ell)$ in the log, only a message labeled with ℓ can be received. The history is anyway updated with a term of the form $\mathsf{rec}(\theta, e, S, p', \{v, \ell\})$. Observe that κ (the *future*) is now bound to the body of the selected clause.
- As for spawning a process, we also distinguish two cases, depending on the process log. If it is empty, then a fresh pid is chosen for the new process. Otherwise, the pid in the process log is used. In both cases, a new term $\mathsf{spawn}(\theta, e, S, p')$ is added to the history of the process. Moreover, κ is bound to the pid of the spawned process.
- Finally, rule *Self* simply binds κ with the pid of the selected process, and adds a new term $\mathsf{self}(\theta, e, S)$ to the process history.

Trivially, when no system log is considered, the reversible semantics is a conservative extension of the standard semantics since we only added some additional information (the history) but imposed no additional restriction to perform a reduction step. Moreover, when a system log is provided, one can easily prove that the reversible semantics is sound and complete w.r.t. the traced computation.

As for the backward (reversible) semantics, it can be easily obtained by reversing the rules of Fig. 2 and, then, removing all unnecessary conditions in the premises. The resulting rules are shown in Fig. 3, where the auxiliary function $\mathcal{D}om$ returns the variables in the domain of a substitution. Note that, in these rules, we *always* take an element from the history and move the corresponding information (if any) to the system log. Therefore, once we go backward, forward steps will be driven by the corresponding log, no matter if we initially considered the log of a computation or not.

The reversible semantics is denoted by the relation $\rightleftharpoons$ which is defined as the union of the forward and backward transition relations $(\rightharpoonup \cup \leftharpoondown)$.

---

[4] Here, we use the auxiliary function $\mathsf{match\_rec}$ to select the matching clause, so that it returns the matching substitution as well as the body of the selected clause.

The main differences with previous versions of the reversible semantics are summarized as follows:

- At the level of expressions, we consider the source language, Erlang, rather than the intermediate representation, Core Erlang. Moreover, we also consider higher-order expressions, which were skipped so far.
- Regarding the reversible semantics, we keep the same structure of previous versions but integrate both definitions, the user-driven reversible semantics of [9] and the replay reversible semantics of [11]. This simplifies the development of a debugging tool that integrates both definitions into a single framework.

Since our changes mainly affect the control aspects of the reversible semantics (and the concurrent actions are the same for both Erlang and Core Erlang), the properties in [9,11] carry over easily to our new approach. Basically, the following properties should also hold in our framework:

- The so-called *loop lemma*: For every pair of systems, s_1 and s_2, we have $s_1 \rightharpoonup_{p,r} s_2$ iff $s_2 \leftharpoondown_{p,r} s_1$.
- An essential property of reversible systems, *causal consistency*, which is stated as follows: Given two coinitial (i.e., starting with the same configuration) derivations d_1 and d_2, then $d_1 \approx d_2$ iff d_1 and d_2 are cofinal (i.e., they end with the same configuration).
- Finally, one could also prove that bugs are preserved under the reversible semantics: a (faulty) behavior occurs in a traced derivation iff the replay derivation also exhibits the same *faulty* behavior, hence replay is correct and complete.

3.2 Controlled Semantics

In this section, we introduce a controlled version of the reversible semantics. The key idea is that this semantics is driven by the user requests, e.g., "go forward until the spawning of process p", "go backwards until the step immediately before message ℓ was sent", etc.

Here, we consider that, given a system s, we want to start a forward (resp. backward) derivation until a particular action ψ is performed (resp. undone) on a given process p. We denote such a request with the following notation: $\llparenthesis s \rrparenthesis_\Phi$, where s is a system and Φ is a sequence of requests that can be seen as a stack where the first element is the most recent request. We formalize the requests as a static stream that is provided to the calculus but, in practice, the requests are provided by the user in an interactive way. In this paper, we consider the following requests:

- $\{p, \mathsf{s}\}$: one step backward/forward of process p;[5]
- $\{p, \ell_\Uparrow\}$: a backward/forward derivation of process p up to the sending of the message tagged with ℓ;

---

[5] The extension to n steps is straightforward. We omit it for simplicity.

- $\{p, \ell_{\Downarrow}\}$: a backward/forward derivation of process p up to the reception of the message tagged with ℓ;
- $\{p, \mathsf{sp}_{p'}\}$: a backward/forward derivation of process p up to the spawning of the process with pid p'.
- $\{p, \mathsf{sp}\}$: a backward derivation of process p up to the point immediately after its creation;
- $\{p, X\}$: a backward derivation of process p up to the introduction of variable X.

When the request can be either a forward or a backward request, we use an arrow to indicate the direction. E.g., $\{p, \overrightarrow{\mathsf{s}}\}$ requires one step forward, while $\{p, \overleftarrow{\mathsf{s}}\}$ requires one step backward. In particular, $\{p, \overleftarrow{\mathsf{sp}}\}$ and $\{p, \overleftarrow{X}\}$ have just one version since they always require a backward computation.

A debugging session can start either with a log (computed using the tracing semantics or, equivalently, an instrumented source program) or with an empty log. If the log is not empty, we speak of *replay* debugging; otherwise, we say that it is a *user-driven* debugging session. Of course, one can start in replay mode and, once all the actions of the log are consumed, switch to the user-driven mode.

The requests above are *satisfied* when a corresponding uncontrolled transition is performed. This is where the third element labeling the relations of the reversible semantics in Figs. 2 and 3 comes into play. This third element is a set with the requests that are satisfied in the corresponding step.

Let us explain the rules of the controlled semantics in Fig. 4. Here, we assume that the computation always starts with a single request. We then have the following possibilities:

- If the desired process p can perform a step satisfying the request ψ on top of the stack, we do it and remove the request from the stack of requests (first rule of both forward and backward rules).
- If the desired process p can perform a step, but the step does not satisfy the request ψ, we update the system but keep the request in the stack (second rule of both forward and backward rules).
- If a step on the desired process p is not possible, then we track the dependencies and add a new request on top of the stack.[6] For the forward rules, either we cannot proceed because we aim at receiving a message which is not in Γ or because the considered process does not exist. In the first case, the label ℓ of the message can be found in the process' log. Then, the auxiliary function *sender* is used to locate the process p' that should send message ℓ, so that an additional request for process p' to send message ℓ is added. In the second case, if process p is not in Π, then we add another request for the parent of p to spawn it. For this purpose, we use the auxiliary function *parent*.
  As for the backward rules, we consider three cases: one rule to add a request to undo the receiving of a message whose sending we want to undo, another rule to undo the actions of a given process whose spawning we want to undo,

---

[6] Note that, if the process' log is empty, only the first two rules are applicable; in other words, the user must provide feasible requests to drive the forward computation.

FORWARD RULES:

$$\frac{\mathcal{W}; \Gamma; \Pi \rightarrow_{p,r,\Psi'} \mathcal{W}'; \Gamma'; \Pi' \ \land \ \psi \in \Psi'}{\llbracket \mathcal{W}; \Gamma; \Pi \rrbracket_{\{p,\vec{\psi}\}+\Psi} \rightsquigarrow \llbracket \mathcal{W}'; \Gamma'; \Pi' \rrbracket_{\Psi}} \qquad \frac{\mathcal{W}; \Gamma; \Pi \rightarrow_{p,r,\Psi'} \mathcal{W}'; \Gamma'; \Pi' \ \land \ \psi \notin \Psi'}{\llbracket \mathcal{W}; \Gamma; \Pi \rrbracket_{\{p,\vec{\psi}\}+\Psi} \rightsquigarrow \llbracket \mathcal{W}'; \Gamma'; \Pi' \rrbracket_{\{p,\vec{\psi}\}+\Psi}}$$

$$\frac{\mathcal{W}[p \mapsto \mathsf{rec}(\ell)+\omega]; \Gamma; \Pi \not\rightarrow_{p,r,\Psi'} \ \land \ sender(\mathcal{W}, \ell) = p'}{\llbracket \mathcal{W}[p \mapsto \mathsf{rec}(\ell)+\omega]; \Gamma; \Pi \rrbracket_{\{p,\vec{\psi}\}+\Psi} \rightsquigarrow \llbracket \mathcal{W}[p \mapsto \mathsf{rec}(\ell)+\omega]; \Gamma; \Pi \rrbracket_{(\{p',\vec{\ell_\Uparrow}\},\{p,\vec{\psi}\})+\Psi}}$$

$$\frac{\not\exists p \text{ in } \Pi \ \land \ parent(\mathcal{W}, p) = p'}{\llbracket \mathcal{W}, \Gamma; \Pi \rrbracket_{\{p,\vec{\psi}\}+\Psi} \rightsquigarrow \llbracket \mathcal{W}, \Gamma; \Pi \rrbracket_{(\{p',\vec{\mathsf{sp}_p}\},\{p,\vec{\psi}\})+\Psi}}$$

BACKWARD RULES:

$$\frac{\mathcal{W}; \Gamma; \Pi \leftharpoonup_{p,r,\Psi'} \mathcal{W}'; \Gamma'; \Pi' \ \land \ \psi \in \Psi'}{\llbracket \mathcal{W}; \Gamma; \Pi \rrbracket_{\{p,\overleftarrow{\psi}\}+\Psi} \rightsquigarrow \llbracket \mathcal{W}'; \Gamma'; \Pi' \rrbracket_{\Psi}} \qquad \frac{\mathcal{W}; \Gamma; \Pi \leftharpoonup_{p,r,\Psi'} \mathcal{W}'; \Gamma'; \Pi' \ \land \ \psi \notin \Psi'}{\llbracket \mathcal{W}; \Gamma; \Pi \rrbracket_{\{p,\overleftarrow{\psi}\}+\Psi} \rightsquigarrow \llbracket \mathcal{W}'; \Gamma'; \Pi' \rrbracket_{\{p,\overleftarrow{\psi}\}+\Psi}}$$

$$\frac{\mathcal{W}; \Gamma; \langle p, \mathsf{send}(\theta, e, S, p', \{v, \ell\})+h, \theta', e'\rangle \mid \Pi \not\leftharpoonup_{p,r,\Psi'}}{\llbracket \mathcal{W}; \Gamma; \langle p, \mathsf{send}(\theta, e, S, p', \{v, \ell\})+h, \theta', e', S'\rangle \mid \Pi \rrbracket_{\{p,\overleftarrow{\psi}\}+\Psi}} \\ \rightsquigarrow \llbracket \mathcal{W}; \Gamma; \langle p, \mathsf{send}(\theta, e, S, p', \{v, \ell\})+h, \theta', e', S'\rangle \mid \Pi \rrbracket_{(\{p',\overleftarrow{\ell_\Downarrow}\},\{p,\overleftarrow{\psi}\})+\Psi}$$

$$\frac{\mathcal{W}; \Gamma; \langle p, \mathsf{spawn}(\theta, e, S, p')+h, \theta', e', S'\rangle \mid \Pi \not\leftharpoonup_{p,r,\Psi'}}{\llbracket \mathcal{W}; \Gamma; \langle p, \mathsf{spawn}(\theta, e, S, p')+h, \theta', e', S'\rangle \mid \Pi \rrbracket_{\{p,\overleftarrow{\psi}\}+\Psi}} \\ \rightsquigarrow \llbracket \mathcal{W}; \Gamma; \langle p, \mathsf{spawn}(\theta, e, S, p')+h, \theta', e', S'\rangle \mid \Pi \rrbracket_{(\{p',\overleftarrow{\mathsf{sp}}\},\{p,\overleftarrow{\psi}\})+\Psi}$$

$$\llbracket \mathcal{W}; \Gamma; \langle p, [\,], \theta', e', S'\rangle \mid \Pi \rrbracket_{\{p,\overleftarrow{\mathsf{sp}}\}+\Psi} \rightsquigarrow \llbracket \mathcal{W}; \Gamma; \langle p, [\,], \theta', e', S'\rangle \mid \Pi \rrbracket_{\Psi}$$

Fig. 4. Controlled forward/backward semantics

and a final rule to check that a process has reached its initial state (with an empty history), and the request $\{p, \overleftarrow{\mathsf{sp}}\}$ can be removed. In this last case, the process p will actually be removed from the system when a request of the form $\{p', \overleftarrow{\mathsf{sp}_p}\}$ is on top of the stack.

The relation "$\rightsquigarrow$" can be seen as a controlled version of the uncontrolled reversible semantics ($\rightleftharpoons$) in the sense that each derivation of the controlled semantics corresponds to a derivation of the uncontrolled one, while the opposite is not generally true.

The controlled semantics is the basis of the implemented reversible debugger CauDEr. Figure 5 shows a snapshot of both the old and the new, improved user interface. In contrast to the previous version of the debugger [10], we show the source code of the program and *highlight* the line that is being evaluated. In contrast, the old version showed the current Core Erlang expression to be reduced, which was far less intuitive. Moreover, all the available information (bindings, stack, log, history, etc) is shown in different boxes, while the previous version showed all information together in a single text box. Furthermore, the user can now decide whether to add a log or not, while the previous version required the use of different implementations of the debugger.

The new version of the reversible debugger is publicly available from https://github.com/mistupv/cauder-v2.

Fig. 5. CauDEr Old User Interface vs New Interface

4   Conclusions and Future Work

In this paper, we have adapted and extended the framework for causal-consistent reversible debugging from Core Erlang to Erlang. In doing so, we have extended the standard semantics to also cope with program constructs that were not covered in previous work [8,9,11], e.g., *if* statements, higher-order functions, sequences, etc. Furthermore, we have integrated user-driven debugging and replay debugging into a single, more general framework. Finally, the user interface of CauDEr has been redesigned in order to make it easier to use (and closer to that of the standard debugger of Erlang). We refer the reader to [9,11] for a detailed comparison between causal-consistent reversible debugging in Erlang and other, related work.

As for future work, we aim at modelling in the semantics different levels of granularity for debugging. For instance, the user may choose to evaluate a function call in one step or to explore the reduction of the function's body step by step. Moreover, we are also exploring the possibility of allowing the user to *speculatively* receive a message which is different from the one in the process' log during replay debugging. Finally, other interesting ideas for future work include the implementation of appropriate extensions to deal with distributed programs and error handling (following, e.g., the approach of [7]).

Acknowledgements. The authors would like to thank Ivan Lanese for his useful remarks that helped us to improve the new version of the CauDEr debugger.

References

1. Carlsson, R.: An introduction to core erlang. In: Proceedings of the PLI 2001 Erlang Workshop (2001). http://www.erlang.se/workshop/carlsson.ps
2. Giachino, E., Lanese, I., Mezzina, C.A.: Causal-consistent reversible debugging. In: Gnesi, S., Rensink, A. (eds.) FASE 2014. LNCS, vol. 8411, pp. 370–384. Springer, Heidelberg (2014). https://doi.org/10.1007/978-3-642-54804-8_26

3. González-Abril, J.J., Vidal, G.: Causal-consistent reversible debugging: improving CauDEr. Technical report, DSIC, Universitat Politècnica de València (2020). http://personales.upv.es/~gvidal/german/padl21/tr.pdf

4. Grishman, R.: The debugging system AIDS. In: American Federation of Information Processing Societies: AFIPS Conference Proceedings: 1970 Spring Joint Computer Conference. AFIPS Conference Proceedings, vol. 36, pp. 59–64. AFIPS Press (1970). https://doi.org/10.1145/1476936.1476952

5. Lamport, L.: Time, clocks, and the ordering of events in a distributed system. Commun. ACM **21**(7), 558–565 (1978)

6. Landauer, R.: Irreversibility and heat generation in the computing process. IBM J. Res. Dev. **5**, 183–191 (1961)

7. Lanese, I., Medic, D.: A general approach to derive uncontrolled reversible semantics. In: Konnov, I., Kovács, L. (eds.) 31st International Conference on Concurrency Theory, CONCUR 2020, 1–4 September 2020, Vienna, Austria (Virtual Conference). LIPIcs, vol. 171, pp. 33:1–33:24. Schloss Dagstuhl - Leibniz-Zentrum für Informatik (2020). https://doi.org/10.4230/LIPIcs.CONCUR.2020.33

8. Lanese, I., Nishida, N., Palacios, A., Vidal, G.: CauDEr: a causal-consistent reversible debugger for Erlang. In: Gallagher, J.P., Sulzmann, M. (eds.) FLOPS 2018. LNCS, vol. 10818, pp. 247–263. Springer, Cham (2018). https://doi.org/10.1007/978-3-319-90686-7_16

9. Lanese, I., Nishida, N., Palacios, A., Vidal, G.: A theory of reversibility for Erlang. J. Log. Algebraic Methods Program. **100**, 71–97 (2018)

10. Lanese, I., Nishida, N., Palacios, A., Vidal, G.: CauDEr website (2019). https://github.com/mistupv/cauder

11. Lanese, I., Palacios, A., Vidal, G.: Causal-consistent replay debugging for message passing programs. In: Pérez, J.A., Yoshida, N. (eds.) FORTE 2019. LNCS, vol. 11535, pp. 167–184. Springer, Cham (2019). https://doi.org/10.1007/978-3-030-21759-4_10

12. Leroy, X., Doligez, D., Frisch, A., Garrigue, J., Rémy, D., Vouillon, J.: The OCaml system release 4.11. Documentation and user's manual. Technical report, INRIA (2020)

13. Nishida, N., Palacios, A., Vidal, G.: A reversible semantics for Erlang. In: Hermenegildo, M.V., Lopez-Garcia, P. (eds.) LOPSTR 2016. LNCS, vol. 10184, pp. 259–274. Springer, Cham (2017). https://doi.org/10.1007/978-3-319-63139-4_15

14. Nishida, N., Palacios, A., Vidal, G.: Reversible computation in term rewriting. J. Log. Algebraic Methods Program. **94**, 128–149 (2018). https://doi.org/10.1016/j.jlamp.2017.10.003

15. O'Callahan, R., Jones, C., Froyd, N., Huey, K., Noll, A., Partush, N.: Engineering record and replay for deployability: Extended technical report. CoRR abs/1705.05937 (2017). http://arxiv.org/abs/1705.05937

16. Svensson, H., Fredlund, L.A., Earle, C.B.: A unified semantics for future Erlang. In: 9th ACM SIGPLAN workshop on Erlang, pp. 23–32. ACM (2010)

17. Undo Software: Increasing software development productivity with reversible debugging (2014). https://undo.io/media/uploads/files/Undo_ReversibleDebugging_Whitepaper.pdf

18. Zelkowitz, M.V.: Reversible execution. Commun. ACM **16**(9), 566 (1973). https://doi.org/10.1145/362342.362360

Declarative Debugging of XML Queries

Jesús M. Almendros-Jiménez[(✉)] and Antonio Becerra-Terón

Department of Informatics, University of Almería, 04120 Almería, Spain
{jalmen,abecerra}@ual.es

Abstract. In this paper we present the elements of an algorithmic debugger for XQuery. Given a XQuery program/query, a debugging tree is built in which the root is the query and the answer, and non-root nodes contain the results of function calls and XPath expressions computed from the query. Using the higher-order capabilities of XQuery several navigation strategies can be defined, enabling the adaptation of the debugging to the program/query and the user needs. Debugging trees and concepts as (partially) incomplete and incorrect answers are formally defined for queries in terms of XQuery semantics. A Web tool has been developed allowing the visualization of the debugging tree and the debugging of a XQuery program/query with the selected navigation strategy.

Keywords: Testing and debugging · Database query languages · XQuery

1 Introduction

Declarative debugging (DD) [8] is a well-known debugging technique enabling to find program bugs. Also known as *algorithmic debugging*, it was proposed for logic programming [19], but it has been adapted to other programming languages (for instance, *Haskell* [10], *Java* [14], *Erlang* [7] *Maude* [17], *Datalog* [5] and *SQL* [6]). DD has been successfully applied to database query languages because they share the declarative nature with logic/functional programming languages.

DD is based on the navigation of the so-called *debugging tree*, where the root of the debugging tree is the main program and the result, and non-root nodes contain *partial computations* (usually, function calls) and their computed values. The children of each node correspond to subcomputations of the parent. The debugging process consists in the navigation of the debugging tree, in which an *oracle* (normally, the user) answers "Yes" or "No" to *debugging questions*, which are questions about the results of the partial computations. When the answers of the oracle to all the children of a given node are "Yes" and the answer to the parent is "No", a bug has been located in the code of the parent. Several strategies have been defined (see [20] for a survey), whose main goal is to reduce the time

This work was supported by UAL/CECEU/FEDER under grant UAL18-TIC-A002-B1 and the State Research Agency (AEI) of the Spanish Ministry of Science and Innovation under grant PID2019-104735RB-C42 (SAFER).

J. F. Morales and D. Orchard (Eds.): PADL 2021, LNCS 12548, pp. 161–177, 2021.
https://doi.org/10.1007/978-3-030-67438-0_10

of the DD. They range from *top-down* to *bottom-up* traversal of the debugging tree, selection strategies of nodes, types of debugging questions, memorization of oracle answers and debugging tree transformations, among others. The number and complexity of debugging questions affect the debugging process time. Additionally, the reduction of the time to be built or the space consumed by the debugging tree have influenced the design of declarative debuggers.

XQuery [18] is a database query language specifically designed for querying XML documents. XQuery is a functional language equipped with *for-let-order by-group by-where-return* expressions, enabling function definitions, and using as base language the *XPath* query language, whose role is the retrieval of paths in XML documents. With XPath, sequences of tags/attributes of the document, combined with Boolean conditions, can be specified. DD is a very good fit for a language like XQuery because, compared with general-purpose programming languages, XQuery programs tend to be fairly small and fairly simple in terms of the abstractions used. Taking functional programming as an example, extensive use of higher-order constructs and monadic code pose significant practical problems not the least in terms of how to present debugging information in a way that questions can be asked and answered in a reasonable way.

In this paper we present the elements of an algorithmic debugger for XQuery. One of the decisions taken about the design of the debugger focuses on the kind of questions the user has to answer. In a logic and functional programming context, the oracle/user answers questions about the success of logic predicates and the results of function calls, respectively. XPath expressions are central in XQuery because they serve to retrieve paths on XML documents. Most of programming errors in XQuery are due to wrong XPath expressions [3,11], and caused by missing/incorrect tags/attributes and unsatisfiable Boolean conditions. Therefore, the debugging of a XQuery program should check XPath expressions. Moreover, XPath expressions can be seen as functions acting on a XML tree and returning a forest of XML trees. For this reason, in our proposal the debugging tree will contain XPath expressions as well as function calls. The second decision we have taken about the design of the debugger is the use of XML/XQuery for the implementation. The debugging tree is represented by a XML tree. Such debugging tree is built from the query to be debugged, using XQuery to trace partial computations of the query. Our implementation has been developed in *BaseX* [12], which has reflection capabilities, enabling to parse any XQuery program/query, and producing a XML tree based representation. This XML representation of the XQuery program/query is traversed with XQuery and the partial results of the query are also computed with XQuery, producing a XML debugging tree. The XML debugging tree can be stored in secondary memory depending on its size. Additionally, once it is computed, the XML debugging tree can be navigated or transformed with XQuery.

With the aim to make more flexible the debugging process, we take advantage of the *higher-order* capabilities of XQuery. A *navigation strategy* is represented in our approach by a XQuery function which can be passed as argument to the (higher-order) debugging tree traversal function. A navigation strategy defines a *selection/ordering criterion of children in a debugging tree node*. Several navigation strategies can be freely defined by the user in order to adapt the debugging to the program/query.

We have formally defined the debugging tree of a XQuery program/query, as well as the concepts of *valid*, *non valid* and *buggy* nodes. To this end, a *formal semantics* for XQuery is given. In order to *classify XQuery bugs*, instead to carry out code analysis, answers analysis is achieved. In terms of the semantics, the concept of *erroneous query* is defined, producing *incomplete* and *incorrect* answers, as well as of *partially incomplete* and *incorrect answers*.

Finally, we have implemented a Web tool[1] for the debugging of XQuery queries. *Vaadin/Java* has been used for the Web tool implementation. The tool allows the selection of a debugging strategy (or to type a new one), and graphically visualizes the debugging tree as a grid. Such a grid is automatically traversed according to the user answers and the selected strategy, until a bug is found (or no questions remain). In order to improve debugging process the Java component of the implementation memorizes user answers to avoid the repetition of questions.

1.1   Related Work

Existing XQuery implementations are usually equipped with some mechanism of program execution tracing as well as with traditional breakpoint/step-by-step debuggers [16]. This is the case of Oxigen XML Editor[2], Stylus Studio[3], Liquid Studio[4], MarkLogic[5], Altova XML Spy[6] and Zorba[7].

Only an early work [13], proposed a declarative debugger called *Rover* for XQuery. This debugger uses the standard built-in function fn:trace() for facilitating the observation of XQuery expressions. It translates XQuery expressions into relational algebra plans, and makes it possible to inspect relational tables obtained from XPath expressions. Our approach outperforms this approach, by directly handling XML documents and XQuery, without an encoding into another language, and also provides richer debugging sessions, allowing also user-defined strategies, and, not at least important, it is equipped with a Web tool.

The current work follows the line of research about XQuery debugging started in [1–3], whose main goal was to detect programming errors in XQuery programs. In [2] a property-based testing method and in [1] a path validation algorithm were proposed, both extended in [3]. Declarative debugging can be seen as complementary of both methods.

The structure of the paper is as follows. Section 2 shows a running example used in the rest of the paper. Section 3 defines the elements of the debugger:

---

[1] http://minerva.ual.es:8090/debxquery/.

[2] https://www.oxygenxml.com/xml_editor/xquery_debugger.html.

[3] http://www.stylusstudio.com/xquery-debugger.html.

[4] https://www.liquid-technologies.com/xquery-debugger.

[5] https://developer.marklogic.com/code/xqdebug/.

[6] https://www.altova.com/xmlspy-xml-editor#xquery_debug.

[7] http://cf.zorba-xquery.com.s3.amazonaws.com/doc/zorba-1.0.0/zorba/html/debugger.html.

```
<mylist>
    <title>TCP/IP Illustrated</title>
    <title>Advanced Programming in the Unix environment</title>
    <title>The Economics of Technology and Content for Digital TV</title>
</mylist>
```

Fig. 1. Running example: dataset I

```
<bstore>
    <book year="1994">
        <title>TCP/IP Illustrated</title>
        <author><last>Stevens</last><first>W.</first></author>
        <publisher>Addison-Wesley</publisher>
        <rate>7</rate><rate>6</rate>
    </book>
    <book year="1992">
        <title>Advanced Programming in the Unix environment</title>
        <author><last>Stevens</last><first>W.</first></author>
        <publisher>Addison-Wesley</publisher>
        <rate>8</rate><rate>2</rate>
    </book>
    <book year="1999">
        <title>The Economics of Technology and Content for Digital TV</title>
        <editor><last>Gerbarg</last><first>Darcy</first><affiliation>CITI</
            affiliation></editor>
        <publisher>Kluwer Academic Publishers</publisher>
        <rate>9</rate><rate>10</rate>
    </book>
</bstore>
```

Fig. 2. Running example: dataset II

formal semantics, debugging sessions and debugging strategies; as well as the experiments. And finally, Sect. 4 discusses improvements and future work.

2 Running Example

Let us suppose the input XML documents of Figs. 1, 2 and 3; and the XQuery program and query of Fig. 4. Here the query extracts the full data of each book of a names list as well as the store offering the lowest price (Fig. 1). The query also filters books with an average rating above five. With this aim, the query uses the following XQuery functions: *local:data* for getting the data of well-rated books (average rating above five), from the document of Fig. 2; and *local:min_price* which returns the store and the lowest price, from the document of Fig. 3. The function *local:min_price* calls to auxiliary functions: *local:min* –for computing the minimum price– and *local:store* – for retrieving the store–. Additionally, *local:data* computes the average rate by calling the function *local:avg*. The answer of the query is as follows:

```
<prices>
    <book>
        <title>Advanced Programming in the Unix environment</title>
        <source>bstore2.example.com</source>
        <price>67.95</price><year>1995</year>
    </book>
    <book>
        <title>Advanced Programming in the Unix environment</title>
        <source>bstore1.example.com</source>
        <price>65.95</price><year>1997</year>
    </book>
    <book>
        <title>TCP/IP Illustrated</title>
        <source>bstore2.example.com</source>
        <price>55.95</price><year>2002</year>
    </book>
    <book>
        <title>TCP/IP Illustrated</title>
        <source>bstore1.example.com</source>
        <price>65.95</price><year>2007</year>
    </book>
    <book>
        <title>The Economics of Technology and Content for Digital TV</title>
        <source>bstore2.example.com</source>
        <price>64.95</price><year>1995</year>
    </book>
    <book>
        <title>The Economics of Technology and Content for Digital TV</title>
        <source>bstore1.example.com</source>
        <price>89.95</price><year>1998</year>
    </book>
</prices>
```

Fig. 3. Running example: dataset III

```
<bib>
  <book>
    <editor>
      <last>Gerbarg</last><first>Darcy</first><affiliation>CITI</affiliation>
    </editor>
    <publisher>Kluwer Academic Publishers</publisher>
    <avg>9.5</avg>
    <minprice title="The Economics of Technology and Content for Digital TV">
        <source>bstore2.example.com</source><price>64.95</price>
    </minprice>
  </book>
</bib>
```

In Fig. 4, both XQuery program and query are free of bugs and, thus, the answer is right. However, a number of mistakes can be made in them. The first kind of error (in fact, the most frequent) is the definition of *wrong paths*. For instance, let us consider:

Bug 1

```
<bib>{
let $mylist := db:open('mylist')
for $t in distinct-values($mylist/title)
let $d := local:data($t) where exists($d) return
<book>{$d,local:min_price($t)}</book>
}</bib>
```

wherein one of the tags of the path *$mylist/mylist/title* is missing. A similar situation happens when an incorrect tag is added, for instance, *$mylist/mylist/-books/title*; or even an spelling mistake of a tag is made, for instance,

```
                              Functions
declare function local:min($t){
let $prices := db:open('prices')
let $p := $prices/prices/book[title = $t]/price
return min($p)};

declare function local:store($t,$p){
let $prices := db:open('prices')
let $p := $prices/prices/book[title = $t and price=$p]
return $p/source};

declare function local:min_price($t){
let $min := local:min($t)
return
<minprice title='{$t}'>
{local:store($t,$min)}
<price>{local:min($t)}</price>
</minprice>};

declare function local:avg($rates){
let $n:= count($rates) return sum($rates) div $n};

declare function local:data($t){
for $b in db:open('bstore')/bstore/book[title=$t]
let $ra := local:avg($b/rate)
where $ra > 5
return
if ($b[editor]) then ($b/editor,$b/publisher,<avg>{$ra}</avg>)
else ($b/author[position()<=1],$b/publisher,<avg>{$ra}</avg>)};
```
```
                               Query
<bib>{
let $mylist := db:open('mylist')
for $t in distinct-values($mylist/mylist/title)
let $d := local:data($t)
where exists($d) return
<book>{$d,local:min_price($t)}</book>}
</bib>
```

Fig. 4. Running example: free of bugs program and query

$mylist/mylist/titles or *$mylist/mylists/title*. In such a case, these XPath expressions have an empty result[8].

The second kind of bug might occur in Boolean conditions. For instance, a wrong definition of a Boolean condition according to the user intention, such as shown as follows:

Bug 2

```
declare function local:data($t){
for $b in db:open('bstore')/bstore/book[title=$t]
let $ra := local:avg($b/rate) where $ra < 5
return
if ($b[editor]) then ($b/editor,$b/publisher,<avg>{$ra}</avg>)
else ($b/author[position()<=1],$b/publisher,<avg>{$ra}</avg>)}
```

where the wrong Boolean condition would probably lead to a non empty result but incorrect: only those books with an average rate below five are retrieved. It could also happen that the Boolean condition leads to correct but incomplete

---

[8] It could be happen that some of them returns a non empty but incorrect result but it does not arise here.

results, for instance, requiring $ra > 8$. In addition, combinations of wrong paths and Boolean conditions can be considered, such as shown as follows:

Bug 3

```
declare function local:min($t){
let $prices := db:open('prices')
let $p := $prices/prices/book[title = $t]/prices
return min($p)}
```

where there exists a spelling mistake in the tag "price". Another kind of bug is due to make a mistake when using arithmetic expressions. Let us consider the following case:

Bug 4

```
declare function local:avg($rates){
let $n := count($rates) return sum($rates)}
```

wherein the average rate is badly computed. Also bugs would be produced by calling functions with wrong arguments. Let us consider the following mistake:

Bug 5

```
declare function local:min($t){
let $prices := db:open('prices')
let $p := $prices/prices/book[title = $t]/year
return min($p)}
```

where the XQuery built-in function *min* is used with a wrong argument (i.e., year instead of price).

2.1 Bugs Classification

In order to classify bugs answer analysis is achieved instead to carrying out code analysis. Answer analysis is mandatory because, for instance, an empty result in a XPath expression does not necessarily mean an incorrect program. XQuery can require, as Boolean condition in an *if/where* expression, the existence of a path and thus both empty and non empty results are valid. In XML query languages, a query answer is usually a forest (sequence) of XML trees –in particular, a unitary tree–, but an answer can also consist in a sequence of values of basic types: integer, string, etc., as well as a mix of them. Taking into account this consideration, we might distinguish the following types of erroneous answers – from the user's point of view–: *incomplete answer*: at least one tree/value is missing; in particular, an *empty answer*; and *partially incomplete answer*: at least one of the non-root nodes of some tree is missing.

In **Bug 1** the wrong path *$mylist/title* leads to the answer *<bib/>* which is a partially incomplete answer produced by the incomplete (empty) answer of *$mylist/title*. Let us remark that such answer can be obtained even though the path is correct, whenever *local:data* returns an empty set of books –in the case of all the books are rated under five–. A partially incomplete answer is also obtained by **Bug 3**, because "prices" does not exist.

We also need to consider two additional types of answers: *incorrect answer*: at least one tree/value is incorrect; *partially incorrect answer*: at least one of the non-root nodes of some tree is incorrect.

Partially incorrect answers are obtained from: (1) Bug 2, because the Boolean condition is incorrect, (2) Bug 4, because the arithmetic expression of *local:avg* produces an incorrect answer, and, finally, (3) Bug 5, given that the actual parameter of the function call *min* is incorrect, even though the path is right.

3   Debugging XML Queries

In this section, we will formally define the elements used in our approach. Starting from a formal semantics of XQuery, we will define the concept of erroneous answer and debugging tree as well as valid, non valid and buggy nodes. Next, we will sketch results of correctness and completeness of the debugging process. Besides, an example of debugging session is shown and debugging strategies are presented. Finally, experiments and benchmarks are reported.

3.1   Debugging Semantics

In the following, empty sequences will be denoted by ϵ, and sequences of n elements will be denoted by $\overline{k}^n$, where $\overline{k}^n[i]$ represents the element k_i.

A XML tree $\mathcal{X}$ contains (tagged) nodes n of the form $<l\ [Attr_1\ \ldots\ Attr_n]>$ $ch_1,\ldots,ch_m </l>$ where ch_i can be literals l_i or nodes n_i, l is the label of n, and $Attr_j$ are attribute nodes of the form $a_j = k_j$, where a_j is the name of the attribute and k_j is a literal. $ch_1,\ldots,ch_m$ are called the child nodes of n. For short, we call items to tagged/attribute nodes and literals. Given a node n of a XML tree $\mathcal{X}$ we can define functions $axis :: p$ where $axis$ can be one of 'self', 'child', 'descendant', 'descendant-or-self', 'parent', 'ancestor', 'ancestor-or-self', 'attribute', 'following', 'following-sibling', 'preceding', 'preceding-sibling' and 'namespace', and p can be one of '*', node(), text() and k, where k is a label or an attribute name. Such $axis :: p$ returns the set of items of $\mathcal{X}$ at the corresponding positions. $axis : p$ can be extended to a sequence of XML nodes $\overline{n}^k$ and a sequence of XML trees $\overline{\mathcal{X}}^k$ as follows: $axis : p(\overline{n}^k, \overline{\mathcal{X}}^k) = \overline{axis : p(n, \mathcal{X})}^k$. Given a node n of a XML tree $\mathcal{X}$, $tree(n)$ denotes $\mathcal{X}$, also can be extended to a sequence of XML nodes $\overline{n}^k$ as follows: $tree(\overline{n}^k) = \overline{tree(n)}^k$. We denote by $\mathcal{X}(nm)$ the XML tree of name nm. Given a XML tree $\mathcal{X}$, we can consider the following operations: *insertion* of a new (non empty) child in any of the non-root nodes; *replacement* of a child in any of the non-root nodes by a new (non empty) child; and *deletion* of a child in any of the non-root nodes.

Now, a XQuery query Q has the syntax of Fig. 5[9], and its semantics is defined in Fig. 6. We have defined two elements: (1) the semantics of a *for/let* definition denoted by $[\![\cdot]\!]_C^\Gamma$ and (2) the semantics of a XQuery expression denoted by

---

[9] We have restricted ourselves to the most known XQuery constructors.

XQuery	::= GFLWR | CElem | If | Quantifier | FuncCall
	:= | Var | XPath | () | literal | XQuery op XQuery
	:= | (XQuery, ... , XQuery) | not(XQuery)
GFLWR	::= GFLWRItem [... GFLWRItem] return XQuery
GFLWRItem	::= For | Let
Let	::= for $v in Query [where XQuery]
For	::= let $v := Query [where XQuery]
CElem	::= <l [CAttr ... CAttr] >XQuery</l>
CAttr	::= a="{XQuery}"
If	::= if XQuery then XQuery else XQuery
Quantifier	::= some $v in XQuery satisfies XQuery
	:= | every $v in XQuery satisfies XQuery
FuncCall	::= f(XQuery ... XQuery)
Var	::= $v
XPath	::= db:open(nm) | XQuery / axis::p | Query[XQuery]

Fig. 5. XQuery syntax

$[\![\cdot]\!]^\Gamma$. In (1), the semantics is a sequence Γ of contexts $\gamma_1, \ldots, \gamma_k$ of the form $\{\$v_1 \to t_1, \ldots, \$v_n \to t_n\}$ where $\$v_i \neq \$v_j$ for $i \neq j$, and $t_1, \ldots, t_n$ are items, and $\{\$v_1, \ldots, \$v_n\}$ variables. Such sequence represents the bindings t_i of variables $\$v_i$ in the *for/let* definition. Note that due to *for* expressions, in general, a variable is bound to k values (one for each γ_k). In (2), the semantics is an *answer*; i.e., a sequence (possibly empty) of items. When a context γ is built from a variable binding, we use the notation $\gamma \oplus \{\$v \to t\}$ assuming that the previous assignment to $\$v$ (if any) is removed from γ. Given $\Gamma = \gamma_1, \ldots, \gamma_k$, we denote by $\gamma_i(\$v_j)$ the value t_j when it exists, and otherwise $\gamma_i(\$v_j) = \epsilon$. *op* represents any XQuery arithmetic operator, Boolean operator as well as XML Union, Intersection and Difference set operators. Finally, let us remark that $f(e_1, \ldots, e_n)$, whenever f is defined as $f(\$x_1, \ldots, \$x_n)\{e\}$, is semantically defined as *let* $\$x_1 := e_1, \ldots, let \$x_n := e_n \ return \ e$.

From now on, we will consider only queries with at least one XPath expression or Function call, for which the concept of erroneous answer has sense. Given a query Q, the *intended answer* of Q is denoted by $\mathcal{I}(Q)$. Such concept corresponds to the idea of intended interpretations usually employed in algorithmic debugging. However, the *computed answer* of Q, denoted by $\mathcal{C}(Q)$ and defined as $\mathcal{C}(Q) = [\![Q]\!]^\emptyset$, can be different from $\mathcal{I}(Q)$.

Definition 1 (Incomplete and Incorrect Answers). *Given a query Q, and an intended answer $\mathcal{I}(Q)$, we say that:*

- *Q has a incomplete answer whenever $\exists k \in \mathcal{I}(Q)$ such that $k \notin \mathcal{C}(Q)$.*
- *Q has a partially incomplete answer whenever $\exists k \in \mathcal{I}(Q)$, $k \notin \mathcal{C}(Q)$ and a sequence of insertions λ such that $\lambda(k) \in \mathcal{C}(Q)$.*
- *Q has an incorrect answer whenever $\exists k \in \mathcal{C}(Q)$ such that $k \notin \mathcal{I}(Q)$.*
- *Q has a partially incorrect answer whenever $\exists k \in \mathcal{C}(Q)$, $k \notin \mathcal{I}(Q)$, and a sequence of replacements/deletions λ such that $\lambda(k) \in \mathcal{I}(Q)$.*

Definition 2 (Erroneous and Correct Query). *Given a query Q, and an intended answer $\mathcal{I}(Q)$, we say that Q is erroneous in $\mathcal{I}(Q)$ whenever Q has either a (partially) incomplete or (partially) incorrect answer, and Q is correct in $\mathcal{I}(Q)$ otherwise.*

(1) $[\![\overline{GFLWRItem}^n \; return \; XQ]\!]^\Gamma \quad = [\![XQ]\!]^{\Gamma'} \; where \; \Gamma' = [\![\overline{GFLWRItem}^n]\!]_C^\Gamma$

(2) $[\![\overline{GFLWRItem}^n]\!]_C^\Gamma \qquad\qquad = \Gamma' \; where \; \Gamma_{i+1} = [\![GFLWRItem_i]\!]_C^{\Gamma_i},$
$\qquad\qquad\qquad\qquad\qquad\qquad 1 \le i \le n, \Gamma_1 = \Gamma \; and \; \Gamma_{n+1} = \Gamma'$

(3) $[\![for \; \$v \; in \; XQ_1 \; [where \; XQ_2]]\!]_C^\Gamma = \Gamma' \; where \; \Gamma = \gamma_1, \ldots, \gamma_m \; \Gamma' = \gamma'_{11}, \ldots, \gamma'_{nm},$
$\qquad\qquad\qquad\qquad\qquad\qquad 1 \le i \le n, 1 \le j \le m, \; \gamma'_{ij} = \gamma_j \oplus \{\$v \to [\![XQ_1]\!]^\Gamma[i]\},$
$\qquad\qquad\qquad\qquad\qquad\qquad if \; [\![XQ_2]\!]^{\Gamma_{ij}} = true \; or \; (\ne () \; and \; \ne false) \; and \; \gamma'_{ij} = \gamma_j,$
$\qquad\qquad\qquad\qquad\qquad\qquad otherwise$
$\qquad\qquad\qquad\qquad\qquad\qquad being \; \Gamma_{ij} = \gamma_1, \ldots, \; \gamma_j \oplus \{\$v \to [\![XQ_1]\!]^\Gamma[i]\}, \ldots, \gamma_m$

(4) $[\![let \; \$v \; in \; XQ_1 \; [where \; XQ_2]]\!]_C^\Gamma = \Gamma' \; where \; \Gamma = \gamma_1, \ldots, \gamma_m \; \Gamma' = \gamma'_1, \ldots, \gamma'_m,$
$\qquad\qquad\qquad\qquad\qquad\qquad 1 \le j \le n, \; \gamma'_j = \gamma_j \oplus \{\$v \to [\![XQ_1]\!]^\Gamma\},$
$\qquad\qquad\qquad\qquad\qquad\qquad if \; [\![XQ_2]\!]^{\Gamma_j} = true \; or \; (\ne () \; and \; \ne false) \; and \; \gamma'_j = \gamma_j,$
$\qquad\qquad\qquad\qquad\qquad\qquad otherwise$
$\qquad\qquad\qquad\qquad\qquad\qquad being \; \Gamma_j = \gamma_1, \ldots, \; \gamma_j \oplus \{\$v \to [\![XQ_1]\!]^\Gamma\}, \ldots, \gamma_m$

(5) $[\![< l \; [\overline{CAttr}^n] > XQ < /l >]\!]^\Gamma \quad =< l[[\overline{CAttr}^n]\!]^\Gamma] > [\![XQ]\!]^\Gamma < /l >$

(6) $[\![a ='' \{XQ\}'']\!]^\Gamma \qquad\qquad = a = [\![XQ]\!]^\Gamma$

(7) $[\![if \; XQ_1 \; then \; XQ_2 \; else \; XQ_3]\!]^\Gamma \; = [\![XQ_2]\!]^\Gamma if \; [\![XQ_1]\!]^\Gamma = true \; or \; (\ne () \; and \; \ne false)$
$\qquad\qquad\qquad\qquad\qquad\qquad and \; = [\![XQ_3]\!]^\Gamma, \; otherwise$

(8) $[\![some \; \$v \; in \; XQ_1 \; satisfies \; XQ_2]\!]^\Gamma = true, \; whenever \; [\![for \; \$v \; in \; XQ_1 \; where \; XQ_2]\!]^\Gamma = \Gamma'$
$\qquad\qquad\qquad\qquad\qquad\qquad and \; some \; \gamma'_i(\$v) \ne \epsilon, \Gamma' = \gamma'_1, \ldots, \gamma'_m$
$\qquad\qquad\qquad\qquad\qquad\qquad = false,$
$\qquad\qquad\qquad\qquad\qquad\qquad otherwise$

(9) $[\![every \; \$v \; in \; XQ_1 \; satisfies \; XQ_2]\!]^\Gamma = true, \; whenever \; [\![for \; \$v \; in \; XQ_1 \; where \; XQ_2]\!]^\Gamma = \Gamma'$
$\qquad\qquad\qquad\qquad\qquad\qquad and \; every \; \gamma'_i(\$v) \ne \epsilon, \Gamma' = \gamma'_1, \ldots, \gamma'_m$
$\qquad\qquad\qquad\qquad\qquad\qquad = false,$
$\qquad\qquad\qquad\qquad\qquad\qquad otherwise$

(10) $[\![f(\overline{XQ}^n)]\!]^\Gamma \qquad\qquad = f(\overline{[\![XQ]\!]^\Gamma}^n)$

(11) $[\![\$v]\!]^\Gamma \qquad\qquad\qquad = \overline{\gamma(\$v)}^n, \Gamma = \gamma_1, \ldots, \gamma_n$

(12) $[\![db : open(nm)]\!]^\Gamma \qquad = \mathcal{X}(nm)$

(13) $[\![XQ/axis :: p]\!]^\Gamma \qquad = axis :: p([\![XQ]\!]^\Gamma, \overline{\mathcal{X}}^n) \; where \; tree([\![XQ]\!]^\Gamma) = \overline{\mathcal{X}}^n$

(14) $[\![XQ_1[XQ_2]]\!]^\Gamma \qquad\quad = [\![for \; \$v \; in \; XQ_1 \; where \; \$v/XQ_2 \; return \; \$v]\!]^\Gamma$

(15) $[\![()]\!]^\Gamma \qquad\qquad\qquad = \epsilon$

(16) $[\![literal]\!]^\Gamma \qquad\qquad = literal$

(17) $[\![XQ_1 \; op \; XQ_2]\!]^\Gamma \qquad = [\![XQ_1]\!]^\Gamma \; op \; [\![XQ_2]\!]^\Gamma$

(18) $[\![(\overline{XQ}^n)]\!]^\Gamma \qquad\qquad = (\overline{[\![XQ]\!]^\Gamma}^n)$

(19) $[\![not(XQ)]\!]^\Gamma \qquad\qquad = not([\![XQ]\!]^\Gamma)$

Fig. 6. XQuery semantics

Let us remark that XPath expressions and Function calls are special cases of queries and thus the concepts of erroneous and correct query can be applied to them. Next, we can formally define debugging trees, as well as valid, non valid and buggy nodes from the defined XQuery semantics.

Definition 3 (Debugging Tree). *The debugging tree of an expression Q, denoted by $DT(Q)$, is built as follows. The root is $(Q, [\![Q]\!]^\emptyset)$ and for each node $(N, \overline{k}^n)$ of $DT(Q)$ the children consist in the $DT(PF)$ of each XPath expression and Function call PF occurring in N.*

Figure 7 partially shows the debugging tree of the running example (without bugs). Green nodes represent XPath nodes, while blue ones are Function calls. For saving space, we have omitted the XML values associated to each node.

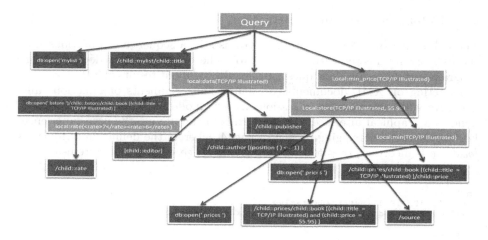

Fig. 7. Debugging tree

Definition 4 (Valid, Non valid and Buggy Nodes). *Let $DT(Q)$ be the debugging tree of a query Q, $\mathcal{I}(Q)$ an intended answer for the nodes in $DT(Q)$ and $(N, \overline{k}^n)$ a node of $DT(Q)$, then we say that N is valid whenever N is correct; non valid whenever it is erroneous, and buggy when it is non valid and all its children are valid.*

Finally, the following theorem states soundness and completeness results of the debugging process.

Theorem 1 (Soundness and Completeness). *Let us suppose a query Q, $DT(Q)$ the debugging tree of Q, and $\mathcal{I}(Q)$ an intended answer for the nodes in $DT(Q)$. If the root T of the tree $DT(Q)$ is non valid then:*

(a) Every buggy node of T corresponds to an erroneous XPath expression or Function call.

(b) T contains a buggy node.

Proof Sketch:
Case (a): Trivial. If N is a buggy node of T then it is non valid, thus, N is erroneous. Case (b): By induction on the height of the $DT(T)$ tree and reasoning as follows. Let $DT(PF)$ be for each XPath expression and Function call PF in T. If T is non valid then T is erroneous, thus, T has either a (partially) incomplete or (partially) incorrect answer. According to Definition 1, in the case of T has an incomplete answer, $\exists k \in \mathcal{I}(T)$ such that $k \notin \mathcal{C}(T)$. Thus, either T is buggy, or T is not buggy, and according to the XQuery semantics, there exists $DT(PF_k)$ of some child of T, producing k, which is non valid. Similar reasoning can be followed for partially incomplete and (partially) incorrect answers.

3.2 Debugging Session

The debugging of a XQuery program consists in a sequence of questions that the user should answer with 'Yes' or 'No'. The debugging tree does not store program variables and, thus, questions are always about results of XPath expressions acting on XML documents, or results and arguments of Function calls. Here, we will show debugging sessions in text mode, however, the Web tool[10] handles a graphical interface, and uses grids for improving the user experience. For instance, the debugging session of Bug 4, wherein the definition of function *local:avg* is incorrect, is as follows –for saving space we omit some items–:

```
Can be db:open(' mylist ')
equal to
<mylist>
  <title>TCP/IP Illustrated</title>
  <title>Advanced Programming in the Unix environment</title>
  ...
</mylist>?
Question (Y/N): Y

Can be
<root>
  <mylist>
    <title>TCP/IP Illustrated</title>
    <title>Advanced Programming in the Unix environment</title>
    ...
  </mylist>
</root>
/child::mylist/child::title
equal to
<title>TCP/IP Illustrated</title>
<title>Advanced Programming in the Unix environment</title>
...?
Question (Y/N): Y

Can be this function call: local:data
with arguments: TCP/IP Illustrated
equal to
<author>
  <last>Stevens</last><first>W.</first>
</author>
<publisher>Addison-Wesley</publisher>
<avg>13</avg>?
Question (Y/N): N

Can be db:open(' bstore ')/child::bstore/child::book [(child::title  =  TCP/
    IP Illustrated) ]
equal to
<book year="1994">
  <title>TCP/IP Illustrated</title>
  <author>
    <last>Stevens</last><first>W.</first>
  </author>
  <publisher>Addison-Wesley</publisher>
  <rate>7</rate><rate>6</rate>
</book>?
Question (Y/N): Y

Can be this function call: local:avg
with arguments:
<rate>7</rate><rate>6</rate> equal to 13?
Question (Y/N): N
```

---

[10] http://minerva.ual.es:8090/debxquery/.

```
Can be
<book year="1994">
  <title>TCP/IP Illustrated</title>
  <author>
    <last>Stevens</last><first>W.</first>
  </author>
  <publisher>Addison-Wesley</publisher>
  <rate>7</rate><rate>6</rate>
</book>
/child::rate
equal to
<rate>7</rate><rate>6</rate>?
Question (Y/N): Y
Error in local:avg
```

Here, the first negative answer is given when the question about *local:data* emerges, since *avg* (i.e., average rate) value is incorrect. It triggers questions about the code of *local:data*. In particular, the debugging session asks about *local:avg*. Now, the answer should be again 'No', but the only child of this node has a positive answer. Therefore, the bug is located at *local:avg*.

3.3 Debugging Strategies

The XML debugging tree contains under the root node a sequence of *question* XML nodes, each one enclosing *p* nodes and *sf* nodes, as well as possibly other *question* XML nodes. *Question* XML nodes store questions about XPath expressions (*p* nodes) and Function calls (*sf* nodes). The XML debugging tree has the following form: $\langle question \rangle..\langle p \rangle...\langle /p \rangle...\langle /question \rangle...\langle question \rangle... \langle sf \rangle... \langle /sf \rangle$ $...\langle /question \rangle$. The user does not directly handle this representation. However, he/she can define from the representation his/her own navigation strategies of the XML debugging tree. These navigation strategies can be defined as XQuery functions, and they define children selection/ordering criteria of tree nodes. Such functions are passed as argument to a (higher-order) top-down traversal function of the debugging tree. For instance, the identity XQuery function:

```
function($x){$x}
```

defines a naive strategy, in which no specific selection/ordering of nodes is performed. Using *p* and *sf* tags, two strategies, called *First Paths* and *First Functions*, can be defined as follows:

```
function($x){($x[p],$x[sf])}     function($x){($x[sf],$x[p])}
```

where the first one prioritizes the debugging of paths against functions (and the second one functions against paths). In some cases, a very useful strategy is the so-called *Only Functions*, in which only function calls are analyzed. It allows us to focus the interest of the debugging session on functions results. This strategy is defined as follows:

```
function($x){$x[sf]}
```

The size of the children can be used for defining the *Heaviest First* strategy [4]; i.e., an strategy in which children are ordered by size:

```
function($x){
for $ch in $x order by count($ch//question)
ascending return $ch}
```

Table 1. Benchmarks.

Strategy	Q1		Q2		Q3		Q4		Q5		Q6		Q7		Q8	
	S	E	S	E	S	E	S	E	S	E	S	E	S	E	S	E
Naive	3	Yes	10	Yes	6	Yes	4	Yes	6	Yes	23	Yes	9	Yes	6	Yes
Paths first	2	Yes	10	Yes	6	Yes	8	Yes	6	Yes	31	Yes	9	Yes	6	Yes
Functions first	6	Yes	2	Yes	4	Yes	4*	No	4	Yes	22	Yes	4*	No	4	Yes
Only functions	4	No	2	Yes	4	Yes	2*	No	4	Yes	4	Yes	4*	No	4	Yes
Heaviest first	5	Yes	6	Yes	4	Yes	3	Yes	7	Yes	22	Yes	6	Yes	4	Yes
Lightest results first	1	Yes	2	Yes	3	Yes	6	Yes	3	Yes	31	Yes	3	Yes	3	Yes
Divide and query	5	Yes	7	Yes	4	Yes	3	Yes	7	Yes	27	Yes	6	Yes	4	Yes
Heaviest paths first	5	Yes	2	Yes	2	Yes	2*	No	2	Yes	22	Yes	2*	No	2	Yes
Heaviest functions first	5	Yes	7	Yes	5	Yes	3	Yes	4	Yes	22	Yes	6	Yes	5	Yes

A size-based strategy is also *Lightest Results First* which orders children by the size of the result:

```
function($x){
for $ch in $x order by count($ch/values//node())
ascending return $ch }
```

in such a way that empty answers are checked first. Additionally, typical *Divide and Query* strategy [19] can also be defined as follows:

```
function($x){
let $w := count($x//question)
let $m := $w div 2
let $bigger := (for $n in $x where count($n//question) > $m
        order by count($n//question) descending return $n)
let $smaller := (for $n in $x where count($n//question) <= $m
        order by count($n//question) descending return $n)
let $pivot := head($smaller)
let $rest := tail($smaller)
return ($pivot,$rest,$bigger)
}
```

Finally, the *Heaviest Functions First* strategy analyzes nodes with the highest number of Function calls first. This strategy is defined as follows:

```
function($x){for $ch in $x order by count($ch//sf) descending return $ch}
```

and similarly, *Heaviest Paths First* strategy analyzes nodes with the highest number of XPath expressions first:

```
function($x){for $ch in $x order by count($ch//p) descending return $ch}
```

3.4   Benchmarks

Table 1 shows the benchmarks obtained analyzing eight queries (they can be found at http://minerva.ual.es:8090/debxquery/). The column "S" indicates the number of debugging steps needed to reach the bug. The column "E" indicates whether the bug is reached or not. We have two cases in which the value of "E" is "no". The first case is when the strategy is not complete. This is the case of *Only Functions* when the bug occurs in a XPath expression, and the XPath expression is not in the scope of a Function call. The second case is when the strategy reaches first another bug which is caused by the bug under study. The latter case is marked "*" in the Table 1.

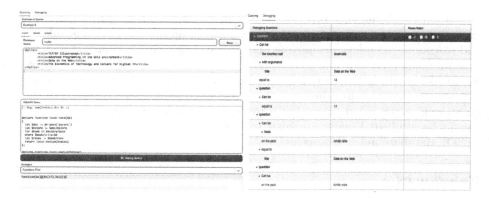

Fig. 8. Web tool: debugging tree

The conclusions of our experiments can be summarized as follows. While the choice of *Paths First* might seem to be a good strategy to find the most frequent bug in XQuery programs, *Functions First* cannot be discarded as good choice, in the presence of numerous Function calls. The user can suspect what the type of bug is by inspecting the answer. Incomplete (and, in particular, empty) answers can be better analyzed by *Lightest Results First*, which serves for early detection of empty answers of XPath expressions and Function calls. However, incorrect answers might be better analyzed with other strategies. For instance, when some Function call has a high number of XPath expressions (respectively, Function calls), *Heaviest Paths First* (resp. *Heaviest Functions First*) significantly reduces the number of debugging steps. The *Only Functions* strategy, even though it is incomplete serves to ignore XPath expressions, reducing drastically the number of debugging steps in some cases. For instance, it is crucial in *Q6* (example taken from [6]) where the checking of a high number of XPath expressions is required. However, this strategy has a low granularity, revealing the function in which the bug is located but not the code point. Fortunately, the developed Web tool enables to define new strategies, which can be combinations of the proposed here, and might help the user to customize his/her debugging session. User defined strategies can be compositions of the proposed here or new ones written from the scratch.

4 Conclusions and Future Work

In this paper we have presented the elements of an algorithmic debugger for XQuery. Using the higher-order capabilities of XQuery several navigation strategies can be defined, enabling the adaptation of the debugging to the program/-query and the user needs. A Web tool (see Fig. 8) has been developed allowing the visualization of the debugging tree and the debugging of a XQuery program/-query with the selected navigation strategy. While the debugger works well in our experiments, some improvements will be added. For instance, features like *"undo"* in the debugging process, *I don't know* user answers [15], handling of *exceptions* and *non-termination*. Another planned improvement is the *indexing* and *storing in secondary memory* [9] of the debugging tree. Currently, it is stored in main memory, and it affects the performance in some cases. Additionally, we would like to study a wider range of strategies, in particular, those ones taking into account the user answers. Currently, once a question is answered, this question is never asked again, but a more sophisticated mechanism of *trusting* should be studied. Finally, we plan to study algorithmic debugging in other NoSQL database query languages.

References

1. Almendros-Jiménez, J.M., Becerra-Terón, A.: Automatic validation of XQuery programs. In: The 17th International Conference on Information Integration and Web-based Applications & Services, pp. 603–607. ACM Press (2015)
2. Almendros-Jiménez, J.M., Becerra-Terón, A.: XQuery testing from XML schema based random test cases. In: Chen, Q., Hameurlain, A., Toumani, F., Wagner, R., Decker, H. (eds.) DEXA 2015. LNCS, vol. 9262, pp. 268–282. Springer, Cham (2015). https://doi.org/10.1007/978-3-319-22852-5_23
3. Almendros-Jiménez, J.M., Becerra-Terón, A.: Automatic property-based testing and path validation of XQuery programs. Softw. Test. Verif. Reliab. **27**(1–2), e1625 (2017)
4. Binks, D.: Declarative debugging in godel. Ph.D. thesis, University of Bristol (1995)
5. Caballero, R., García-Ruiz, Y., Sáenz-Pérez, F.: A theoretical framework for the declarative debugging of datalog programs. In: Schewe, K.-D., Thalheim, B. (eds.) SDKB 2008. LNCS, vol. 4925, pp. 143–159. Springer, Heidelberg (2008). https://doi.org/10.1007/978-3-540-88594-8_8
6. Caballero, R., García-Ruiz, Y., Sáenz-Pérez, F.: Algorithmic debugging of SQL views. In: Clarke, E., Virbitskaite, I., Voronkov, A. (eds.) PSI 2011. LNCS, vol. 7162, pp. 77–85. Springer, Heidelberg (2012). https://doi.org/10.1007/978-3-642-29709-0_9
7. Caballero, R., Martin-Martin, E., Riesco, A., Tamarit, S.: Declarative debugging of concurrent Erlang programs. J. Log. Algebraic Methods Program. **101**, 22–41 (2018)
8. Caballero, R., Riesco, A., Silva, J.: A survey of algorithmic debugging. ACM Comput. Surv. (CSUR) **50**(4), 1–35 (2017)
9. Davie, T., Chitil, O.: Hat-delta: one right does make a wrong. In: Seventh Symposium on Trends in Functional Programming, TFP 2006, pp. 1–9. Intellect (2006)
10. Faddegon, M., Chitil, O.: Algorithmic debugging of real-world haskell programs: deriving dependencies from the cost centre stack. ACM SIGPLAN Not. **50**(6), 33–42 (2015)
11. Groppe, J., Groppe, S.: Filtering unsatisfiable XPath queries. Data Knowl. Eng. **64**(1), 134–169 (2008)
12. Grün, C.: BaseX. The XML Database (2020). http://basex.org
13. Grust, T., Rittinger, J., Teubner, J.: Data-intensive XQuery debugging with instant replay. In: Proceedings of the 4th International Workshop on XQuery Implementation, Experience and Perspectives, pp. 1–6 (2007)
14. Insa, D., Silva, J.: An algorithmic debugger for Java. In: 2010 IEEE International Conference on Software Maintenance, pp. 1–6. IEEE (2010)

15. Nilsson, H.: How to look busy while being as lazy as ever: the implementation of a lazy functional debugger. J. Funct. Program. **11**(6), 629–671 (2001)
16. Petrovay, G.: XQuery (scripting) debugging: IDE and engine support. Master's thesis, ETH, Swiss Federal Institute of Technology Zurich, Department of CS (2008)
17. Riesco, A., Verdejo, A., Martí-Oliet, N., Caballero, R.: Declarative debugging of rewriting logic specifications. J. Log. Algebraic Program. **81**(7–8), 851–897 (2012)
18. Robie, J., Chamberlin, D., Dyck, M., Snelson, J.: XQuery 3.0: an XML query language. W3C Proposed Recommendation (2014)
19. Shapiro, E.Y.: Algorithmic program diagnosis. In: Proceedings of the 9th ACM SIGPLAN-SIGACT Symposium on Principles of Programming Languages, pp. 299–308 (1982)
20. Silva, J.: A survey on algorithmic debugging strategies. Adv. Eng. Softw. **42**(11), 976–991 (2011)

Author Index

Printed in the United States
By Bookmasters